MW00446113

MASTERING SPACE WAR

THE ADVANCED STRATEGIES, TECHNOLOGIES, AND THEORIES NEEDED FOR VICTORY

EDITOR: PAUL SZYMANSKI

MICHAEL S. DODGE AND BRYANT A.M. BAKER
CHRISTOPHER KUKLINSKI
COLONEL CHRISTOPHER R. DINOTE
COLONEL RYAN SANFORD
LIEUTENANT COLONEL (R) BRAD TOWNSEND, PhD
JOHNATHON MARTIN AND BRANDON BAILEY
MICHAEL UNBEHAUEN
DAINIUS T. BALČYTIS

NIMBLE BOOKS LLC

Copyright © 2023 Paul Szymanski
All rights reserved.

ISBNs:

9781934840122 (hardcover)

This book is composed in Adobe Skolar (body) and Proxima Nova (headings). Emojis and wingdings are from Mac OS.

This book is dedicated to the classical military strategists, such as Sun Tzu, Clausewitz, Jomini, Liddell Hart, Fuller, Corbett, and Mahan. May this book be a significant addition to the literature of warfare that has been written before and in the future for the new environment of military outer space warfare.

Publisher's Notes

Human militaries have been operating in space since June 20, 1944, when a German V-2 rocket reached an altitude of 175 km (109 miles).[1] For most of that period space power has been vitally important to the military activities of spacefaring powers. While there have been as yet no declared or disclosed space wars, with every year that goes by the chances seem higher, as the potential payoff of achieving space dominance increases.

Publishers seek to anticipate trends and events. One of the ways we do this is by observing, and stimulating, the creation of new categories and genres of books. The formation of the US Space Force on December 20, 2019, convinced me that the study of military activity in space was here to stay on an equal footing with enduring publishing categories such as naval history and aviation history. Paul Szymanski is a world-leading expert, and he has brought together here all the information you need to understand how nations will fight and win space wars. If you are someone who would be affected by the outcome of a space war—which is nearly everyone—you may benefit from reading this book. If your daily work life relies upon space or services that depend on access to space, it becomes essential reading. I am confident you will enjoy it as much as I have.

Fred Zimmerman
Ann Arbor, Michigan, USA

---

[1] Neufeld, Michael J. *The Rocket and the Reich: Peenemünde and the Coming of the Ballistic Missile Era.* New York: Free Press, 1995.

For technical and cost reasons, we retained certain known inconsistencies in the way that citations and bibliographies are rendered in different parts of the book.

- In the footnotes in Chapter 4 (only), citations are rendered in (date/author) format with full citations available in a bibliography at the end of the chapter, whereas in other chapters, citations appearing within footnotes are shown with full bibliographic information on first appearance, which is the normal practice.
- In Chapters 3, 4, and 9 (only), full bibliographies are provided as the final section of the chapter.

CONTENTS

ABBREVIATIONS

ABM	Anti-ballistic missile
BMD	Ballistic Missile Defense
BS	Biological Sciences
CIWS	Close-in weapon systems
COTS	Commercial Orbital Transportation Services
CRAF	Civil Reserve Air Fleet
CSLA	Commercial Space Launch Act as Amended
CSLCA	Commercial Space Launch Competitiveness Act
DEW	Directed-energy weapons
EKV	Exo-atmospheric Kill Vehicle
EU	European Union
EW	Electronic warfare
FAI	Fédération Aéronautique Internationale
FEP	Front-end processors
GIUK	Greenland-Iceland-United Kingdom
GMD	Ground-Based Midcourse Defense
GNSS	Global Navigation Satellite Systems
GSD	Ground sample distance
HPM	High-powered microwaves
ICBM	Intercontinental ballistic missiles

ICJ	International Court of Justice
KKV	Kinetic-kill vehicle
LEO	Low Earth Orbit
LOAC	Laws of Armed Conflict
MDA	Missile Defense Agency
NADA	National Aerospace Development Administration
NDAA	National Defense Authorization Act
NGI	New Ground-based Interceptor
NMCC	National Military Command Center
NOAA	National Oceanic and Atmospheric Administration
NOTAM	Notice to Airmen
NOTSP	Notice To Space Personnel
NRO	National Reconnaissance Office
NSC	National Security Council
NSS	National Security Strategy
ODNI	Office of the Director of National Intelligence
OODA	Observe, Orient, Decide, Act
OPIR	Overhead Persistent Infrared
OST	Outer Space Treaty
PLA	People's Liberation Army
QDR	Quadrennial Defense Review
RPO	Rendezvous and proximity operation
SAR	Synthetic Aperture Radar
SBIRS	Space Force through its legacy Space-Based Infrared System
SBX	Sea-based X-Band
SCP	Space Capstone Publication

SDA	Space Domain Awareness
SMC	Space and Missile Systems Center
SOF	Special operations forces
SSA	Space Situational Awareness
SSF	Strategic Support Force
SWIR	Shortwave Infrared
TT&C	Telemetry, tracking, and control
UN-COPUOS	United Nations Committee on the Peaceful Uses of Outer Space
ZPO	Zero-proximity operation

Figures

Tables

CHAPTER 1: INTRODUCTION

The chapter on China's People's Liberation Army (PLA) Space Doctrine in *Chinese Aerospace Power* by Andrew Erickson shows that Chinese space warfare doctrine closely resembles German strategic doctrine in the 20th Century. The Germans believed they were surrounded by neighbors who could ultimately beat them in any protracted conflict, so their doctrine emphasized quick, lightning strikes to knock out their opponents before they could bring the full weight of their military upon them. That is why the very brightest military thinkers on the German general staff spent whole careers devising optimized railway schedules for mobilization of their forces before World War I, and why they also embraced blitzkrieg warfare during World War II to force a quick end to any conflict.

The Chinese have the same strategic outlook, as they believe that the United States would beat them in any protracted conflict due to its superior technology. Thus, the stage is set for space blitzkrieg warfare at the beginning of any major conflict between China and the United States. Would the Chinese strike US space assets in a lightning-quick surprise attack, or just position themselves to threaten US space assets so we hesitate in our responses and self-deter? If the US also positions their space control assets that threaten Chinese space systems, does this create a hair-trigger strategic impasse? Poor Space Situational Awareness (SSA) and Space Domain Awareness (SDA) could quickly, and inadvertently devolve into general space war. Does the side who attacks first generally win future space wars? Does all this sound similar to the hair-triggers of nuclear war, but without the self-deterrence of mutual mass destruction?

Looking at the history of new military technologies, it's interesting how quickly the Germans developed the doctrine and strategies that blew France and Great Britain off the battlefield. General Heinz Guderian, the proponent and leader of German combined arms blitzkrieg warfare, did not even ride in a tank until 1929, just ten years before his tanks began to conquer Europe. Germany's first tank, the very weak MK I, was not fully deployed to their troops until 1935, just four years before the start of World War II. (Due to the Versailles Treaty, Germany was not allowed to build tanks.) Guderian's book, *"Achtung - Panzer!"*, on the theory of armored warfare, was not even published until 1937, just two years before his tanks invaded Poland. It's amazing that with so short a time period for development of armored warfare theory, doctrine, equipment and training the Germans were so successful in knocking out the French and British forces so early in the invasion of France that began on May 10, 1940. At the start of that invasion, the Allies had a 17 to 1 advantage in number of tanks over the Germans, and their tanks were better armored and had better armament than the Germans. And the Allies had eight months to prepare defenses and train forces during the Phony War of September 1939 to May 1940. So why did the Germans beat the Allies so soundly and so quickly?

The simple answer was the Germans had the advantage of starting from scratch due to being defeated in World War I. The Allies did the Germans a favor by destroying their weapons capabilities immediately after WW I, forcing them to begin anew not just with equipment but with training and doctrine as well. Their situation required new, original thinking. Their superior maneuver warfare doctrine at the beginning of World War II led to their spectacular victories over the Allies in the early phrases of WW II.

The lesson to be learned here? The Chinese are starting from scratch in developing space warfare theory and doctrine and are not hindered by long space traditions. There is a lot of writing on this subject in their open literature, but I see almost no discussions in the United States on these topics. We had the Program 437 nuclear Anti-Satellite (ASAT) on Johnston Island in the 1960's and the F-15 ASAT program in the 1980s, but over these last fifty years we have not yet felt the need to develop space warfare doctrine.

The Germans developed their winning armored warfare doctrine in just a few years without much testing or training. Their soldiers in the war were mostly raw recruits. Similarly, China's space forces today may be new to this subject area, but this may allow them to be more agile and to have more flexible and innovative attack plans. They enjoy the additional advantage of being able to conduct surprise attacks because of our poor space situational awareness capabilities. And they have a more realistic leadership structure that does not worship "political correctness" dogmas that encourage self-deterrence.

The US has many advantages, just as the French and British did. We may have better and more numerous space forces than any potential adversary, but if we lack the proper doctrine, strategies and tactics, then we are open to defeat by a resurgent power with fresh doctrine. I am reliably informed that senior leadership in Washington would require absolute proof of attribution before they would allow any counter-strikes when US satellites are destroyed. Since attacking anti-satellites (ASAT) systems do not have big red stars painted on their sides (and are probably constructed by mainly Western parts), then quick verification will be quite problematic, and will essentially cause self-deterrence and paralysis of national leadership. Currently, if a satellite stops working it takes weeks and months for the cause to be determined, and many times this is only a big guess as to the root causes, since these space systems cannot generally be directly imaged, being tens of thousands of miles from Earth sensors. A space war will be over before we even know what hit us!

CHAPTER 2: THE WARFIGHTER'S GUIDE TO SPACE LAW

BY MICHAEL S. DODGE AND BRYANT A.M. BAKER[2]

WHY SPACE LAW?

What does the law have to do with a discussion of how to secure space? There are some who would argue that the law cannot practically, or even ultimately should not be, a part of the discussion because when it comes to protecting a nation and its interests in space, there should be no limits. But while the fullest extent of a war in space has not yet been tested, let alone the extents that a nation would be willing to go to win such a war, the fact is that space law has had and will continue to have a vital role in deciding and preventing conflicts in space. To understand this, one need look no further than the first ever venture into space.

In 1957, the Soviet Union famously changed the world by technologically leapfrogging the United States when it launched Sputnik into orbit, becoming the first human-made satellite. History has consistently labeled this event as a blatant failure of the US to understand the importance that space would play in the world of global politics. How could the US have allowed this embarrassment to have taken place? While from the technical perspective this list of reasons has long since been postulated and debated among scholars, interestingly, there was one

---

[2] *The views expressed are those of the authors and do not reflect the official guidance or position of the United States Government, the Department of Defense or of the United States Air Force.*

group in the Eisenhower administration that was decidedly not disappointed: the attorneys.

While the Soviets had succeeded in forever claiming their place in the history books, they also had perhaps inadvertently helped the US shape the future utilization of space; arguably, a Soviet misstep whose impacts have lasted to this day. And how did that happen? Through space law.

Prior to Sputnik, the US and Russia had entered a cold war whose outcomes were shaped by perceptions of superiority and secrecy. It became clear to the Eisenhower administration that lifting the fog of war which hovered over the communist regime was of vital importance to US success. So, under the guise of peace Eisenhower suggested that national sovereignty over airspace be amended to allow air-based reconnaissance between the two superpowers. This of course the Kremlin refused.

The law of the air had by that point in history been made clear. Nation-states owned outright the airspace above their nations. But did that ownership have an upper limit? Or did it in fact rise to infinitum? If direct observation of Soviet territory from the air was off the table, what about from space? This unanswered question was finally provided by Sputnik. And it was decided in the US's favor.

By flying over the US and other nations, Sputnik the law would protect a nation's right to fly objects in space with or without permission of the other nations the object may fly over. From that moment, the entire space-reconnaissance mission became proper and possible. And because of that legal precedent, US national satellite systems have been able to provide over 60 years of valuable service from space.

Understanding not only how this process works, but why it works and how it can be utilized is vital for the space fighter. In this chapter, we will describe what space law is, where it comes from, what it has to say about war, and how it will shape the future of space conflicts.

WHAT IS SPACE LAW?

Ultimately, international law is the collection of rules that bind States to certain kinds of behaviors toward one another or governs their obligations to other types of entities (e.g., 'the environment', 'the economy', etc.). Put differently, international law "covers relations between states in all their myriad forms, from war to satellites, and regulates the operations of the many international institutions."[3] The sources of international law, and their global impact, are often accessed through the lens of the Statute of the International Court of Justice (ICJ), colloquially known as the World Court.' This Statute describes three categories of international law used by justices to make their decisions when there is conflict between States.[4] There is also a fourth tool in their kit used for interpretive means that they may employ if and when the first three legal categories fail them in resolving the matter before them. The three primary types of international law may be roughly described as: 1) international accords or conventions (i.e., treaties and other instantiations of 'hard' or binding law); 2) customary international law (a more elusive concept that conveys legal authority especially important when more typical, written means elude the Court); and 3) principles of 'civilized' nations[5] (a catch-all category that covers international norms not readily shelved into one of the prior types, but which nevertheless guide the actions of States). The fourth category used by the ICJ may broadly be described as the writings or teachings of eminent scholars (typically

---

[3] Malcolm N. Shaw, International Law 2 (2008).

[4] Article 38, Statute of the International Court of Justice, Signed June 26, 1945, 59 Stat. 1055, T.S. 993.

[5] Note: contemporary international law holds that all legitimate States are equal in the eyes of the law. The language 'civilized' was written at a time when the major powers of the world held sway over law formation, and this term was used to distinguish these States from less developed powers.

law scholars or professors) who may have erudite views on the meaning of international law, or the applicability of law to novel scenarios before the Court.

While the first three categories of international law represent the vast majority of norms, cases, conflicts, and emerging theories of law as applied to States, treaties are by far the most respected and influential. In outer space, a series of treaties have been written, signed, ratified, and generally adopted by a host of nations, and their primacy in space has been proven through the hold they have on State actions in that particular lex *spacialis*. In laymen's terms, a treaty may be thought of as "in its nature a contract between two nations."[6], or "primarily a compact between independent nations."[7] Thus, States that properly ratify a treaty become *bound* to that treaty and are not free to deviate from its provisions unless and until the State officially withdraws. This is why treaties are so important to the ICJ in resolving disputes between States—they represent incontrovertible evidence of what each party meant to be bound by at a particular point in time. It is also why a series of five United Nations treaties, discussed below, are so critical in examining the relationship of States in outer space.

WHERE DOES SPACE LAW COME FROM?

As we know it, Space Law originates primarily from two sources: international law, and domestic legislation. The former concerns various types of arrangements between States, ranging from "hard law" treaties (which bind States) to "soft law" principles and declarations (which influence State behavior, but which also grant them wide discretion in their actions). In contrast, domestic legislation creates laws for one State

---

[6] Comments of Chief Justice Marshall, U.S. Supreme Court, Foster v. Nelson, 2 Pet. 253, at 314 (1829).

[7] Comments of Justice Miller, U.S. Supreme Court, Head Money Cases, 112 U.S. 589, at 598 (1884).

alone, though it may impact a host of other nations through its implementation. In both instances, the need for laws governing space emerged with the advent of the Space Age, arguably begun by the successful orbiting of the Earth by the Soviet Union's Yuri Gagarin on October 4th, 1957.

After Gagarin's flight, the world quickly recognized the need for rules and regulations regarding human activity beyond the atmosphere. The geopolitical ramifications of the Soviet Union's feat were substantial, and not only spurred the United States to ramp up its own nascent space program (which did not yet include NASA, formed by Act of Congress in 1958), but also agitated legislators in Congress to such a degree that calls were put out to act, and to do so quickly. There was a real fear that if the Soviets were allowed to claim all the successes in space, they would move beyond the United States in the brinkmanship of the Cold War. Historian Walter McDougall referenced the excited reaction of some politicians, including that of Overton Brooks, Sam Rayburn, and John W. McCormack—not to mention Lyndon Johnson, who chaired the newly created Special Committee on Science and Astronautics.[8] If Sputnik could orbit the Earth, lawmakers reasoned that something like it could just as easily be co-opted for the sake of warfare, hence the need to create committees capable of passing legislation to handle space topics. From that time on, Congress has passed numerous laws governing US activities in space, from the creation of NASA to remote sensing laws, and even to encourage private activities like launch and resupply missions.

Globally, Sputnik encouraged forward thinking individuals to collaborate in the halls of the United Nations to draft a series of rules applicable to all States in space. In 1959, the UN Generally Assembly created the United Nations Committee on the Peaceful Uses of Outer Space

---

[8] Walter A. McDougall, ...the Heavens and the Earth 169-170 (1985).

(UNCOPUOS)[9], which created the currently governing series of five space treaties. While this Committee still labors toward the creation of new rules and norms in space, the bulk of its work was completed between 1967 and 1979, when the space treaties were adopted. The ultimate goal of international law is to promote stable relationships between nation-states. In this respect, space law is simply the extension of this ambition into the realm of outer space and the celestial bodies subject to current or future human exploration and use.

WHAT DO THE TREATIES SAY?

There are five extant space law treaties. Each of these have been crafted to address particular issues respecting activities of nation-states or their nationals in the environs of space and its celestial bodies. The treaties began with the Outer Space Treaty of 1967[10], and continued with the Return and Rescue Agreement (1968)[11], the Liability Convention (1972)[12], the Registration Convention (1974)[13], and the Moon Agreement (1979)[14].

Of particular relevance to space warfare are the Outer Space Treaty (OST) and the Registration Convention. The latter is important because

---

[9] See COPUOS History, *available at* https://www.unoosa.org/oosa/en/our-work/copuos/history.html.

[10] Treaty on Principles Governing the Activities of States in the Exploration and Use of Outer Space, including the Moon and Other Celestial Bodies, opened for signature Jan. 27, 1967, 18 U.S.T. 2410, 610 U.N.T.S. 205.

[11] Agreement on the Rescue of Astronauts, the Return of Astronauts and the Return of Objects Launched into Outer Space, *opened for signature* April 22 1968, 19 U.S.T. 7570, 672 U.N.T.S. 119.

[12] Convention on International Liability for Damage Caused by Space Objects, *opened for signature* Mar. 29 1972, 24 U.S.T. 2389, 961 U.N.T.S. 187.

[13] Convention on the Registration of Objects Launched into Outer Space, *opened for signature* Nov. 12 1974, 28 U.S.T. 695, 1023 U.N.T.S. 15.

[14] Agreement Governing the Activities of States on the Moon and Other Celestial Objects, 18 I.L.M. 1434, 1363 U.N.T.S. 3.

of the wealth of information that States are meant to provide to the Secretary General respecting their space assets (such as information about what objects are in space, when they got there, which State launched them, and what they do), and the former because the OST sets the norms of State cooperation and due regard, as well as forms the foundation of international law in space. The Outer Space Treaty mandates that space is free for the exploration and use of all States (Art. I), that States cannot nationally appropriate space or celestial objects (Art. II), that extant international law follows States into outer space (Art. III), and that States must use celestial objects in particular exclusively for peaceful purposes (Art. IV). Article IV also tells us that States cannot set up military installations on the Moon, for instance, nor may they test weapons of any kind on celestial objects; further, they cannot orbit weapons of mass destruction around the Earth, up to and especially including nuclear weapons. Article VI dictates that States are internationally responsible for their nationals' activities in outer space, whether or not these were governmental or private activities. Further, Article IX mandates that States operate with "due regard" toward one another and seek out opportunities to cooperate in space. Most if not all of these principles have been so widely accepted by the international community that not only have they been accepted by over 100 signatory states, but they have become a part of customary international law. Because of this, it would be difficult if not impossible for States to argue that they are not subject to these laws even if they have not signed the OST or abdicated from it.

So with that understanding of Space Law, next we will move on to the Law of War to better understand how these fields interact with one another.

WHAT IS THE LAW OF WAR?

The US Department of Defense defines the "Law of War" as being "that part of international law that regulates the resort to armed force;

the conduct of hostilities and the protection of war victims in both inter-national and non-international armed conflict; belligerent occupation; and the relationships between belligerent, neutral, and non-belligerent States."[15] To understand this somewhat esoteric definition, we have to break down exactly what is being referred to.

We have already established what international law is, but what of the use of armed force? There is plenty that the warfighter does and is responsible for in her day-to-day life that does not directly involve the use of armed force. Equipment and materials have to be transported, training has to be performed and skills must be honed, and the future of war must be developed. All are vital to the warfighter's purpose, but do not involve the use of armed force. But when violence (force) is carried out against another party, the use of force has been invoked. And as the name implies, the use of "armed" force usually implies at least some level of kinetic injury causing harm to people or property.

Finally, the term "Belligerent" refers to a group, country or other en-tity which is engaged in a war.[16] Therefore, it is not necessary that the entity be in fact a recognized nation, nor that an official declaration of war be declared for the label of "belligerent" to apply nor for the law of war to apply.[17]

WHERE DID IT COME FROM?

The bad news for the interested scholar is that the history of the law of war is as vast and multi-directional as the history of war itself. The good news is, as in the study of warfare, in the history of the law of war there are principles and themes that have run through from the

---

[15] Office of General Counsel, *Department of Defense Law Of War Manual* 7–8 (2016).

[16] Belligerency, *Oxford Public International Law*, https://opil.ou-plaw.com/view/10.1093/law:epil/9780199231690/law-9780199231690-e249 (last vis-ited Sep 14, 2021).

[17] Keith E. Puls & Derek Grimes, *Law of War Handbook* (2005) 9 (2005).

beginning. Ever since humankind became advanced enough to bring violence against one another in any sort of organized fashion there has been discussion about what that violence is supposed to mean and what should and should not be included in such violence.

The Old Testament contains multiple passages citing limitations on waring activities of the Israelites.[18] Sun Tzu famously discussed not only strategies for defeat of one's enemies but wrote of the need to follow conduct conducive with reaping the benefits of such success in war. And from the time of Greece and Persia to the present day, history is littered with examples of discussions and conclusions on the acceptable conducts of war (and yes, the breaches of such conflict). Thus, the key principles discussed below have long appeared in one form or another throughout history, but the modern understanding of the law of war came about as a result of the end of the great wars!

Attempts began to be made by the end of the 19th century to begin an international effort to limit the atrocities of war.[19] Discussions began concerning protections for medical personnel, followed by rules against slaughter of non-combatants at the end of the century, and the limitations of the use of certain weapons as a result of World Wars I and II.[20] This all culminated in the creation of the United Nations in 1945, whose

---

[18] See *Judges* 1: 28-32; 2 *Kings* 6:22-23; *Proverbs* 25:21; *Deuteronomy* 20: 19-20; *Exodos* 23: 29; see also Guy B. Roberts, *Judaic Sources of and Views on the Laws of War*, 37 *Naval L. Rev.* 221, 231 (1988); Leslie C. Green, The Law of War in Historical Perspective, 72 *International Law Studies* (1998), https://digital-commons.usnwc.edu/cgi/viewcontent.cgi?article=1468&context=ils (last visited Sep 14, 2021).

[19] Howard S. Levie, *History Of The Law Of War On Land* ICRC (2000), https://www.icrc.org/en/doc/resources/documents/article/other/57jqhg.htm (last visited Sep 14, 2021); it is not coincidental that these efforts came near the end of the American Civil War which demonstrated in explicit detail the capability of newer advancing technologies to be used for the mass devastation of warfighters as well as local populations.

[20] Id.

charter, in a bold historical move which would shape the law of war from that point onward, declared war effectively illegal.[21] The charter declares that "All Members shall *refrain* in their international relations from the *threat or use of force* against the territorial integrity or political independence of any state, or in any other manner inconsistent with the Purposes of the United Nations.".[22]

WHAT DOES THE LAW OF WAR SAY?

If the nations of the world were capable of eliminating armed conflicts with a swift swish of the pen back in 1945, however, our present day may have looked very differently. Instead, the law has evolved to answer two key legal questions: (1) when can we go to war (known as *jus ad bellum*); and (2) when war does happen, what are the rules (known as *jus in bello*).[23]

Jus ad Bellum

In its simplest form, Article 2(4) of the UN Charter states there are two times when a nation is justified in the use of warfare: (1) when such use of force is sanctioned by the UN Security Councill; or (2) when it constitutes a legitimate act of individual or collective self-defense. By far the more common reason cited for the use of force is the latter.

Self-defense has historically arisen in one of four forms: individual self-defense, collective self-defense, anticipatory self-defense, and

---

[21] U.N. Charter art. 2, para.4.

[22] *Id.* (emphasis added).

[23] See, e.g., William O'Brien, *The Conduct Of Just And Limited War* 9 (1981) (defining jus ad bellum as the "doctrines concerning permissible recourse to war" and jus in bello as "the just conduct of war"); Michael Walzer, *Just And Unjust Wars 21* (1977); Office of General Counsel, *Department of Defense Law of War Manual* 39 (Ann Arbor: Nimble Books, 2017). But see Robert Kolb, Origin of the twin terms jus ad bellum/jus in bello, 37 *International Review Of The Red Cross* 553 (Sept.-Oct. 1997).

preemptive self-defense.[24] Of these, individual self-defense is likely the most straight forward and the one that an average person would probably imagine as being what "self-defense" means. Individual self-defense involves the use of force to protect a nation's territorial integrity, its political independence, and its people and their property. Collective self-defense takes the bubble of protection to the next step by allowing for the defense of ally States.[25] Anticipatory self-defense, rooted in a case from 1837 between US and British forces near the falls at Niagara, is the idea that a State need not wait until after an attack has taken place to use force to defend itself.[26] Instead, a nation can justify the use of force in anticipation of an "imminent armed attack."[27] Finally, and most controversially, in the 2002 National Security Strategy (NSS), the US government published an expansion of the doctrine of anticipatory self-defense into a concept labeled the Preemptive Use of Force. While drawing various levels of agreement and consternation internationally, the US has held strongly to this concept which expands the definition of "imminent" to include any point in which evidence shows that an aggressor has committed itself to an armed attack and delaying a response would hinder the defender's ability to mount a meaningful defense.

Jus in Bello

After the decision to engage in the use of force is made, that force must be tempered by adherence to the Laws of Armed Conflict (LOAC).

---

[24] Operational law handbook, 5-7 (17 ed. 2017).

[25] See also U.N. Charter art. 51.

[26] The case involved an international incident in which a merchant riverboat, the Caroline, was ferrying supplies to Canadian rebels. British forces seized the vessel and destroyed it. A series of letters between the US Secretary of State and British Foreign Office established the common international understanding of anticipatory self-defense. See Operational law handbook, 6 (17 ed. 2017).

[27] Id.

The main purposes of the LOAC are to protect both combatants and non-combatants from unnecessary suffering, safeguard persons who fall in the hands of the enemy, and facilitate the restoration of peace.[28] To do this, each use of force employed must adhere to four broad principles: (1) the Principle of Military Necessity; (2) the Principle of Distinction; (3) the Principle of Proportionality; and (4) the Principle of Unnecessary Suffering.

The principle of military necessity simply stands for the idea that targets of the use of force must not be destroyed or seized unless such action is demanded by the necessities of war.[29] In other words, that destruction must not take place without reason or without a military benefit being sought. The principle of distinction requires that armed forces distinguish the difference between civilians and military objectives.[30] The purpose here is to prevent the indiscriminate destruction of both military and civilian targets. Third, the principle of proportionality requires states to refrain from attacks in which the expected harm incidental to the attacks would be excessive in relation to the concrete and direct military advantage anticipated to be gained.[31] And finally, the somewhat self-explanatory principle of unnecessary suffering requires that States minimize superfluous injury or violence on its targets.[32]

While none of these principles of law are new, the challenges which exist at present have arisen in attempting to answer the controversial question of how to apply them to the space environment. The following sections will attempt to answer what role the law has had in preventing

---

[28] Id. at 9.

[29] Id.

[30] Id. at 10.

[31] Id. at 11.

[32] Id. at 12.

war in space, and what challenges it will have as humankind continues to branch out into space.

WHAT ROLE HAS SPACE LAW PLAYED IN WAR?

While the OST shapes international actions in space, it is a generalized treaty that leaves much room for interpretation. Further, the Treaty leaves many gaps in the law to be filled by States through their own legislative actions. With respect to the domain of war, the United States has crafted several laws which have direct or indirect applicability, such as laws related to remote sensing (the Land Remote Sensing Act of 1992[33]), the Commercial Space Launch Act as Amended (CSLA of 1984)[34], and the US Commercial Space Launch Competitiveness Act (CSLCA of 2015)[35], or the authorization that created the United States Space Force[36]. Because these laws must respect the US obligation to the OST, it should be noted that any and all military actions in space, especially during times of peace, must conform to the Treaty's provisions. Also relevant is the preamble and other articles within the OST, which stress the need to use space for peaceful purposes. Many of the activities in space that are applicable to national security or strategic planning have military overtones, from remotely sensing potential adversaries, to launching Global Navigation Satellite Systems (GNSS) satellites for positioning, navigation, and timing purposes. Consequentially, when States like the United States perform these activities in space, they send the signal (their *opinio*

---

[33] Land Remote Sensing Act of 1992, Pub. Law No. 98-365, 98 Stat. 451 (1984).

[34] Commercial Space Launch Act, Pub. L. 98-575 (1984); *see generally*, 51 U.S.C. § 50902 et seq.

[35] U.S. Commercial Space Launch Competitiveness Act, Pub. L. 114-90, 129 Stat. 704 (2015).

[36] National Defense Authorization Act for Fiscal Year 2020, Public Law 116-92, Sec. 951-961 (creating the United States Space Force).

juris) that these activities are in fact in conformity with international obligations under the treaty system.

Remote sensing was arguably the primary motivator for developing and launching space technologies in the post Sputnik-1 world. The military and intelligence applications for viewing the Earth from space are immense, and President Eisenhower saw developing remote sensing technology as a solution to the problem of obtaining data regarding Soviet nuclear weapon placement. Since the Soviets rejected his Open Skies proposal, all that (legally) remained was finding a way to view the USSR from space. Since that time, operations like Corona, the first US reconnaissance satellite program, led the way to obtain information critical to the United States in times of peace or war. Subsequently, remote sensing technology became critical to warfare from the time of the Six-Day War of 1967 onward, with the Gulf War representing a conflict on which the United States depended strongly on space assets like remote sensing. For decades, this technology has been a critical aspect of strategic planning, and this has been acknowledged through the drafting of domestic legislation. The Land Remote Sensing Act of 1992 was created at the end of the Cold War, and its language showcases the deep and abiding value of remotely-sensed data to the US government. Since that time, the government has worked to update the remote sensing regulations to better appreciate the concurrent need to promote private remote sensing actors, many of whom may use the United States Government as an anchor client for whom they provide valuable data. Internationally, the United Nations Remote Sensing Principles[37] recognized the value of this technology for all States, though it shied away from making proclamations on reconnaissance or military operations.

---

[37] Principles Relating to Remote Sensing of the Earth from Outer Space, G.A. Resolution 41/65, adopted without vote on Dec. 3, 1986.

For launch policy, the CSLAA was created in the mid-1980s as a way of encouraging private actors to operate in space, with the intent of commercializing as many space activities as could be passed off to the private sector. The idea meshed with the governmental philosophy espoused by President Reagan, which in this case promoted that the private sector could do things in space more efficiently and affordably than the government, and therefore both the private and public sectors could benefit from commercialization. For instance, the US Air Force and other branches have long used private space actors to launch military payloads into outer space, which lessens the burden on the taxpayers to have such launches done in-house and provides opportunities for the private sector. This sort of public-private partnership between the military client and the civilian service provider continues to define many current launch operations.

More recently, the CSLCA of 2015 extensively overhauled domestic space legislation. Of particular relevance to warfighting was the emphasis of that law on stressing the need to locate an authority within the halls of the United States Government to take a long-term handle on tracking orbital debris and other elements in space situational awareness, as well as which authorities would regulate space traffic management. Both fields have direct applicability to the warfighter, who needs to know where things are in space in order to properly craft security strategies.

When the Space Force was created as the latest branch of the US military, it demonstrated the bipartisan belief that space activities are becoming increasingly important to how warfare is conducted. The new branch is a recognition of the value of space to national defense for all space powers, as well as an update to national security infrastructure. Since the Outer Space Treaty regime leaves much to States to determine, it seems that there are many things the Space Force may do in space, ranging from remote sensing to sending military personnel into space. Operating military bases on Earth, maneuvering spacecraft in the void of space (but not on celestial bodies) and launching military satellites into orbit are all legally permissible activities for Space Force. So long as certain prohibitions (like those against WMDs) are respected, the existence of the Space Force is not an affront to international space law.

How does Space Law help prevent war?

Perhaps the greatest value of the Outer Space Treaty regime is the stability it provides space actors. States know the basic rules of the road, what generally is or is not permissible, and which parties are responsible for particular activities in space. The treaties repeatedly emphasize the value of international cooperation, and stress how States ought to work together where possible during their exploration and use of space. Article IX of the OST creates two obligations—one for giving "due regard" to other States acting in space, and one to engage in international consultations with a State when there will be possible interference with that State's peaceful uses of space. Further, the OST and its progeny promote the sharing of data, activities, and locations in space, all with the idea of enhancing the knowledge of each State actor. Presumably, such data help States to pursue cooperation, and prevent engaging in hostile actions due to ignorance of standard activities.

The second greatest value of the Outer Space Treaty is its exceptional flexibility. Article I gives States the ability to use and explore space as they see fit, within certain conditions laid out in subsequent clauses. More often than not, a State will find itself with the ability to do whatever it deems necessary in space. Several key elements in national defense planning require the use of space, such as gathering remotely-sensed data, settling GPS satellites into orbit, or testing spacecraft viability in the orbital space around the Earth. Each of these is permitted by the OST regime, so long as States pursue them with due regard to others. In turn, these activities help assist defense planners to avoid unnecessary warfare.

So with this general understanding of the substance and background of the law of war and space, let us look briefly at a few examples of the application of these laws in two key space environments: Earth orbit, and on the lunar surface.

WHAT DOES SPACE LAW SAY ABOUT CONFLICTS IN ORBIT?

Of the dozens of legal questions that will need to be answered for wars in Earth orbit, three of the most important involve the use of nuclear weapons, military action and utilization, and the limits imposed by the law of war in space.

WHAT DOES SPACE LAW SAY ABOUT NUCLEAR WEAPONS IN SPACE?

The most significant limitation on the military's use of outer space in the OST is Article IV, which prohibits States from "[placing] in orbit around the Earth any objects carrying nuclear weapons or any other kinds of weapons of mass destruction ... or station such weapons in outer space in any other manner." Before moving on to the implications of this prohibition, it is important to point out that this prohibition in no way prohibits weapons of ALL kinds from being in space. The only limitations mentioned are nuclear weapons and weapons of mass destruction.

But even the limitations on the weapons mentioned are not as strict as it may at first seem. There are important limiters to this ban which the warfighter needs to understand. Article IV specifically prohibits placing nuclear weapons "in orbit," thus implying that for the limitation to apply it would require a nuclear weapon to complete at least a single orbit around the Earth to be in violation. Therefore, it is widely accepted that intercontinental ballistic missiles (ICBMs), which frequently launch far higher than the Kármán Line [38] are not in violation of Article IV because they are not designed to complete a full orbit around the Earth before reentering airspace to hit their intended targets.

Two interesting questions which have not yet been answered still exist on this point. The first is the definition of a nuclear weapon, and the second regards nuclear weapons sent in transit to other locations. For illustration purposes, we can refer to the somewhat farcical notion some have suggested of using the launching of nuclear bombs to Mars to vaporize enough material to replenish Mars' atmosphere and make it habitable for human life. Would the use of nuclear explosions, not for the destruction of human life or property but of natural phenomena be considered the use of a nuclear weapon? What if it was to destroy an asteroid headed toward Earth? And second, during the several month-long journey such a nuclear bomb would require traveling from the Earth to Mars, would that device be "station[ed] ... in outer space"? These are questions for serious debate and the warfighters of today are likely destined to play a key role in the final decision-making.

WHAT MILITARY ACTS ARE ALLOWED IN ORBIT?

As discussed above, the OST allows for a tremendous amount of freedom for the use of space. But until hostilities arise such that the laws of jus ad bellum authorize the use of armed force in space, the admonition of Article I of the OST to maintain space for peaceful purposes remains in place. Although debates began even earlier than 1957 on whether space can or should be reserved for non-military use, after sixty years of

---

[38] At approximately 100 km in altitude, this is the point at which airplanes are not able to maintain lift without the use of rocket propulsion and is widely used as an approximator of the boundary of space. It has also been established as the point in which US Space Command assumes warfighting jurisdiction. However, it should be noted that there is no internationally recognized legal definition for the boundary between air space and outer space, despite the international recognition that such boundary must, of legal necessity, exist.

precedence it seems clear that "peaceful purposes" cannot be properly interpreted as meaning "non-military."

But it is also important to note a legal principle which may cause some space lawyers discomfort; and that is that if and when hostilities do arise in orbit, it will likely not be the OST that governs, but the laws of war outlined above under the UN charter. Article III of the OST specifically incorporates international law, including the law of war, into the use and activities occurring in space. What this means, is though the OST binds the US and its other more than 100 signatory States to the use of space for peaceful purposes, the OST does not and cannot prevent States from utilizing the laws available to them to justify the use of force for the purposes of the various forms of self-defense described above.[39]

HOW DO WE DEFINE "AGGRESSIVE?"

As space becomes internationally recognized as a warfighting domain, the space law field will face challenges in be in defining specific instances of justification for the use of force. The term the US has chosen to describe such justifiable instances is "aggressive" uses of space by another party. But what does "aggressive" use of space mean? Despite the long history and precedent for defining aggressive behavior on Earth, the effort to define it is ongoing and challenging because of the differences in the application of physics in the orbital environment. Does a satellite flying close-by constitute a threat in the same way that a warship floating close to a frigate would? (See figure below.) Irresponsible designs can lead to serious issues from orbital debris, but is this an environmental concern or does it constitute an actionable security threat? Although the same legal analysis that would apply to wars on the Earth,

---

[39] See U.N. charter, art. 103: "In the event of any conflict between the obligations of the members of the United Nations under the present Charter and their obligations under any other international obligation, their obligations under the present Charter shall prevail."

i.e., application of the principles of jus ad bellum and jus in bello, would be applied in space, how that application would take place is a yet-to-be-determined mystery. The space warfighter will play a vital role in distinguishing answers to these questions.

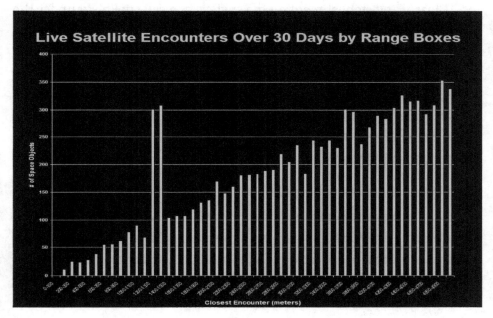

Figure 1. Space Objects Come Close to Each Other Many Times a Month Due to Natural Orbital Motions

WHAT DOES SPACE LAW SAY ABOUT CONFLICTS ON CELESTIAL BODIES LIKE THE MOON AND MARS?

Similar questions arise as we travel to celestial bodies like the Moon or Mars which, while the superiority of the law of self-defense above the OST provisions still prevails, nevertheless enjoy an implication of a higher standard of anti-warlike protections. In contrast to Article I of the OST which calls for the use of space to be for "peaceful purposes," Article IV reserves celestial bodies for "*exclusively* peaceful purposes." The article further prohibits the "establishment of military bases, installations and fortifications" or "the testing of any type of weapons and the conduct of military maneuvers."

What are the challenges in defining "military base?"

Clearly an establishment on the surface of a celestial body under the full control and jurisdiction of a military officer seems to fit the definition. But this was the case for every human landing on the Moon to date! The Apollo missions at a very minimum establish that the term "military base" cannot mean any place where there are military personnel, or even some form of military control. But what is the line between a civilian establishment with military personnel on it (Apollo) and a military base with civilian involvement?

What are the challenges in defining "military maneuver?"

Similar vagaries exist in Article IV's prohibition of military maneuvers. Some may argue that any movement of military personnel or equipment from one location of a celestial body to another constitutes a prohibited maneuver. And while this would be an obvious over-application of the intent of Article IV, exactly what the difference is between a "military maneuver" and an allowable movement of personnel or equipment may be simple in concept but will be difficult in application. The key distinguishing factor will likely be the intent of the parties. If the purpose of the movement is to gain military advantage or to strike, then the prohibition will most likely apply. But if it is not, then there is no such prohibition.

What could lead to conflict on the Moon and Mars?

There is an increasing desire to treat the Moon and Mars as potential grounds for national economic and technological advantage rather than as traditional wonders of space. NASA's Artemis program and China's published strategy of lunar settlements show that humans of various national origin are likely to be on the surface of the Moon (and hopefully

Mars) in the not-too-distant future. Considerations such as local re-sources, advantageous launch and landing sites, locations for communi-cation arrays, as well as the integrity and historical significance of these sites are all factors in which one may imagine contention arising. Article IX of the OST requires that States conduct their activities on celestial bodies with "due regard" for others, but what happens when either States don't do so; or merely when States act in a way that a negatively affected State *believes* was not done with "due regard?" The first shot has not yet been fired on the Moon or any other celestial body, but if humans are involved it is unlikely that such a record will remain intact indefi-nitely.

CONCLUSION

Space law has helped the proliferation of space activities from the early days of the Space Age to the present day. By creating a foundation for the peaceful uses of space, the OST regime enabled the USA and USSR, and many other nations to follow, to impact the future of space. The motivation to enhance national security and defense has promoted the creation and use of technologies like remote sensing and GNSS, in addition to telecommunication satellites and private space launches with defense agencies as key clients. The general legal sense imparted by the OST is one of permissibility; consequentially, States are now and will continue to be mostly free to do as they wish in space—within lim-its. Since this regime suits the needs of the major space powers, it is un-likely that the OST will be amended any time soon to impose new re-strictions or create new concerns, so the paradigm established in 1967 will continue to provide guidance for space actors, be they defense plan-ners or corporate interests.

The possibility of disruption is present, especially given concerns over the proliferation of orbital debris. However, outside of a major im-pact to current satellite constellations or space stations, there will be minimal international pressure to change current international space law. In contrast, space law will continue to grow at a healthy clip at the domestic level, with States around the world passing legislation, or crafting policy, to promote or enable their own activities. Thus, much of the future of space law, and its impact on security, will be seen from domestic legislative actions across the globe.

CHAPTER 3: DETERRING STRATEGIC ATTACKS IN THE SPACE DOMAIN

BY CHRISTOPHER THOMAS KUKLINSKI

In March 2021, the president of the United States, Joseph Biden, signed the *Interim National Security Guidance*. Within this interim guidance, President Biden defined the national security landscape this way:

> *"We face a world of rising nationalism, receding democracy, growing rivalry with China, Russia, and other authoritarian states, and a technological revolution that is reshaping every aspect of our lives."*

The People's Republic of China and the Russian Federation are identified as those hoping to keep the influence of the United States in check. The *Guidance* states:

> *"China, in particular, has rapidly become more assertive. It is the only competitor potentially capable of combining its economic, diplomatic, military, and technological power to mount a sustained challenge to a stable and open international system. Russia remains determined to enhance its global influence and play a disruptive role on the world stage."*

In addition to peer-competitors such as China and Russia, President Biden's guidance adds regional actors "... like Iran and North Korea [who] continue to pursue game-changing capabilities and technologies, while threatening US allies and partners and challenging regional stability." Some of the "game-changing capabilities and technologies" possessed by China, Russia, Iran, and North Korea reside within the space domain·[40] and may enable strategic attacks·[41] on all instruments of the national power·[42] of the United States. Possessing such capabilities provides one nation the ability to conduct strategic attacks, either intentionally or unintentionally, to deny, disable, or destroy another nation's space capabilities. The confluence of Great Power Competition and regional hegemony with the introduction of advanced technologies creates an unprecedented international security dilemma, and the need to deter irresponsible behavior within the space domain from escalating to conflict.

Before positing a strategy to deter irresponsible behavior in space, this paper provides insight into the space domain, highlights actions by China, Russia, North Korea, and Iran which potentially challenged the 'unfettered access to and freedom to operate in space," and discusses a deterrence strategy establishing the safeguards necessary to deter irresponsible behavior in the space domain.

---

[40]Domains are the physical areas (land, sea, air, and space) and information environment (cyberspace) in which military operations are conducted. Along with the composite of conditions, circumstances, and influences affect how decisions are made and capabilities employed (Joint Staff 2017, Change 1 2018)

[41] Strategic attacks are designed to weaken an adversary's ability and will to fight by attacking systems and centers of gravity to include leadership, critical processes, popular will and perception, and fielded forces with the intent to drive an early end to conflict (LeMay Center for Doctrine 2017).

[42] Joint Publication-1 list four fundamental 'instruments of national power': Diplomatic, Informational, Military, and Economic (DIME) (Joint Publication 1-0: Doctrine for the Armed Forces of the United States 2017).

"History consists of a series of accumulated imaginative innovations...."

Voltaire

INSIGHT

To understand the space domain, it is important to discuss its origins, national security objectives, strategic benefits, physical boundaries, legal protections, critical components, and inherent vulnerabilities.

ORIGINS

Voltaire's comment proves true in modern warfare as imagination and innovation led man beyond the land, sea, and air domains to compete for the ultimate high ground, outer space. On 4 October 1957, the Union of the Soviet Socialist Republic launched Sputnik[43] from the Baikonur Cosmodrome near Tyuratam Kazakhstan. This great technological innovation led Lyndon B. Johnson, then a United States Senator from Texas and future president, to say that "the sky seemed almost alien" (Launius, *Sputnik and the Origins of the Space Age* 2019). Sputnik introduced the world to the Space Age. It marked an accomplishment of "considerable technical and scientific importance" that "will, for a long time, be highly problematic" according to John Foster Dulles, then the United States Secretary of State (Launius, *Prelude to the Space Age* 1995).

---

[43] Sputnik was the first man-made object to exist outside the Earth's atmosphere and orbit the planet. It was 58 cm or 22.8 inches in diameter, weighed 83.6 kilograms or 183.9 pounds, and took about 98 minutes to complete an orbit around the planet (NASA 2007).

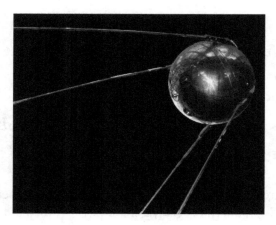

Figure 1. Replica of Sputnik 1, http://nssdc.gsfc.nasa.gov/database-/MasterCatalog?sc=1957-001B.

After initially failing to beat the Soviets to space[44], the United States in the years and decades to follow embarked on an epic journey to become the world's leader in space, launching satellites into a variety of orbits[45] around the planet, putting a man on the Moon, and sending

---

[44] On 28 July 1955, the USA announced plans to launch "small earth-circling satellites as part of the United States participation in the International Geophysical Year 1957-1958 (NASA 2005).

[45] Joint Publication 3-14 *Space Operations* identifies four commonly used satellite orbits along with potential satellite mission assigned to each.

Geosynchronous Earth Orbit (GEO) places the satellite in a position where it rotates Earth at the same rate the Earth rotates on its axis (approximately 22,300 nautical miles (nm) above the equator). In some cases, this allows the satellite to see approximately one-third of the planet's surface. This orbit is best suited for worldwide communications, surveillance, reconnaissance, weather, and missile warning.

Highly Elliptical Orbit (HEO) mimic the benefits of GEO by employing elliptical orbits over the planet. It places the highest point of the ellipse (apogee) over the area of concern and the lowest point (perigee) at a point closest to the planet. In some cases, the apogee is 25,000 nm above the planet and the perigees is as close as a few hundred miles. The spacecraft operates over its area of concern for about 10-12 hours per day. HEO is typically used for communications, surveillance and weather satellites by nations at higher latitudes such as the RF and Scandinavian nations.

exploration probes throughout our Solar system and beyond. Neither Johnson nor Dulles could have imagined how "alien" and how "problematic" the space domain would become over the next six decades.

NATIONAL SECURITY CONCERNS

Just as in the nuclear arms race in the late 1950s and early 1960s, the Soviets and Americans dominated the space domain by inserting mostly military intelligence and communications satellites into orbit. Today, the orbital planes around the planet are now congested and contested with over 1,957 operational satellites owned by sixty-four nations and a variety of corporate consortia (Union of Concerned Scientists 2018), a number that has increased drastically in the last five years with the launch of constellations composed of hundreds or thousands of smaller satellites. The collective global dependence on satellites reaches beyond strictly military applications to civil, diplomatic, and commercial applications ranging from emergency response communications to treaty compliance to environmental surveillance to support a variety scientific and commercial purposes. The United States now considers "Any harmful interference with or an attack upon critical components of our space architecture that directly affects this vital US interest will be met with a deliberate response at the time, place, manner, and domain of our choosing" (Trump, National Security Strategy of the United States of America 2017).

Medium Earth Orbit (MEO) does not have a set distance from the planet but is estimated to midway between Low Earth Orbit (a few hundred miles) to GEO (22,300 nm). HEO enables a satellite to cover the same portion of the Earth every 12 hours. The GPS constellation uses this orbit, as do some communications satellites.

Low Earth Orbit (LEO) is within a few hundred miles of the Earth surface (the International Space Station (ISS) orbits at 248 nm or 400 kilometers). They are in view of an area of concern for approximately 90-100 minutes. LEO is ideal for intelligence, surveillance, and reconnaissance (ISR), environmental monitoring, and communications (Joint Staff 2018).

Boundaries

Like land, maritime, and air, the space domain is a physical domain. Unlike the other physical domains, space does not have a universally accepted boundary. The strictest definition establishes space at the point where one escapes all the Earth's atmospheric effect, ~521 nm or 965 km. The Fédération Aéronautique Internationale (FAI) recognizes the Kármán Line [46] set at ~54 nm or 100 km, whereas National Aeronautics and Space Administration (NASA) sets the boundary at ~44nm or ~80km (NOAA 2016). Even within the American government a clearly defined definition does not exist as its military sets the space boundary at the point where "the atmospheric effect on airborne objects becomes negligible" (Joint Staff 2018).

Some, like Jonathan McDowell of the Harvard-Smithsonian Center for Astrophysics, believe it is important to define where airspace ends, and space begins. It is their belief that "Once you agree on a boundary of space, you agree on a boundary where space law applies." Although the USA does not support a formal delineation of space, it recognizes "spaceflight is a global challenge" and encourages other spacefaring nations to behave in a "safe and responsible" manner (Trump, Space Policy Directive-3, National Space Traffic Management Policy 2018). Those supporting a formal demarcation of space believe "maintaining a distinct boundary will be crucial, given an increase in the number of national space programs and in private spaceflight endeavors that are boosting the amount of suborbital traffic" (Drake 2018).

---

[46] Kármán Line, named after Theodore von Kármán, a Hungarian-American mathematician, aerospace engineer, and physicist, is the point where the atmosphere becomes too thin to support aeronautical flight. Vehicles flying above this point are no longer considered airplanes but spacecraft (MessageToEagle.com 2017).

LEGAL PROTECTIONS

Boundaries and laws affecting the space domain did not exist when the Soviets launched Sputnik in October 1957. According to Donald A. Quarles, former Secretary of the Air Force (1955-1957), "the Russians have ... done us a good turn, unintentionally, in establishing the concept of freedom of international space" (McDougall 1985). As the Soviets and Americans continued to build and launch satellites, the United Nations acted upon the need to protect space for all humanity. Over the next several decades, these protections manifested themselves in five international treaties [47] and five sets of principles [48]. They address a variety of issues to include:

> "... the preservation of the space and Earth environment, liability for damages caused by space objects, the settlement of disputes, the rescue of astronauts, the sharing of information about potential dangers in outer space, the use of space-related technologies, and international cooperation. A number of fundamental principles guide the conduct of space activities, including the notion of space as the province of all humankind, the freedom of exploration and use of

---

[47] Treaties: Treaty on Principles Governing the Activities of States in the Exploration and Use of Outer Space, including the Moon and Other Celestial Bodies (1967); Agreement on the Rescue of Astronauts, the Return of Astronauts and the Return of Objects Launched into Outer Space (1968); Convention on International Liability for Damage Caused by Space Objects (1972); Convention on Registration of Objects Launched into Outer Space (1976); and Agreement Governing the Activities of States on the Moon and Other Celestial Bodies (1979)

[48] Principles: Declaration of Legal Principles Governing the Activities of States in the Exploration and Uses of Outer Space (1963); The Principles Governing the Use by States of Artificial Earth Satellites for International Direct Television Broadcasting (1982); The Principles Relating to Remote Sensing of the Earth from Outer Space (1986); The Principles Relevant to the Use of Nuclear Power Sources in Outer Space (1992); The Declaration on International Cooperation in the Exploration and Use of Outer Space for the Benefit and in the Interest of All States, Taking into Particular Account the Needs of Developing Countries (1996)

*outer space by all states without discrimination, and the principle of
non-appropriation of outer space" (United Nations Office of Outer
Space Affairs 2019).*

The 1967 Outer Space Treaty, formally known as the 1967 "Treaty on
Principles Governing the Activities of States in the Exploration and Use
of Outer Space, including the Moon and Other Celestial Bodies" and the
"Principles Relating to the Remote Sensing of Earth from Outer Space"
became particularly important as others joined the elite club of spacefaring nations. The Outer Space Treaty, signed and ratified by 107 nations to include the United States, China, Russia and North Korea [49]
guarantees all nations equal opportunity to conduct activities for
"peaceful purposes" in space, an environment that "is not subject to national appropriation by claim of sovereignty, by means of use or occupation, or by any other means" (United Nations 1967). The Principle protected the rights of all nations to use man-made orbiting satellites to
make "use of electromagnetic waves emitted, reflected, or diffracted
from the sensed object" (United Nations 1986).

STRATEGIC BENEFITS

The space domain provides military, civil, and corporate users within
the international community access to its inherent benefits of worldwide coverage for communications, navigation, timing sources, and access to denied areas within a nation's geographic boundaries. They enable functions such as intelligence collection, environmental surveillance, reconnaissance, and command and control (C2) of globally dispersed resources. When applied to military operations, space is a force
multiplier providing "speed, precision, accuracy, and clarity ... making
the force more lethal at less cost in lives and resources" (DOD 2018).

---

[49] Iran signed but did not ratify the 1967 Outer Space Treaty.

CRITICAL COMPONENTS

Although no formal internationally approved list exists, space critical components include those resources enabling access to space (i.e., space launch vehicles, telemetry sites, and command centers), the on-orbit satellite itself, the means to control the satellite (uplink) and access collected data (downlink) through ground stations transmitting commands and receiving data from satellites across the electromagnetic spectrum; and the processing, exploitation and dissemination of the data to users (Elbert 2014).

THREATS

The threats to the critical space components can be presented in a variety of means. They can be executed as a temporary, reversible, and non-destructive means of *denying* capability or permanently *destroying* it (Wright, Grego and Gronlund 2005). A variety of means are available to deny or destroy space capabilities to include electromagnetic interference, high energy weapons, and physical kinetic attacks.

Non-kinetic denial attacks include electromagnetic interference (i.e., jamming [50] and spoofing [51] of uplink and downlink radio frequencies) and attacks using high energy weapons (i.e. lasers to dazzle [52] electro-optical sensors or destroy them and high-power microwaves to disrupt electronics on spacecraft). Kinetic attacks employ the physical means to permanently destroy or disable ground stations and satellites.

---

[50] Jamming interferes with the satellite's communications by overpowering uplink and downlink communication on its operating frequency (Wright, Grego and Gronlund 2005).

[51] Spoofing mimics the true signal to fool the user to use it instead of the real one (Wright, Grego and Gronlund 2005).

[52] Dazzling a satellite with a high-powered ground-based laser is intended to deny imagery satellites the ability to collect over a nation's territory. Lasers with enough power could permanently damage the on-board sensors or solar arrays used to generate the spacecraft's power. (Secure World Foundation 2018)

They range from persons employing a variety of means from sabotage to an assault of a ground station to the use of ground-based direct-ascent[53] and co-orbital[54] anti-satellite (ASAT) weapons to attack satellites in space. This also includes "maintenance" satellites that have manipulator arms that can cut, saw, drill, or bend satellite components, or simply pull an attacked satellite out of its intended orbit. Also see Trevithick 2021 for a description of Russia's "space cannon."[55]

"Satellites have no mothers." - Maj. Gen. Roger G. DeKok (deceased), Air Force Space Command's Director of Operations and Plans

---

[53] Direct ascent ASAT is a weapon launched from the surface of the planet intended to intercept a satellite in its orbit (Harrison, Johnson and Roberts 2018).

[54] Co-orbital ASAT is a weapon placed in an orbit that remains idle until commanded to autonomously maneuver to strike its intended target satellite. A variant of a co-orbital satellite includes an existing on-orbit satellite that is repurposed to intercept the target satellite in its orbit (Harrison, Johnson and Roberts 2018).

[55] Joseph Trevithick. "Here's Our Best Look Yet At Russia's Secretive Space Cannon, The Only Gun Ever Fired In Space," February 16, 2021. https://www.thedrive.com/the-war-zone/39277/heres-our-best-look-yet-at-russias-secretive-space-cannon-the-only-gun-ever-fired-in-space.

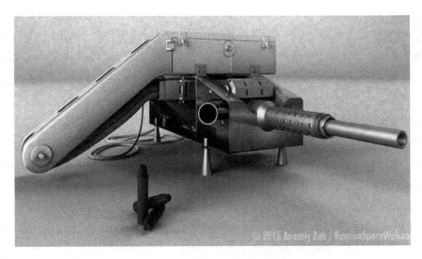

Figure 2. Russian Space Cannon 1975. Anatoly Zak.

ACTIONS BY CHALLENGERS

The *Interim National Security Guidance* published by the Biden administration specified four nations of concern, China, Russia, North Korea, and Iran. This section provides insight into their intentions as captured in national policy, technological capabilities, and cites specific examples of their use of that technology.

CHINA

China's Military Strategy published in 2015 stated "Outer space has become the commanding heights in international strategic competition" and that China "advocated [for] the peaceful use of outer space" and "opposed the weaponization of and arms race in outer space" (The State Council Information Office of the People's Republic of China 2015). The strategy continues assigning China's armed forces with the responsibility "to safeguard China's security and interests in new domains" to include space. It also states the China will "endeavor to realize the Chinese Dream of great national rejuvenation."

Like the United States and Russia, China views its space programs as a source of great national prestige. On 15 October 2003 it joined them as the only nations ever to independently launch an astronaut into orbit around the Earth (Space.com Staff 2005). Less than two decades later, China became the first nation to land a spacecraft [56] on the dark side of the Moon (Wall, Space.com 2019). Although this is a considerable accomplishment, according to Lieutenant General Zhang Yulin with the People's Liberation Army's (PLA) Strategic Support Force (SSF), "The Earth-Moon space will be strategically important for the great rejuvenation of the Chinese nation." He continues that "The future of China's manned space program, is not a Moon landing, which is quite simple, or even a manned Mars program which remains difficult, but continual exploration of the Earth-Moon space with ever developing technology" (Goswami 2018).

China has 284 satellites in space supporting military, civil, scientific, and commercial ventures. Some of these satellites, such as the Beidou, Haiyang, and Chuangxin, serve multiple purposes. Beidou navigation satellites which, like its US sister, has interwoven its services with military precision missile applications to commercial support to a full range of businesses from taxi drivers to ranchers (Jakhar 2018). While the Haiyang satellite supports the development of ports in coastal regions and resource exploration through environmental monitoring of the oceans (Barbosa 2018). Chuangxin satellites support China's disaster relief and economic development needs by collecting hydrological, meteorological, and electric power civil data (N2YO.com 2019).

China's space ground infrastructure stretches from tracking and control centers within its homeland to ground stations around the globe in

---

[56] The Chinese robotic spacecraft *Chang'e 4* is the first spacecraft to successfully touchdown on the dark side of the Moon.

both the Northern and Southern Hemispheres[57]. It is augmented by Yuan Wang tracking ships deployed to the Atlantic, Indian, and Pacific Oceans (GlobalSecurity.org n.d.).

China launched its first satellite on 24 April 1970 using a CSS-3 intercontinental ballistic missile (House of Representatives 1999). In 2018, China launched a total of thirty-eight successful space launch vehicles from its three launch sites, XiChang, Jiuquan, and Taiyaun. In comparison with the United States and Russia, this is nine and eighteen more than each nation respectively (Kyle 2018).

China is equally aggressive in its pursuit of capabilities to deny competitors' use of space. These counter-space capabilities include jammers, directed-energy weapons, and anti-satellite capabilities. (Office of the Secretary of Defense 2015). Open-source reporting does not provide much on China's suspected jamming and direct energy counter-space weapons. Though, considerable amounts of data are available on multiple anti-satellite capabilities. In 2007, China used a direct-ascent anti-satellite interceptor to destroy a Feng Yun-1 weather satellite in low Earth orbit (LEO) resulting in over 3,000 pieces of debris in orbit. Additionally in 2013, China launched the Dong Neng-2 followed by a Dong Neng 3 in 2015. These flight tests are believed to be direct-ascent weapons capable of destroying satellites in MEO and GEO such as GPS and ISR satellites respectively (Vasani 2017). Another variant of a potential Chines anti-satellite capability is a satellite able to inspect and repair on-orbit assets with an additional capability to clean-up space debris. The American Defense Intelligence Agency warns "this technology is dual-use because it could be used to damage another satellite" (Defense Intelligence Agency 2019). The Chinese Foreign Ministry called these allegations "groundless" (Capaccio 2019).

---

[57] Chinese ground stations are in Argentina, Australia, Chile, Kenya, Kiribati, Sweden, Namibia, and Pakistan (GlobalSecurity.org n.d.)

RUSSIA

Russia's space program is a source of great national pride and is a significant contributor to its national identity (A. A. Siddiqi 2010). In the early days of the Cold War, the Soviets achieved a number of firsts in space: the first man-made satellite in space (Sputnik, 4 October 1957); first animal in orbit (Laika, 3 November 1957); the first lunar fly-by (Luna-1, 2 January 1959); first lunar impact (Luna-2, 12 September 1959), the first man in space (Yuri Gagarin 12 April 1961); and the first woman in space (Valentina Tereshkova, 16 June 1963) (Howell 2018).

Today, as then, space provides Russia a means to achieve its national security objectives. According to the 2015 *Russian National Security Strategy*, its national security objectives include "safeguard[ing] its sovereignty" and "strengthen[ing] positions in the sphere of the exploration of space" (V. Putin 2015). In order to meet these objectives, Russia identified both the development of space technologies and space launch capabilities as national-level priorities (V. Putin 2011; amended 2015).

Unfortunately, Russia's lofty aspirations are balanced against the reality that its space program is, in the words of Pavel Luzin, a space analyst and university professor in the Russian city of Perm, in "decline [and in a] long-term crisis that is based on our inability to adapt our economics and scientific policy to a contemporary world" (Brown 2018). A major driver behind its decline is Russia's economic dependence on petroleum and gas exports and Western sanctions imposed on the Russian Federation following its annexation of Crimea. Russia's space budget in 2014 was $5 billion and in 2016 it was $1.6 billion (Karash 2016). Simply, Roscosmos is operating with expected budget shortfalls in the 100s of millions of dollars making it hard for Russia to afford space (Bodner 2017). Other factors negatively impacting the Russian space program include corruption, mismanagement, and launch failures (A. Siddiqi 2017).

Russian current capabilities in space include on-orbit satellites, an international ground architecture, space launch services, and counter-space capabilities. Russia possesses over 150 on-orbit military, commercial, and civil satellites (Union of Concerned Scientists 2018) providing electronic, optical, and radar intelligence collection needs, early warning, communications, navigation, and scientific research.

The Command and Measurement Complex operates and supports Russia's on-orbit assets. This ground infrastructure established in the 1950s supported the Soviet's intercontinental ballistic missile (ICBM) development and the launch of Sputnik. The original network consisted of thirteen stations extending from Saint Petersburg in the West to the Kamchatka Peninsula in the East. Today, the system extends beyond Russia's national borders across the globe to include Nicaragua (sputniknews.com 2015) and Antarctica with potential sites in South Africa and Australia (Zak 2018). It includes assets to command and control satellites, support missile tests, and conduct space situational awareness[58].

Russia operates space launch facilities within its territory to include Plesetsk, Dombarovskiy, and Vostochny and externally at Baikonur in Kazakhstan and from Guiana Space Center is French Guiana (ROSCOSMOS 2019). In 2018, Russia conducted twenty space launches while China and the United States successfully launched 38 and 29 respectively. Russia possesses of family of Soyuz space launch vehicles able to place a variety of satellites in LEO, HEO, and GEO.

Russian counter-space capabilities include both kinetic and non-kinetic capabilities as well as ground, air and space-based assets. Kinetic

---

[58] Space situational awareness (SSA) "the requisite current and predictive knowledge of space events, threats, activities, conditions and space system (space, ground, link) status capabilities, constraints and employment -- to current and future, friendly and hostile-- to enable commanders, decision makers, planners and operators to gain and maintain space superiority across the spectrum of conflict." (Curtis E. LeMay Center 2018)

capabilities include co-orbital and direct-ascent assets. One example of a possible co-orbital anti-satellite, identified as Kosmos-2519 was launched 23 June 2017. According to Russian authorities, the satellite deployed a satellite which later maneuvered to inspect another on-orbit satellite. According to the United States Assistant Secretary of State for Arms Control, Verification, and Compliance, the satellites behavior is "inconsistent with anything seen before from on-orbit inspection or space situational awareness capabilities" (Wolfgang 2018).

The PL19 Nudol direct-ascent anti-satellite complements Russian co-orbital capabilities. On 26 March 2018, a Nudol was test launched from a mobile launcher from the Plesetsk Cosmodrome (Panda 2018). Other anti-satellite capabilities include ground-based and airborne high-powered lasers such as the one deployed aboard the Beriev A-60 jet. The airborne variant has reportedly completed testing and has reported illuminated, but not destroyed a Japanese satellite at 810 nm or 1500 km (Cenciotti 2016).

Non-kinetic space capabilities include ground-based radar, communications, and navigation jammers. Reports indicate Russia used its jamming capabilities in the Ukraine and Syria. These jammers such as the R-330Zh and R-381T2 effect satellite communications. Other jammers such as the Pole-21 interact with GPS navigation and timing signals (Harrison, Johnson and Roberts 2018).

North Korea: The North Korean space program is managed by the National Aerospace Development Administration (NADA). Although NADA announced an ambitious National Space Development plan which included a satellite communications system by 2019 (Persio 2017), and a mission to the Moon (Ghoshal 2018), DPRK has no operational satellites on-orbit [59]. Although North Korea possesses ballistic missile and

---

[59] North Korea has attempted to place satellites on orbit six times since 1998. Of those six attempts, only two resulted in orbital insertion of a satellite. In both instances,

space launch technology, it is assessed to not possess either a direct-ascent or co-orbital ASAT. It is believed they are limited to jamming civilian GPS signals (Secure World Foundation 2018) localized to the Korean peninsula. In 2016, GPS jamming was reported near the North Korea-South Korea border (Evans 2016).

IRAN

Iran views its space program as a source of national pride. Although the nation possesses ballistic missile and space launch technology it has yet to place a satellite on-orbit. Iran intends to launch its first satellite in 'near future' but a specific date has not been announced. Additionally, the head of the Iranian Space Agency, Morteza Barari announced in December 2018 his nation's intent to manufacture telecommunications satellites (FARS News Agency 2018). Iran's counter-space capabilities are limited to inference with GPS and possibly commercial satellites (Defense Intelligence Agency 2019).

DETERRENCE STRATEGY

Creating and implementing a strategy to deter irresponsible behavior in the space domain relies primarily on all parties understanding what is at risk. Irresponsible actions in the space domain, driven by miscalculation, misinterpretation, or initiated purely accidentally, place at risk capabilities nations consider critical to their instruments of national power. Depending on the severity, these acts may drive unintended responses by the nation impacted by the act to the nation initiating the infraction.

The modern American military definition of deterrence is "the prevention of action by the existence of a credible threat of unacceptable

---

the satellites failed to transmit (Jones 2017). The latest attempt came in December 2017 with the launch of the Kwangmyongsong-5 Earth-exploration satellite (Ghoshal 2018).

counteraction and/or belief that the cost of action outweighs the perceived benefits" (Joint Staff 2018). But this definition simply creates a contingent threat. General Selva, a former Vice Chairman of the Joint Chiefs of Staff reinforced this definition stating "If you attack me, I have the capacity to return that attack, and I will return it with a degree of violence that is commensurate with the violence you've done to me. If you can accept that, then we reach a state of equilibrium" (Garamone 2017). General Selva's definition highlights the need for technological resilience to attack. But to prevent an aggressive act from initiating unrestricted escalation, deterrence strategies must reinforce technology with relationships between nations to establish the "conditions under which deterrence will succeed" (Zagare 1985).

TECHNOLOGICAL SAFEGUARDS

In the early days of the Space Age, access to space was restricted by how much treasure a nation was going to invest. Given the restrictive nature of space access and the relative lack of competition with the domain, spacefaring nations operated with an accepted level of mutual vulnerability. As access to space became less fiscally restrictive the mutual vulnerability between rivals became more complicated as more spacefaring nations entered the domain. This new dynamic within the space domain meant that a nation must worry about the ability of multiple parties to deny, degrade, or destroy its space assets. A nation possessing capabilities has the ability to attack--the intent to use these capabilities depends on the state of nature between nations. Some like Kenneth Waltz believe the state of nature is the state of war" and "because some states may at any time use force, all states must be prepared to do so or live at the mercy of their militarily more vigorous neighbors" (Waltz 1979 reissued 2010). It is this realist approach that drives the need for constant readiness to defend oneself from attack as well as respond to an attack.

Resilient space architectures provide the safeguards to deliver defensive and offensive capabilities. It integrates defense of vulnerable critical components using encryption and firewalls to protect data and access, new jam and intercept resistant waveforms for up- and downlink communications, and maneuverable satellites to avoid anti-satellite capabilities. The intent of these efforts is to increase the cost of entry for would-be aggressors to deny, disable, or destroy critical components and the services they provide. In the words of a former United States Air Force Space Commander General Shelton, "Resilience is the ability of a system architecture to continue providing required capabilities in the face of system failures, environmental challenges, or adversary actions" (Air Force Space Command 2013).

CONFIDENCE BUILDING MEASURES

In addition to resilient architectures, deterrence in the space domain depends upon implementing confidence building measures. The intent of these measures is to resolve misunderstandings, clarify misinterpretations, and explain accidents from inadvertently escalating a situation to actual conflict.

The global nature of the space domain emphasizes the need to balance the conflicting demands of national sovereignty and international interests. To address these demands, the international community, specifically the United Nations and the other international bodies, must engage and deliver diplomatic mechanisms establishing norms of acceptable behavior and forums to peacefully resolve issues before conflicts emerge.

Confidence building measures create decision space for leaders. By creating decision space, leaders can more accurately measure risk to ensure proportionality of a response. This prevents the absurdity of temporary low-scale space activities such as satellite jamming or the denial of service resulting in retaliatory strikes disabling or destroying critical components.

CONCLUSION

Today, strategic attack is no longer restricted to the confines of combat operations. In the words of General Gerasimov, the Russian Chief of the General Staff, "there is no longer a clear delineation between war and peace" (Kramer 2019). If this is the case, then the belief that war occurs when deterrence fails is no longer true. Instead, the concepts put forth by Waltz emphasizing the realpolitik idea that we are always at some level of war exists. Among the many benefits of operations in the space domain, the assets used to achieve one objective can be used for several others. This attribute allows the asset owner to maneuver within the ambiguity while pausing the actions of their competitors.

To counter the effects of a constant state of war, deterrence in space must be executed as a campaign through all phases of conflict including nominal "peace.". The fundamental strategy is to assume a position of strength. This is achieved by building a resilient architecture complemented by confidence building measures designed to prevent inadvertent escalation by creating channels to resolve issues stemming from the misinterpretation of an action, miscommunication of intent, and inadvertent or accidental application of effects. These measures also serve to resolve incidents purposefully initiated either by hubris or fear at the lowest phases of conflict. These confidence building measures include the need for productive relationships between rivals, the establishment of norms of behavior, and the exercising of restraint to prevent emotions from clouding the judgment of decision makers. Through the combination of these measures, harmful momentum is dampened allowing a state of strategic stability to flourish. In this state, sovereign nations can pursue national interests while adhering to established international norms.

Bibliography

Air Force Space Command. 2013. *Resiliency and Disaggregated Space Architectures.* White Paper, Colorado Springs: United States Air Force Space Command.

Anderson, Collin, and Karim Sadjadpour. 2018. *Iran's Cyber Threat.* Washington DC: Carnegie Endowment for International Peace.

Andrewes, A. 1962. "The Mytilene Debate: Thucydides 3.36-49." *Phoenix* (Classical Association of Canada) 16 (2): 64-85. Accessed December 5, 2018. www.jstor.org/stable/1086942.

Babb, Robin, David DellaVolpe, Nick Miller, and Gordon Muir. 2014. *War Gamers' Handbook.* Edited by Shawn Burns. Newport, RI: War Gaming Department, U. S. Naval War College.

Barbosa, Rui C. 2018. "Haiyang-1C launched by China's Long March 2C." *NASAspaceflight.com,* 6 September. Accessed February 18, 2019. https://www.nasaspaceflight.com/2018/09/haiyang-1-launched-by-chinas-long-march-2c/.

Barlow, John P. 1996. "A Declaration of the Independence of Cyberspace." Accessed March 5, 2019. http://editions-hache.com/essais/pdf/barlow1.pdf.

Barros, Andrew. 2009. "Bombing and Restraint in 'Total War', 1915-1918." *The Historical Journal* (Cambridge University Press) 52 (2): 413-431. https://www.jstor.org/stable/40264177.

Becker, Jeff. 2021. *A STARCRUISER FOR SPACE FORCE: THINKING THROUGH THE IMMINENT TRANSFORMATION OF SPACEPOWER.* Texas National Security Review. 19 May. Accessed May 19, 2021. https://warontherocks.com/2021/05/a-starcruiser-for-space-force-thinking-through-the-imminent-transformation-of-spacepower/.

Berger, Eric. 2021. "The US military is starting to get really interested in Starship." *ars technica.* 1 June. Accessed June 1, 2021. https://arstechnica.com/science/2021/06/the-us-military-is-starting-to-get-really-interested-in-starship/.

Blair, Dennis C., and Jon M. Huntsman. 2013. *The Report of the Commission on the Theft of American Intellectual Property.* National Bureau of Asian Research.

Bodner, Matthew. 2017. "60 years after Sputnik, Russia is lost in space." *SpaceNews,* 4 October. Accessed February 23, 2019. https://spacenews.com/60-years-after-sputnik-russia-is-lost-in-space/.

Bolger-Cortez, Philip S. 2018. "Principles of Game Design." *Military Operations Research Society.* Washington, District of Columbia: MORS, 23 July.

Brodie, Bernard. 1958. *"The Anatomy of Deterrence".* U. S. Air Force Project Rand Research Memorandum, RAND Corporation.

Brodie, Bernard. 1957. "More About Limited War." *World Politics* 10 (1): 112-122. Accessed October 25, 2018. https://www.jstor.org/stable/2009228.

Brown, Chris. 2018. "Russian space program in 'crisis' as David Saint-Jacques set to balst off." *CBC News,* 28 November. Accessed February 23, 2019. https://www.cbc.ca/news/world/russian-space-program-in-crisis-as-david-saint-jacques-set-to-blast-off-1.4922114.

Bullough, Vern L. 1963. "The Roman Empire vs. Persia: A Study of Successful Deterrence." *The Journal of Conflict Resolution* (Sage Publications, Inc) 7 (1): 55-68. ttps://www.jstor.org/stable/172830.

Bury, John Bagnell. 1889. *A History of the Later Roman Empire: From Arcadius to Irene (AD 395 to AD 800).* London: MacMillian and Company.

Butterfield, John H. 2018. "SpaceCorp: 2025-2300 A.D." GMT Games. https://www.gmtgames.com/p-904-spacecorp-2nd-printing.aspx.

Caffrey, Matthew B. Jr. 2019. *On Wargaming: How Wargames Have Shaped History and How They May Shape the Future.* Newport: Naval War College Press.

Capaccio, Anthony. 2019. "China's Space Debris Cleanup May Be Cover Story, Pentagon Says." *Bloomberg,* 11 February. Accessed February

18, 2019. https://www.bloomberg.com/news/articles/2019-02-11/china-s-space-debris-cleanup-may-be-cover-story-pentagon-says.

Cenciotti, David. 2016. "Russia has completed ground tests of its high-energy airborne combat laser system." *The Aviationist*, 5 October. Accessed February 27, 2019. https://theaviationist.com/2016/10/05/russia-has-completed-ground-tests-of-its-high-energy-airborne-combat-laser-system/.

Chickering, Roger, and Stig Förster. 2005. "A World at Total War: Global Conflict and the Politics of Destruction 1937-1945." Edited by Roger Chickering, Stig Förster and Bernd Greiner. Cambridge: Cambridge University Press.

—. 2003. *Shadows of Total War*. Cambridge: Cambridge University Press.

Clausewitz, Carl von. 1984. *On War*. Princeton: Princeton University Press.

Coats, Daniel R. 2018. *Worldwide Threat Assessment of the US Intelligence Community*. Statement for the Record, Washington DC: Office of the Director of National Intelligence.

Compton, Jon. n.d. "Toward an Epistemology of Wargaming: A Drunkard's Walk."

Conn, Stetson. 1968. "Examples of Total War." Memorandum. https://history.army.mil/documents/misc/ocmh26.htm.

Connell, Michael, and Sarah Vogler. 2017. *Russia's Approach to Cyber Warfare*. Washington DC: CNA.

Curry, John. 2012. *The History of Wargaming Project*. Accessed April 4, 2021. http://www.wargaming.co/index.htm.

Curtis E. LeMay Center. 2018. *Annex 3-14 Counterspace Operations*. Maxwell Air Force Base, Alabama. Accessed February 25, 2019. https://www.doctrine.af.mil/Portals/61/documents/Annex_3-14/3-14-D04-SPACE-SSA.pdf.

Defense Intelligence Agency. 2019. *Challenges to Security in Space.* Washington DC: Defense Intelligence Agency. Accessed February 18, 2019. https://media.defense.gov/2019/Feb/11/2002088710/-1/-1/1/SPACE-SECURITY-CHALLENGES.PDF.

Defense Science Board. 2016. *Summer Study on Autonomy.* Washington DC: DOD.

2018. *Dictionary.com.* December. Accessed December 5, 2018. https://www.dictionary.com/browse/trireme.

DiNote, Christopher R. 2017. "Operation AZURE OSPREY: Wargaming Intelligence, Surveillance, and Reconnaissance." *Vigilance Horizons: ISR Research Task Force.* Maxwell AFB, AL: Air University, 29 August. https://www.airuniversity.af.edu/Portals/10/ISR/student-papers/AY16-17/Operation_AZURE_OSPREY--Wargaming_ISR.pdf.

DoD. 2018. "Interim Report on Organizational and Management Structure for the National Security Space Components of the Department of Defense." Accessed February 15, 2019. https://media.defense.gov/2018/Mar/07/2001887047/-1/-1/1/Interim-Report-on-Organizational-and-Management-Structure-for-the-National-Security-Space-Components-of-the-Department-of-Defense.PDF.

DOD. 2017. *Military Securiy Developments involving the Democratic People's Republic of Korea.* Report to Congress, Washington DC: Department of Defense (DOD).

DOD. 2018. *Summary of the 2018 National Defense Strategy of the United States of AMerica.* Washington DC: Department of Defense.

—. 2018. *Summary: Department of Defense Cyber Strategy.* Washington DC: Department of Defense.

Douhet, Giulio. 1942. *The Command of the Air.* Translated by Dino Ferrari. New York: Coward-McCann.

Downes-Martin, Stephen. 2013. "Adjudication: The Diabolus in Machina of War Gaming." *Naval War College Review* 66 (3): 67-81.

—. 2012. "Speakers Notes: Your Boss, Players, and Sponsor: the Three Witches of Wargaming." *Connections 2012 Conference, Panel: Wargaming in Support of Defense Decision Making.* Washington, District of Columbia: National Defense University. 1-10.

Drake, Nadia. 2018. "Where, exactly, is the edge of space? It depends on who you ask." *National Geographic.* 20 December. Accessed February 16, 2019. https://www.nationalgeographic.com/science/2018/12/where-is-the-edge-of-space-and-what-is-the-kármán-line/.

Dunnigan, James F. 2000. *Wargames Handbook, Third Edition: How to Play and Design Commercial and Professional Wargames.* Lincoln: Writers Club Press.

Edwards, Jane. 2021. *Gen. John Raymond: Space Force Seeks to 'Move at Speed' Through Partnerships.* ExecutiveMosaic. 10 May. Accessed May 10, 2021. https://www.executivegov.com/2021/05/gen-john-raymond-space-force-seeks-to-move-at-speed-through-partnerships/.

Eklund, Phil. n.d. "High Frontier 4 All." ION Game Design/Sierra Madre Games. https://ionsmg.com/products/high-frontier-4-all.

Elbert, Bruce R. 2014. *The Satellite Communications Ground Segment and Earth Station Handbook.* Second Edition. Boston: Artech House.

Erwin, Sandra. 2019. *Trump formally reestablishes US Space Command at White House ceremony.* 29 August. Accessed December 11, 2020. https://spacenews.com/usspacecom-officially-re-established-with-a-focus-on-defending-satellites-and-deterring-conflict/.

Esper, Mark T. 2020. *Defense Space Strategy Summary (Unclassified).* Unclassified Summary Report of Classified Strategy, Department of Defense, Office of the Secretary of Defense, Pentagon: Department of Defense. Accessed April 3, 2021. https://media.defense.gov/2020/Jun/17/2002317391/-1/-1/1/2020_DEFENSE_SPACE_STRATEGY_SUMMARY.PDF?source=email.

Evans, Stephen. 2016. "North Korea 'jamming GPS signals' near South border." *BBC News*, 01 April. Accessed February 17, 2019. https://www.bbc.com/news/world-asia-35940542.

Everts, Sarah. 2015. "A Brief History of Chemical War." *Distillations*, Spring. Accessed December 16, 2018. https://www.sciencehistory.org/distillations/magazine/a-brief-history-of-chemical-war.

FARS News Agency. 2018. *MSN Middle East.* 19 December. Accessed February 18, 2019. https://www.msn.com/en-xl/middleeast/top-stories/minister-iran-to-launch-1st-operational-satellite/ar-BBRaHx9.

Federal Research Division. 2012. *Iran's Ministry of Intelligence and Security: A Profile.* Washington DC: The Library of Congress.

Fielder, James "Pigeon." 2020. "Reflections on Teaching Wargame Design." *War on the Rocks.* 1 January. Accessed January 4, 2020. https://warontherocks.com/2020/01/reflections-on-teaching-wargame-design/.

—. 2020. *Start on Day 3: Liminality in High-Stress Wargames.* 5 November. Accessed January 4, 2021. https://www.ludogogy.co.uk/article/start-on-day-3-liminality-in-high-stress-wargames/.

Fixler, Annie, and Frank Cilluffo. 2018. *Evolving Menace: Iran's Use of Cyber-Enabled Economic Warfare.* Washington DC: Foundation for Defense of Democracies. Accessed February 28, 2019. https://www.fdd.org/wp-content/uploads/2018/11/REPORT_IranCEEW.pdf.

Floridi, Luciano. 2014. *The 4th Revolution: How the Infoshere is Reshaping Human Reality.* Oxford: Oxford University Press.

Fowlkes-Childs, Blair. 2003. *The MET: The Sasanian Empire (224–651 A.D.).* October. Accessed December 3, 2018. https://www.metmuseum.org/toah/hd/sass/hd_sass.htm.

Friedman, George. 2009. *The Next 100 Years: A Forecast for the 21st Century.* New York: Anchor Books.

Garamone, Jim. 2017. "Selva Discusses Nature of Nuclear Deterrence at Mitchell Institute Forum." *DoD News, Defense Media Activity.* 3 August. Accessed December 4, 2018. https://www.jcs.mil/Media/News/News-Display/Article/1266853/selva-discusses-nature-of-nuclear-deterrence-at-mitchell-institute-forum/.

Gertz, Bill. 2021. "Space Force general: Chinese lasers, jammers threaten GPS satellites." *The Washington Times.* Washington, District of Columbia, 10 May. Accessed May 10, 2021. https://www.washingtontimes.com/news/2021/may/10/air-force-gen-john-w-raymond-chinese-lasers-jammer/.

Ghoshal, Debalina. 2018. "North Korea's Toxic Space Program." *Gatestone Institute*, 22 October. Accessed February 17, 2019. https://www.gatestoneinstitute.org/13157/north-korea-space-program.

Gibson, William. 2000. *Neurmancer.* New York: ACE.

GlobalSecurity.org. n.d. *Chinese Space Facilities.* Accessed February 18, 2019. https://www.globalsecurity.org/space/world/china/facility.htm.

—. n.d. *Yuan Wang tracking ship.* Accessed February 18, 2019. https://www.globalsecurity.org/military/world/china/yuan-wang.htm.

Goswami, Namrata. 2018. "Waking Up to China's Space Dream." *The Diplomat*, 15 October. Accessed February 18, 2019. https://thediplomat.com/2018/10/waking-up-to-chinas-space-dream/.

Gov.UK. 2018. *Gov.UK.* 4 October. Accessed March 14, 2019. https://www.gov.uk/government/news/uk-exposes-russian-cyber-attacks.

Haines, Avril. 2021. *2021 Annual Threat Assessment of the US Intelligence Community.* Unclassified Analysis Report, April, Office of the Director of National Intelligence, Washington: Director of National Intelligence. Accessed April 13, 2021.

https://www.dni.gov/files/ODNI/documents/assessments/ATA-2021-Unclassified-Report.pdf.

Harrison, Todd, Kaitlyn Johnson, and Thomas G. Roberts. 2018. *Space Threat Assessment 2018*. Assessment, Washington DC: Center for Strategic and International Studies.

Herman, Mark, Mark Frost, and Robert Kurtz. 2009. *Wargaming for Leaders*. New York: McGraw-Hill.

Hilgers, Philipp von. 2012. *War Games: A History of War on Paper*. Translated by Ross Benjamin. Cambridge, MA: The MIT Press.

Hobbes, Thomas. 1660, first digital edition 2017. *The Leviathan*. Edited by Anna Ruggieri. Kindle Edition.

House of Representatives. 1999. *Report of the Select Committee on U. S. National Security and Military/Commercial Concerns with the People's Republic of China*. 105-851, Washington DC: Government Printing Office (GPO).

Howell, Elizabeth. 2018. "Roscosmos: Russia's Space Agency." *Space.com*, 30 January. Accessed February 23, 2019. https://www.space.com/22724-roscosmos.html.

Huth, Paul K. 1999. "Deterrence and International Conflict: Empiracle Findings and Theoretical Debates." *Annual Review of Political Science*, June: 25-48. https://www.annualreviews.org/doi/pdf/10.1146/annurev.polisci.2.1.25.

ICJ. 1996. "Legality of the Threat or use of Nuclear Weapons." *International Court of Justice*. 8 July. Accessed April 2, 2018. http://www.icj-cij.org/files/case-related/95/095-19960708-ADV-01-00-EN.pdf.

ICRC. 2010. *Protocols Additional to the Geneva Conventions of 12 August 1949*. Geneva: International Committee of the Red Cross (ICRC).

Jabbari, Cyrus. 2018. *UNODA*. 25 October. Accessed March 6, 2019. https://www.un.org/disarmament/update/the-application-of-international-law-in-cyberspace-state-of-play/.

Jakhar, Pratik. 2018. "How China's GPS 'rival' Beidou is plotting to go global." *BBC News*, 20 September. Accessed February 18, 2019. https://www.bbc.com/news/technology-45471959.

Johnson-Freese, Joan. 2019. "China launched more rockets into orbit in 2018 than any other country." *MIT Technology Review*, 19 December. Accessed February 18, 2019. https://www.technologyreview.com/s/612595/china-launched-more-rockets-into-orbit-in-2018-than-any-other-country/.

2017. *Joint Publication 1-0: Doctrine for the Armed Forces of the United States*. Washington DC: Department of Defense.

Joint Staff. 2018. *Joint Publication 3-0: Joint Operations*. Washington District of Columbia: Department of Defense.

—. 2018. *Joint Publication 3-12: Cyberspace Operations*. Washington DC: Department of Defense.

—. 2018. *Joint Publication 3-14 Space Operations*. Washington DC: Department of Defense.

—. 2017, Change 1 2018. *Joint Publication-1: Joint Operations*. Washington DC: Department of Defense.

Jones, Morris. 2017. "North Korea's space program aims higher." *The Interpreter*, 31 October. Accessed February 17, 2019. https://www.lowyinstitute.org/the-interpreter/north-korea-space-program-aims-higher.

Jun, Jenny, Scott LaFoy, and Ethan Sohn. 2015. *North Korea's Cyber Operations: Strategy and Responses*. Lanham: Rowman and Littlefield.

Kahn, Herman. 2017. *On Escalation: Metaphors and Scenarios*. New York: Routledge.

Kahn, Herman. 1960. *The Nature and Feasibility of War and Deterrence*. Santa Monica : The Rand Corporation.

Karash, Yuri. 2016. "Russian Space Program: financl state, current plans, ambitions and cooperation with the United States." The Space Congress Proceedings. Accessed February 26, 2019.

https://commons.erau.edu/cgi/viewcontent.cgi?article=3648&cont
ext=space-congress-proceedings.

Kimball, Darryl, and Kingston Reif. 2012. *Arms Control Association.* 1
August. Accessed January 20, 2019.
https://www.armscontrol.org/factsheets/abmtreaty.

Kissinger, Henry. 1969. *Nuclear Weapons and Foreign Policy.* New York:
W. W. Norton & Company, Inc.

Koblentz, Gregory D. 2014. *Strategic Stability in the Second Nuclear Age.*
Council Special Report, Council on Foreign Relations.

Kramer, Andrew E. 2019. "Russian General Pitches 'Inofrmation'
Operations as a Form of War." *The New York Times*, 02 March.
Accessed March 4, 2019.
https://www.nytimes.com/2019/03/02/world/europe/russia-
hybrid-war-gerasimov.html.

Krauthammer, Charles. 1990. "The Unipolar Moment." *Foreign Affairs*
70 (1): 23-33. http://www.jstor.org/stable/20044692.

Kyle, Ed. 2018. *Space Launch Report.* 29 December. Accessed February
25, 2019. http://www.spacelaunchreport.com/log2018.html#site.

Langham, Gary. 2013. *Threat v's Risk.* IMSL.
http://intelmsl.com/insights/other/threat-vs-risk/.

Launius, Roger D. 1995. "Prelude to the Space Age." In *Exploring the
Unknown: Selected Documents in the History of the US Civil Space
Program, Volume I,* by John M. Logsdon, Linda J. Lear, Jannell
Warren-Findley, Ray A. Williamson and Dwayne A. Day.
Washington DC: NASA.

—. 2019. *Sputnik and the Origins of the Space Age.* Accessed February 09,
2019. https://history.nasa.gov/sputnik/sputorig.html.

LBS Consultancy. n.d. *Professional Wargaming Explains: What is
Wargaming?* http://lbsconsultancy.co.uk/our-approach/what-is-it.

Lebow, Richand Ned. 2007. "Thucydides and Deterrence." *Security
Studies* 163-188. Accessed December 5, 2018.
doi:10.1080/09636410701399440.

Lebow, Richard Ned, and Janice Gross Stein. 1995. "Deterrence and the Cold War." *Political Science Quarterly* (The Academy of Political Science) 110 (2): 157-181. doi:10.2307/2152358.

Lee, Connie, and Jon Harper. 2020. *BREAKING: Pentagon Unveils New Defense Space Strategy.* 17 June. Accessed May 2, 2021. https://www.nationaldefensemagazine.org/articles/2020/6/17/pen tagon-unveils-new-defense-space-strategy.

Leiner, Barry M., Vinton G. Cerf, David D. Clark, Robert E. Kahn, Leonard Kleinrock, Daniel C. Lynch, Jon Postel, Larry G. Roberts, and Stepher Wolff. 1997. "Brief History of the Internet." *Internet Society.* Accessed March 3, 2019. https://www.internetsociety.org/internet/history-internet/brief-history-internet/?gclid=Cj0KCQiAk-7jBRD9ARIsAEy8mh7jDjUh1dLUlb1xEw0-hf58A4F0FCjoWFZavExENbweTvthobRTv0kaAirPEALw_wcB.

LeMay Center for Doctrine. 2017. *Annex 3-70 Strategic Attack.* Maxwell Air Force Base: United States Air Force.

Levy, Jack S. 1985. "Theories of General War." *World Politics* (Cambridge University Press) 37 (3): 344-374. https://www.jstor.org/stable/2010247.

Lillard, John M. 2016. *Playing War: Wargaming and US Navy Preparations for World War II.* Lincoln: Potomac Books.

Luscombe, Richard, and Ian Sample. 2020. "SpaceX successfully launches Nasa astronauts into orbit." *The Guardian.* 30 May. Accessed November 11, 2020. https://www.theguardian.com/science/2020/may/30/spacex-nasa-crewed-spaceflight-launch-dragon-capsule-elon-musk-trump.

Magnuson, Stew. 2014. *US Military Stepping Up Space Cooperation with Japan, Australia.* 18 July. Accessed May 10, 2021. https://www.nationaldefensemagazine.org/articles/2014/7/18/us-military-stepping-up-space-cooperation-with-japan-australia.

Mattis, James N. 2018. *Nuclear Posture Review.* Washington DC: Department of Defense.

Mattis, JIm. 2018. *Summary of the 2018 National Defense Strategy of the United States of America.* Washington District of Columbia: Department of Defense.

McDougall, Walter A. 1985....*The Heavens and the Earth: A Political History of the Space Age.* New York: Basic Books.

McGrady, E.D. 2019. "GETTING THE STORY RIGHT ABOUT WARGAMING." *War on the Rocks.* 8 November. Accessed January 4, 2020. https://warontherocks.com/2019/11/getting-the-story-right-about-wargaming/.

MessageToEagle.com. 2017. "What is the Kármán Line?" *MessageToEagle.* 16 February. Accessed February 16, 2019. http://www.messagetoeagle.com/what-is-the-kármán-line/.

Mitchell, William "Billy." 1925. *Winged Defense: The Development of Modern Air Power--Economic and Military.* Tuscaloosa: University of Alabama.

Morag, Nadav. 2014. "Cybercrime, Cyberespionage, and Cybersabotage: Understanding Emerging Threats." College of Security Studies, Colorado Technical University. Accessed March 9, 2019. https://www.coloradotech.edu/media/default/CTU/documents/resources/cybercrime-white-paper.pdf.

Mukhatzhanova, G. 2017. "The Nuclear Weapons Prohibition Treaty: Negoiations and Beyond." *Arms Control Today* 47. https://www.armscontrol.org/act/2017-09/features/nuclear-weapons-prohibition-treaty-negotiations-beyond.

Murphy, Julia, and Max Roser. 2019. ""Internet."" *Published online at OurWorldInData.org.* Accessed March 2, 2019. https://ourworldindata.org/uploads/2018/09/Internet-users-by-world-region.png.

Murray, Andrew. 2012. "Uses and Abuses of Cyberspace: Coming to Grips with the Present Dangers." In *Realizing Utopia: The Future of International Law,* by Antonio Cassese, 496-507. Oxford: Oxford University Press.

N2YO.com. 2019. *Chuang Xin.* 18 February. Accessed February 18, 2019. https://www.n2yo.com/satellite/?s=40137.

NASA. 2005. "International Geophysical Year (IGY)." *NASA.* 02 February. Accessed February 15, 2019. https://history.nasa.gov/sputnik/usannounce.html.

—. 2013. *NASA.* 26 September. Accessed February 09, 2019. https://www.nasa.gov/mission_pages/station/news/orbital_debris. html.

—. 2007. *Sputnik adn the Dawn of the Space Age.* 10 October. Accessed February 15, 2019. https://history.nasa.gov/sputnik/.

NCSC. 2018. *Foreign Economic Espionage in Cyberspace.* Washington DC: National CounterIntelligence and Security Center.

Nebehay, Stephanie. 2008. "China, Russia to offer treaty to ban arms in space." *Reuters*, 25 January. Accessed February 27, 2019. https://www.reuters.com/article/us-arms-space/china-russia-to-offer-treaty-to-ban-arms-in-space-idUSL2578979020080125.

—. 2018. "Reuters World News." *Reuters.* 14 August. Accessed December 18, 2018. https://www.reuters.com/article/us-russia-usa-space/u-s-warns-on-russias-new-space-weapons-idUSKBN1KZ0T1.

NOAA. 2016. *National Oceanic and Atmospheric Administration (NOAA).* 22 February. Accessed February 10, 2019. https://www.nesdis.noaa.gov/content/where-space.

North, Robert C., Howard E. Koch, and Dina Z. Zinnes. 1960. "The Integrative Functions of Conflict." *The Journal of Conflict Resolution* 3: 355-74.

Norton. 2019. *Symantec Corporation.* Accessed March 11, 2019. https://us.norton.com/internetsecurity-malware-what-is-a-botnet.html.

Office of the Secretary of Defense. 2015. *Annual Report to Congress: Military and Security Developments Involving the People's Republic of China 2015.* Annual Report, Washington DC: Department of Defense. Accessed February 18, 2019.

https://dod.defense.gov/Portals/1/Documents/pubs/2015_China_M
ilitary_Power_Report.pdf.

Ohlin, Jens David, Kevin Govern, and Claire Finkelstein. 2015. "Cyber
War: Law and Ethics for Virtual Conflicts." *Oxford Scholarship Online.*
doi:10.1093/acprof:oso/9780198717492.003.0008.

ORF. 2014. *Observer Research Foundation (ORF).* 01 February. Accessed
March 6, 2019. https://www.orfonline.org/article/the-un-and-
cyberspace-governance/.

Overy, R. J. 1992. "Air Power and the Origins of Deterrence Theory
before 1939." *The Journal of Strategic Studies* 15 (1): 73-101.
doi:10.1080/01402399208437474.

Panda, Ankit. 2018. "Russia Conducts New Test of 'Nudol' Anti-Satellite
System." *The Diplomat,* 02 April. Accessed February 27, 2019.
https://thediplomat.com/2018/04/russia-conducts-new-test-of-
nudol-anti-satellite-system/.

Perla, Peter P. 1990. *Peter Perla's The Art of Wargaming: A Guide For
Professional's and Hobbyists.* 2011. Edited by John Curry. Middletown,
DE: The History of Wargaming Project.

Perla, Peter P., and E. D. McGrady. 2011. "Why Wargaming Works."
Naval War College Review 64 (3): 111-130.

Persio, Sofia Lotto. 2017. "Star Wars: North Korea Unveils Five Year
Plan to Conques Space." *Newsweek,* 30 October. Accessed February
17, 2019. https://www.newsweek.com/star-wars-north-koreas-
unveils-5-year-plan-conquer-space-695896.

Peterson, Jon. 2016. "A Game Out of All Proportions: How a Hobby
Miniaturized War." In *Zones of Control: Perspectives on Wargaming,*
edited by Pat Harrigan and Matthew G. Kirschenbaum, 3-31.
Cambridge, MA: The MIT Press.

Pifer, Steven, Richard C Bush, Vanda Felbab-Brown, Martin S. Indyk,
Michael O'Hanlon, and Kenneth M. Pollack. 2010. *US Nuclear and
Extended Deterrence: Considerations and Challenges.* Brookings.

Poole, Carl A., and Robert A. Bettinger. 2021. "Black Space versus Blue Space: A Proposed Dichotomy of Future Space Operations." Edited by Richard T. Harrison. *Air and Space Power Journal* (Air University) 35 (1): 4-18. Accessed April 11, 2021. https://www.airuniversity.af.edu/Portals/10/ASPJ/journals/Volume-35_Issue-1/F-Poole.pdf.

Popescu, Nicu. 2018. "Russia cyber sins and storms." European Council on Foreign Relations. Accessed March 4, 2019. https://www.ecfr.eu/article/commentary_russian_cyber_sins_and_storms.

Protalinski, Emil. 2012. "NSA: Cybercrime is 'the greatest Transfer of Wealth in History'." *ZDNet*, 10 July. http://www.zdnet.com/article/nsa-cybercrime-is-the-greatest-transfer-of-wealth-in-history/.

Putin, Vladimir. 2011; amended 2015. "Priority Directions Decree Number 899: Development of Science, Technologies and Technology in the Russian Federation." Moscow. Accessed February 23, 2019. https://policy.asiapacificenergy.org/node/2238.

Putin, Vladimir V. 2014. *The Miltary Doctrine of the Russian Federation.* Moscow: Russian Federation.

Putin, Vladimr. 2015. "Russian National Security Strategy." Moscow. Accessed February 2019, 2015. http://www.ieee.es/Galerias/fichero/OtrasPublicaciones/Internacional/2016/Russian-National-Security-Strategy-31Dec2015.pdf.

RAND. n.d. *Paul Baran and the Origins of the Internet.* Accessed March 3, 2019. https://www.rand.org/about/history/baran.html.

Raymond, John W. 2020. *Space Capstone Publication, Space Power: Doctrine for Space Forces.* Doctrine, Department of the Air Force, Pentagon: United States Space Force. https://www.peterson.spaceforce.mil/Portals/15/Space%20Capstone%20Publication_10%20Aug%202020.pdf.

Recorded Future. 2017. *North Korea Cyber Activity.* Recorded Future.

Reed, John. 2019. "Chinese hackers target Cambodia opposition ahead of elections." *Financial Times*, 10 July. Accessed March 14, 2019. https://www.ft.com/content/4d4482e6-84a0-11e8-96dd-fa565ec55929.

ROSCOSMOS. 2019. *ROSCOCMOS*. Accessed February 23, 2019. http://en.roscosmos.ru/119/.

—. 2019. *ROSCOSMOS Space Centers*. Accessed February 26, 2019. http://en.roscosmos.ru/30/.

Sabin, Philip. 2015. *Simulating War: Studying Conflict Through Simultion Games*. New York: Bloomsbury Academic.

Scardera, Michael P., and B T Cesul. 2021. "Media Interaction Warfare Theory." Edited by Richard T. Harrison. *Air and Space Power Journal* (Air University) 35 (1): 37-59. Accessed April 11, 2021. https://www.airuniversity.af.edu/Portals/10/ASPJ/journals/Volume-35_Issue-1/F-Scardera.pdf.

Schelling, Thomas C. 1981. *The Strategy of Conflict*. Cambridge: Harvard University Press.

Schelling, Thomas C., and Morton H. Halperin. 1961. *Strategy and Arms Control*. New York: The Twentieth Century Fund.

Schultz, George P., and Eduard A. Shevardnadze. 1988. *Agreement Between the United States of America and the UNion of the Soviet Socialist Republics on Notifications of Launches of Intercontinental Ballistic Missiles and Submarine-Launched Ballistic Missiles (Ballistic Missile Launch Notification Agreement)*. Treaty, Moscow: US Governemnt. https://www.state.gov/t/isn/4714.htm.

SCIO. 2015. *China's Military Strategy*. The State Council Information Office of the People's Republic of China (SCIO).

Secure World Foundation. 2018. *Global Counterspace Capabilities: An Open Source Assessment*. Assessment, Secure World Foundation.

Segal, Adam. 2017. "The Development of Cyber Norms at the United Nations Ends in Deadlock. Now What?" *Council on Foreign Affairs*.

Accessed March 6, 2019. https://www.cfr.org/blog/development-cyber-norms-united-nations-ends-deadlock-now-what.

Siddiqi, Asif A. 2010. "Competing Technologies, National(ist) Narratives, and Universal Claims: Toward A Global History of Space Exploration." *Technology and Culture* 51 (2): 425-443. Accessed February 23, 2019. https://www.jstor.org/stable/pdf/40647107.pdf?refreqid=excelsior%3A1f79f65913fb46c7eaf31f711f4ed6ad.

Siddiqi, Asif. 2017. "Russia's Space Program is Struggling Mightily." *Slate*, 21 March. Accessed February 25, 2019. https://slate.com/technology/2017/03/russias-space-program-is-in-trouble.html.

Simpson, William L., Jr. 2017. "A Compendium of Wargaming Terms." *US Naval War College, Research and Wargaming, Publications and Journals.* 20 September. Accessed April 24, 2021. https://dnnlgwick.blob.core.windows.net/portals/0/NWCDepartments/Wargaming%20Department/A%20Compendium%20of%20Wargaming%20Terms%2020%20Sept%202017.pdf?sr=b&si=DNNFileManagerPolicy&sig=BEh3XmMzUbqnHm2SIms6QAWn5YWCMWBWnU8Ira1Oud8%3D.

Smith, Malcolm. 1980. "A Matter of Faith: British Strategic Air Doctrine Before 1939." *Journal of Contemporary History* (Sage Publications, Ltd) 15 (3): 423-442. https://www.jstor.org/stable/260412.

Smith, Rich. 2021. "How SpaceX Could Become Space Force's No. 1 Defense Contractor." *The Motley Fool.* 1 June. Accessed June 1, 2021. https://www.fool.com/investing/2021/06/01/how-spacex-could-become-space-forces-no-1-defense/.

Soldatov, Andrei, and Irina Borogan. 2015. *The Red Web: The Struggle Between Russia's Digital Dictators and the New Online Revolutionaries.* New York: Pubic Affairs.

Space.com Staff. 2005. "Space.com." *Making History: China's First Human Spaceflight.* 28 September. Accessed February 16, 2019.

https://www.space.com/1616-making-history-china-human-spaceflight.html.

Speller, Elizabeth. 2003. *Following Hadrian: A Second Century Journey through the Roman Empire.* Oxford: Oxford University Press.

sputniknews.com. 2015. "Russia Establishes Satellite Ground Station on US Doorstep-German Media." *sputniknews.com*, 5 February. Accessed February 25, 2019. https://sputniknews.com/latam/201505021021637618/.

Staff of Strategy and Tactics Magazine. 1977. *Wargame Design: The History, Production, and Use of Conflict Simulation Games.* New York: Simulations Publications, Inc.

Stevens, Jon. 2018. *Internet Stats & Facts for 2019.* 17 December. Accessed March 02, 2019. https://hostingfacts.com/internet-facts-stats/.

2013. *Strategic Stability: Contending Interpretations.* Strategic Studies Institute and the U. S. Army War College Press.

Sunstein, Cass R. 2001. *Probability Neglect: Emotions, Worst Cases, and.* Working Papers, Chicago: University of Chicago Law School. https://chicagounbound.uchicago.edu/law_and_economics?utm_source=chicagounbound.uchicago.edu%2Flaw_and_economics%2F385&utm_medium=PDF&utm_campaign=PDFCoverPages.

Tabansky, Lior. 2011. "Basic Concepts of Cyber Warfare." *Military and Strategic Affairs* 3 (1): 75-92.

The State Council Information Office of the People's Republic of China. 2015. "China's Military Strategy." Strategy. https://jamestown.org/wp-content/uploads/2016/07/China%E2%80%99s-Military-Strategy-2015.pdf.

Theohary, Catherine A., and Anne I. Harrington. 2015. *Cyber Operations in DOD Policy and Plans: Issues for Congress.* Washington DC: Congressional Research Service.

Thucydides. 1954. *The History of the Peloponnesian War.* Translated by Rex Warner. London: Penguin Classics.

Trenchard, Hugh M. 1928. "Note by the First Sea Lord." London (PRO), AIR 9/8 COS 156,: Public Record Office.

2019. *Trend Micro.* March. Accessed March 11, 2019. https://www.trendmicro.com/vinfo/us/security/definition/distrib uted-denial-of-service-temp.

Trump, Donald J. 2020. *Establishment of United States Space Command as a Unified Combatant Command: Memorandum to the Secretary of Defense.* Presidential Document - Memorandum, Executive Office of the President, Executive Branch of the U.S Federal Government, Washington: Federal Register. Accessed May 30, 2021. doi:83 FR 65483.

—. 2018. *National Cyber Strategy of the United States of America.* Washington DC: White House.

Trump, Donald J. 2017. *National Security Strategy of the United States of America.* Washington DC: US Government.

Trump, Donald J. 2018. *Space Policy Directive-3, National Space Traffic Management Policy.* Presidential Memoranda, Washington DC: White House.

U. S. Department of State. 2018. "Outlaw regime: A Chronicle of Iran's Destructive Activities." U. S. Department of State, 31. https://www.state.gov/documents/organization/286410.pdf.

Union of Concerned Scientists. 2018. *UCS Satellite Database.* 30 November. Accessed February 09, 2019. https://www.ucsusa.org/nuclear-weapons/space-weapons/satellite-database#.XF8X_lxKiUk.

Union of Concerned Scientists. 2017. "Whose Finger Is on the Button? Nuclear Launch Authority in the United States and Other Nations." Accessed March 4, 2019. https://www.ucsusa.org/nuclear-weapons/us-nuclear-weapons-policy/sole-authority.

United Nations. 1945. *Charter of the United Nations and Statute of the International Court of Justice.* San Francisco: United Nations.

United Nations. 1945. *Charter of the United Nations and Statute of the International Court of Justice.* Charter, San Francisco: United Nations.

United Nations Office of Outer Space Affairs. 2019. *United Nations Office of Outer Space Affairs Space Law.* Accessed February 18, 2019. http://www.unoosa.org/oosa/en/ourwork/spacelaw/index.html.

United Nations. 1967. "United Nations Office of Outer Space Affairs." *Treaties and Principles.* 10 October. Accessed February 10, 2019. http://www.unoosa.org/oosa/en/ourwork/spacelaw/treaties/intro outerspacetreaty.html.

—. 1986. "United Nations Office of Outer Space Affairs." *Treaties and Principles.* Accessed February 10, 2019. http://www.unoosa.org/oosa/oosadoc/data/resolutions/1986/gener al_assembly_41st_session/res_4165.html.

United States Space Force. 2019. *About the United States Space Force.* 20 December. Accessed November 11, 2020. https://www.spaceforce.mil/About-Us/About-Space-Force/.

n.d. "UNOOSA." *United Nations.* Accessed December 14, 2018. http://www.unoosa.org/oosa/en/ourwork/spacelaw/nationalspacel aw/russian_federation/decree_5663-1_E.html.

US Department of Defense. 2010. *Nuclear Posture Review Report.* Washington DC: US Governemnt.

Vasani, Harsh. 2017. "How China is Weaponizing Outer Space." *The Diplomat,* 19 January. Accessed February 18, 2019. https://thediplomat.com/2017/01/how-china-is-weaponizing-outer-space/.

Verizon. 2013. *2013 Data Breach Investigation Report.* Verizon.

Wall, Mike. 2019. *Space.com.* 03 January. Accessed February 16, 2019. https://www.space.com/42883-china-first-landing-moon-far-side.html.

—. 2018. "Spaceflight." *Space.com.* 16 August. Accessed December 14, 2018. https://www.space.com/41511-weird-russian-satellite-not-so-abnormal.html.

Walter, Phil. 2016. "What is an Existential Threat." *Real Clear Defense.* 09 February. Accessed January 26, 2019.

https://www.realcleardefense.com/articles/2016/02/10/what_is_a
n_existential_threat_109009.html.

Walton, C. Dale. 2007. *Geopolitics and the Great Powers in the Twenty-first Century.* Abingdon: Taylor & Francis.

Waltz, Kenneth N. 1979 reissued 2010. *Theory of International Politics.* Long Grove: Waveland.

Weinzierl, Matt, and Mehak Sarang. 2021. "The Commercial Space Age Is Here." *Harvard Business Review.* 12 February. Accessed February 12, 2021. https://hbr.org/2021/02/the-commercial-space-age-is-here.

Wells, H. G. 1911/1913. *Floor Games and Little Wars.* 2016. Springfield, IL: Monroe St. Press.

Wells, Herbert George. 1908. *The War in the Air and Particularly how Mr. Bert Smallways Fared While It Lasted.* London: George Bell and Sons.

Welsh, Mark A. III. 2015. *Volume 1: Basic Doctrine of the United States Air Force.* Curtis E. LeMay Center. https://www.doctrine.af.mil/Portals/61/documents/Volume_1/Volume-1-Basic-Doctrine.pdf.

Werrell, Kenneth P. 1986. "The Strategic Bombing of Germany in World War II: Costs and Accomplishments." *The Journal of American History* (Oxford University Press on Behalf of Organization of American Historians) 73 (3): 702-713. https://www.jstor.org/stable/1902984.

Weuve, Christopher A., Peter P. Perla, Michael C. Markowitz, Robert Rubel, Stephen Downes-Martin, Michael Martin, and Paul V. Vebber. 2004. *Wargame Pathologies.* Analysis Paper, War Gaming Department, US Naval War College, Alexandria: The CNA Corporation. Accessed November 6, 2016. doi:CRM D0010866.A1/Final.

White House. 2015. *The White House President Barack Obama.* 25 September. Accessed March 17, 2019. https://obamawhitehouse.archives.gov/the-press-office/2015/09/25/fact-sheet-president-xi-jinpings-state-visit-united-states.

Wilson, Heather A., David L. Goldfein, John W. Raymond, and Samuel A. Greaves. 2017. "Department of the Air Force Presentation to the Subcommittee on Strategic Forces." *Military Space Policy.* Washington, District of Columbia: House of Representatives Armed Services Committee, 17 May. Accessed April 30, 2021. https://armedservices.house.gov/_cache/files/a/6/a64b0c4d-bf42-4ca7-862c-e67efdbe9412/2FC8F8210148E95EF3115A6C82AA9CDD.hmtg-116-as00-wstate-goldfeind-20190402.pdf.

Wolfgang, Ben. 2018. "US official raises alarm on Russia's satellites." *The Washington Times*, 14 August. Accessed February 27, 2019. https://www.washingtontimes.com/news/2018/aug/14/yleem-ds-poblete-raises-alarm-on-russias-satellite/.

Wright, David, Laura Grego, and Lisbeth Gronlund. 2005. *The Physics of Space Security: A Reference Manual.* Cambridge: American Academy of Arts and Sciences.

Wright, Gordon. 1968. *The Ordeal of Total War: 1939-1945.* New York: Harper & Row.

Xinhua. 2017. *New China.* 17 October. Accessed March 14, 2019. http://www.xinhuanet.com//english/2017-10/17/c_136686770.htm.

Yu, Jess Macy. 2018. "Chinese cyber-attacks on Taiwan government becoming harder to detect: source." *Reuters*, 15 June. Accessed March 14, 2019. https://www.reuters.com/article/us-taiwan-china-cybersecurity/chinese-cyber attacks-on-taiwan-government-becoming-harder-to-detect-source-idUSKBN1JB17L.

Zagare, Frank C. 1985. "Toward a Reformation of the Theory of Mutual Deterrence." *International Studies Quarterly* 29 (2): 155-169. https://www.jstor.org/stable/2600504?seq=1#metadata_info_tab_contents.

Zak, Anatoly. 2018. *RussianSpaceWeb.com.* 20 February. Accessed February 25, 2019. http://www.russianspaceweb.com/kik.html.

Zhang, Laney. 2018. "China: New Regulation on Police Cybersecurity Supervision and Inspection Powers Issued." *Library of Congress.* 13

November. Accessed March 14, 2019.
http://www.loc.gov/law/foreign-news/article/china-new-regulation-on-police-cybersecurity-supervision-and-inspection-powers-issued/.

CHAPTER 4: AN INTRODUCTION TO WARGAMING SPACE POWER: THREE DESIGN CONSIDERATIONS.[61]

BY COLONEL CHRISTOPHER R. DINOTE

INTRODUCTION

The first quarter of the twenty-first century has seen tremendous changes in military space policy, as we well as growth in space capabilities with major implications for national security. In May 2017 testimony before the Senate Subcommittee on Strategic Forces, then-Secretary of the Air Force Heather Wilson and then-Chief of Staff of the Air Force General David Goldfein formally named space a contested warfighting domain.[62] Joined by other space senior military leaders, they declared the era of unimpeded freedom of action enjoyed by the United States essentially over, going so far as to state that the benign environment the US took for granted for decades "no longer exists."[63] This assertion was reinforced by the unclassified 2020 Defense Space Strategy Summary, which highlighted the high vulnerability of the US defense

---

[61] The views expressed are the author's own and do not reflect the official positions of the United States Government, Department of Defense, or the United States Air Force.

[62] (Wilson, et al. 2017), 2.[Full bibliographic record for this and succeeding citations appearing in this chapter's footnotes may be found in the bibliography at the end of the chapter.]

[63] Ibid., 2.

space enterprise to the emerging capabilities of potential adversaries.[64] The open and public acknowledgment of this new strategic reality, where the US no longer enjoys uncontested access and exploitation of space, has led a multitude of changes in US defense policy.

The elevation of space into a warfighting domain coequal to land, maritime, air, and cyberspace was among the first of a rapid series of developments. In a memorandum to the Secretary of Defense dated December 18, 2018, then-President Trump directed the reestablishment of United States Space Command as the eleventh unified warfighting combatant command.[65] which formally activated on August 29, 2019.[66] This was followed quickly by the creation of the United States Space Force from Air Force Space Command on December 20, 2019.[67] In addition to this very public and at times controversial step, the other US armed services, as well as those of allies, partners, and major competitors Russia and the People's Republic of China are changing doctrine, creating new organizations, and developing new capabilities that will shape warfare for decades to come.

My motivation for writing this chapter is the fact that the Space Force's first doctrinal publication, the *Space Capstone Publication (SCP)* published in 2020 does not mention "wargame" or "wargaming" even once. However, the doctrine it describes, as well as its description of the space domain and the desired characteristics of military space forces, lend themselves very well to professional wargaming. Addressing the

---

[64] "The U.S. defense space enterprise was not built for the current strategic environment. The intentions and advancements of potential adversaries in space are threatening the ability of the United States to deter aggression, to protect U.S. national interests, and to fight and win future conflicts." (Esper 2020), 3.

[65] (Trump, Establishment of United States Space Command as a Unified Combatant Command: Memorandum to the Secretary of Defense 2020), 1.

[66] (Erwin 2019).

[67] (United States Space Force 2019).

key operational and strategic military problems inherent to this new world requires the full spectrum of cognitive tools available to military professionals, leaders, and policy makers. Wargaming should be one of the premier tools put to the task.[68]

PURPOSE

This chapter introduces foundational concepts about military wargaming, and how it may be used to explore novel and emerging space warfare problems. As this is a broad overview designed to spark further discussion and research, I first provide a very brief historical overview of wargaming useful to the layperson or those unfamiliar with professional wargaming. I will also define wargame and wargaming for purposes of this chapter, as well as some underlying theory about wargame utility. Out of respect for the newness of the Space Force, United States Space Command, and the concept of space power, this discussion will bias toward analytical or discovery wargames, rather than wartime training or educational games which may be more familiar to many readers. Explanation and definitions for these terms are included below.

The core of this chapter discusses three "design considerations" that can greatly impact the creation and effectiveness of space warfare games. These design elements are inferred by the unique topography of space as well as the characteristics of space-based capabilities, historical space norms, present and future disruptions of those norms, emerging doctrine, and emerging concepts of the Space Force's unique roles. This short list is not exhaustive but reflects research and analysis of both

---

[68] Readers will note that there is no consensus spelling on "war game" versus "wargame," or "war gaming" versus "wargaming." For simplicity's sake, the author has opted in favor of "wargaming" throughout this chapter, except where a direct citation uses "war game" or "war gaming." In the case of "space power," the author has opted to use the style and definition found throughout *Space Capstone Publication, Space Power: Doctrine for Space Forces* (Raymond 2020).

professional and commercial wargaming.[69] Furthermore, the design considerations are intended as a point of departure for further research and wargaming practice.

HISTORICAL NOTE: ORIGINS OF WARGAMING.[70]

Games about war are probably almost as old as war itself. Archaeological evidence implies that many ancient peoples created toys and games with a military theme that could conceivably have been used for more than just child's play.[71] The ancient Indian game of *chaturanga* dates to the sixth century Common Era, and featured horses, elephants, wagons, and foot soldiers.[72] In Europe chess reached its recognizable form by the sixteenth century, however it was already considered obsolete from the standpoint of a useful military training tool.[73] Many efforts to modify and modernize chess in attempt to restore its value for military training occurred throughout the seventeenth and eighteenth

---

[69] See especially (Dunnigan 2000), as well as *(Fielder, Reflections on Teaching Wargame Design* 2020).

[70] This section draws heavily on my previous work "Operation Azure Osprey," (DiNote 2017).

[71] "Wargames are probably only slightly younger than organized warfare. Archeologists have uncovered a group of Sumerian warriors marching in miniature phalanx, and a similar group of Egyptian miniatures has been found arrayed in full panoply. It is probable that the sons of the nobility...received their initial training with such miniatures. At some point, the play associated with these miniatures became stylized. From this stylized pastime sprang the true games that we play today, often without recognizing their military origins. Chess, Go, and kindred games. As a result of their development, wargames developed along dual lines, as a means for both military training and amusement." *(Staff of Strategy and Tactics Magazine* 1977), 2.

[72] See (DiNote 2017), 5-6, paraphrasing (Hilgers 2012), 166, note 82.

[73] "Throughout the seventeenth and eighteenth centuries, soldiers, scholars, even clergymen attempted to expand chess into a more complex form to restore its relevance." (DiNote 2017), 6, citing (Peterson 2016), 4-7.

centuries.[74] The most ambitious of these was by German academic Johann Hellwig in 1780, creating what was essentially a monster-sized version of chess with expanded types of pieces, terrain, and other features.[75] Hellwig's newly-coined word *kriegsspiel* became "the term by which games descending from Hellwig's work are still known to this day.".[76]

The major turning point, creating what we now recognize as a proper wargame, occurred in the early nineteenth century when Prussian nobleman Georg Leopold von Reisswitz, influenced by Prussia's defeat and humiliation by Napoleon, created his own *kriegsspiel* and broke with the tradition of attempting to refine chess.[77] His son Georg Heinrich developed the game much further, drawing on his experiences as a cavalry officer. He produced a revision in 1824 using topographic terrain on a sand table and wooden blocks bearing symbology to represent units. The younger von Reisswitz introduced many critical innovations that still influence and inform game design into the present. Chief among these

---

[74] "Late in the in the seventeenth century, the philosopher G. W. Leibniz hypothesized that 'one could represent with certain game pieces certain battles and skirmishes, also the position of the weapons and the lay of the land, both at one's discretion and from history' in a game that might be played by 'military colonels and captains' who would 'practice it instead of the chessboard." (Peterson 2016), 4-5.

[75] "In 1780, German academic Johann Hellwig created one of the most successful and influential attempts to substantially modify chess, with a larger board (1,617 squares), more pieces (208), gunpowder weapons, and movement-affecting terrain (mountains, forests, bodies of water). Even though this game could approximate a specific battle, he still faced the enduring design dilemma of all wargaming: realism versus playability." (DiNote 2017), 6, paraphrasing (Peterson 2016), 5.

[76] The term *kriegsspiel* first appears in Johann Christian Ludwig Hellwig, *Versuch eins aufs Schnachspiel gebauten taktischen Spiels von zwey und mechern Personen zu spielen* (Attempt to build upon chess a tactical game which two or more persons might play), 1780. (Peterson 2016), 5.

[77] Specifically in response to the Prussian defeat at Jena-Auerstadt and eight years of French occupation. (Peterson 2016), 7.

is the double-blind "fog of war," meaning that neither player has omniscient awareness of the disposition of enemy forces or strength without making contact or collecting intelligence. The treasure trove of statistical weapons performance data from the late Napoleonic wars combined with mathematically based combat resolution, provided a hitherto unseen level of simulation and realism. The use of probability tables and a neutral umpire to implement the orders of each player established the familiar form and flow of professional military wargaming and helped create its lexicon.[78]

Despite generating enthusiasm in the Prussian general staff, the von Reisswitz *kriegsspiel* produced mixed results in actual use and did not see widespread adoption in the Prussian military.[79] However, it greatly influenced the growth and development of professional military wargaming in the Western world throughout the late nineteenth and early twentieth centuries and became commonly used by many of the great powers. No less an authority than Fleet Admiral Chester Nimitz attributed success against the Japanese in the Second World War to the Naval War College games iterated again and again throughout the decades leading up to the war.[80]

We will conclude this section with a brief introduction to commercial wargaming. Commercial gaming has "crossed over" and influenced the development of professional wargaming in various waves over the twentieth and now twenty-first centuries. H.G. Wells can be named the originator of commercial wargaming, publishing *Floor Games* in 1911

---

[78] Adapted from (DiNote 2017), 6, paraphrasing (Peterson 2016), 7-9.

[79] (DiNote 2017), 7.

[80] (DiNote 2017), 7. My text and note summarize the following: "From an October 1960 speech given at the Naval War College: "[T]he war with Japan had been reenacted in the game rooms [at the Naval War College] by so many people and in so many different ways that nothing that happened during the war was a surprise—absolutely nothing except the kamikaze tactics towards the end of the war." (Lillard 2016) 1.

followed by *Little Wars* in 1913.[81] Both are easily recognizable to modern day wargamers as tabletop (or floor played) miniatures wargames. However, one must acknowledge the 1953 publication of Charles S. Roberts's *Tactics*, a combined arms land combat game, as the industry's founding moment.[82] For nearly seventy years now, the correspondence between commercial and professional wargaming brings to light methods, practices, and standards that provide a foundational understanding of what wargames are and what wargaming is, and how and why wargaming works.[83] Understanding these terms, despite a lack of consensus on their precise meaning, establishes a framework for applying wargaming to space power.

DEFINING CONTEMPORARY WARGAMES[84]

Despite the production and playing of thousands of professional and commercial wargames and the slow but steady growth of university courses, departments, and literature, one will not find a single agreed upon definition of "wargame," or "wargaming." Extant definitions run the gamut from practical and concrete to esoteric and psychological. The most referenced and accepted definitions were created by acknowledged masters in the art of designing, adjudicating, playing, and studying wargames, including Jim Dunnigan, Philip Sabin, ED McGrady, John Curry, and Peter Perla. For reference, I highly recommend McGrady's

---

[81] "They tell me – what I had already a little suspected – that Kriegspiel, as it is played by the British Army, is a very dull and unsatisfactory exercise, lacking in realism, in stir and the unexpected, obsessed by the umpire at every turn, and of very doubtful value in waking up the imagination, which should be its chief function." Wells, 54. (H. G. Wells 1911/1913), 54.

[82] (DiNote 2017), 8.

[83] See (Dunnigan 2000), and (Bolger-Cortez 2018).

[84] This section draws heavily on my previous work "Operation Azure Osprey," (DiNote 2017).

2019 *War on the Rocks* article, "Getting the Story Right about Wargaming," as an excellent primer on the definition of wargames, utility of wargaming, uses, and abuses.[85] For now we will look to the definitions.

Dunnigan's definition of wargame focuses on recreating military history and future extrapolation. He calls it "an attempt to get a jump on the future by obtaining a better understanding of the past. A wargame is a combination of 'game,' history, and science."[86] In contrast, Sabin's uses the phrase "military simulation games" that consist of two components: an "underlying mathematical model of reality," and an "iterative set of active decision inputs by one or more players" to achieve a set of victory criteria. The players' decision inputs direct simulated forces to optimize their performance. The focus is on data-driven learning, trial, and error.[87]

Peter Perla presented the most accepted definition of wargame in 1990 and revised in 2008: "A wargame is a warfare model or simulation in which the flow of events shapes, and is shaped by, decisions made by a human player during the course of those events."[88] Perla focuses on the decision-making process, and the experiences of the players dealing with the consequences of those decisions.[89] This concept of wargame as a "synthetic group narrative experience".[90] inspired my own inelegant attempt at a definition of wargame: "cognitive warfare, mathematically

---

[85] (McGrady 2019).

[86] (Dunnigan 2000), 1. These sentiments are echoed by Herman, et. al, "[wargaming is] "creative tool for replaying military history or trying to anticipate battles to come." (Herman, Frost and Kurtz 2009), 3.

[87] (Sabin 2015), 4.

[88] (Perla, Peter Perla's The Art of Wargaming: A Guide For Professional's and Hobbyists 1990), 279.

[89] Ibid., 279.

[90] (Perla and McGrady, Why Wargaming Works 2011), 113.

modeled and simulated by literal or abstract means, experienced both collectively and individually by its participants as a narrative story.".⁹¹

However, rising authority James Fielder provides an elegant distillation and synthesis of giants John Curry, ⁹² Perla, Dunnigan, and Sabin. Fielder defines a wargame as a "synthetic decision-making test under conditions of uncertainty against thinking opponents, which generates insights but not proven outcomes, engages multiple learning types, and builds team cohesion in a risk-free environment.".⁹³ We will use this definition of wargame from here out.

The constant thread of human cognitive activity should resonate with would-be space wargamers, whether one considers a wargame as a simple tool, or in Fielder's view, a "ritual space" in which "all actions and consequences are real to the players.".⁹⁴ Beyond the artifact of the game, the act of wargaming is a method and a process.⁹⁵ This cognitive nature hearkens to the concept of the space domain as consistent of three unique "dimensions," physical, network, and cognitive, first articulated in June 2020's inaugural Space Capstone Publication, *Spacepower (SCP).*⁹⁶ The cognitive dimension "encompasses the perceptions and mental processes of those who transmit, receive, synthesize, analyze, report, decide, and act on information coming from and to the space domain." Furthermore, the *SCP* highlights the unique role of remote operations, in that space operators execute and interpret their missions

---

⁹¹ (DiNote 2017), 11.

⁹² While I don't reference much of Curry's work directly in this piece, I highly encourage readers to investigate his *History of Wargaming* publication effort. "The Project aims to research and publish key works in the development of professional, hobby and educational use of wargaming." (Curry 2012).

⁹³ Ibid.

⁹⁴ (Fielder, Start on Day 3: Liminality in High-Stress Wargames 2020).

⁹⁵ (Compton n.d.), 10-11.

⁹⁶ (Raymond 2020), 5.

through "virtual stimuli."[.97] In other words, the space domain inherently resembles a gaming space. As games are synthetic cognitive experiences that abstract and simulate reality, space operators must work in their domain via synthetic means just to work at all. Space is a domain ripe for wargaming, and space professionals can be tailor-made for wargames.

THE UTILITY OF WARGAMING

Contemporary wargaming is much more than a hobby or an analytical method.[98] It has grown into an expansive field with both civil and military purposes. It has developed a literature and grown into a field of academic study.[99] It has developed uses as a classroom tool and a crossdisciplinary approach to political science, psychology, and history among other fields.[100]

Additional reading, in particular works by Stephen Downes-Martin, James Fielder, and ED McGrady is essential to understanding what makes a good game versus a bad one, and what constitutes proper expectations versus flawed, and what constitutes uses versus abuses, but is a discussion beyond this scope of this chapter.[101] Suffice to say, well-constructed and well-executed wargaming (including adjudication)

---

[97] Ibid., 8.

[98] *"Method* is a way of doing something. Wargaming is a method." (Compton n.d.), slide 10.

[99] This evolution is not complete yet. "Epistemology is a theory of knowledge. What Wargaming lacks, and thereby suffers for, is a theory of knowledge." (Compton n.d.), 10.

[100] See (Perla and McGrady, Why Wargaming Works 2011), and (Fielder, Reflections on Teaching Wargame Design 2020), (Fielder, Start on Day 3: Liminality in High-Stress Wargames 2020).

[101] (Downes-Martin, Adjudication: The Diabolus in Machina of War Gaming 2013), (Downes-Martin, Speakers Notes: Your Boss, Players, and Sponsor: the Three Witches of Wargaming 2012), (McGrady 2019).

enables military professionals, senior leaders, and policy makers to explore hypotheses, experiment, and train for given scenarios.

They can tell us why commanders make the decisions they make, as well as what decisions are even available depending on the scenario. They can recommend where to spend resources, what tactics, techniques, and procedures (TTPs) are effective, design reactions to enemy TTPs, evaluate strengths and weaknesses, especially ones that are not intuitive or obvious.[102] According to Philip Bolger-Cortez, designer and professional wargamer for Headquarters Air Force, wargames are best used for *"complex problems,* especially involving human input," as opposed to *complicated problems,* such as whether a special weapon system can hit a specific target given a set of variables,"[103] something more appropriate for a pure mathematical model. This distinction informs how we ought to build space wargames.

THEORETICAL FRAMEWORK FOR WARGAMING SPACE

A brief discussion of the types of professional wargames is useful before delving into the depth of space-related design considerations. Broadly, wargames and wargaming fall under the umbrella of Decision Support Modeling, to improve the ability to make decisions or to make better decisions.[104] Under this rubric, we acknowledge two types of wargames: Research and Analysis or "Discovery" games, and Training and Education games.[105] Discovery games are built around a research question,[106] something "previously unknown about a novel operational or strategic problem," where other methods are unable to provide the

---

[102] (Bolger-Cortez 2018), 5.

[103] Ibid., 6. Emphasis added is mine.

[104] (DiNote 2017), 14.

[105] (LBS Consultancy n.d.).

[106] (Bolger-Cortez 2018), 14.

needed insights.[107] Discovery wargames are what we use when we do not possess the requisite experience or data to accurately predict outcomes or train to test TTPs based on historical contexts.[108] As McGrady describes this, "Wargames are the front-end, door-kicking tool of new ideas, dangers, and concepts."[109] This approach should be applied to wargaming the new and emerging military space environment in the early twenty-first century.

This newness demands intellectual humility. The youth of the Space Force as a separate service, the newness of a space environment that is no longer the benign "big sky" of decades past, as well as the potential for explosive growth in the exploration and exploitation of space, far beyond the familiar "blue space" region under the influence of Earth's gravity and into the cislunar and interplanetary regions of "black space" demonstrate how much remains unknown at this time.[110] Because of these factors, many attempts at detailed predictive analyses or high-end learning/decision-making run great risk of either failure to produce usable results, or producing exceedingly flawed results resulting in poor

---

[107] "...something that cannot be better discovered by other methods, such as seminars, work groups, modeling and simulation, or operations research." (Downes-Martin, Adjudication: The Diabolus in Machina of War Gaming 2013), 67.

[108] "...commonly used war-game adjudication methods break down and create unreliable results when addressing novel operational or strategic problems for which we have little experience or data (for example, information warfare or a regional nuclear conflict) and when we wish to explore situations rather than educate officers about well-understood situations." Ibid., 67.

[109] (McGrady 2019).

[110] This terminology comes from the fantastic article "Black Space versus Blue Space: A Proposed Dichotomy of Future Space Operations," in *Air and Space Power Journal*. Recommend to be read in its entirety for the theoretical concept of two distinct components of the space domain's geography, as well as adding to the lexicon of space power theory. (Poole and Bettinger 2021).

strategic and operational military decisions.[111] Instituting wargaming into the Space Force's culture should fall in quite successfully on the values articulated by Space Force senior leaders. These include "measured risk-taking," "organizational agility, innovation, and boldness" as desired traits in the Space Force.[112]

THREE DESIGN CONSIDERATIONS FOR WARGAMING SPACE

Even though humankind has over sixty years of experience exploring space and exploiting the benefits of space technology, the space environment has largely been benign, seen as an avenue for scientific and economic growth and to produce cooperation among rival powers.[113] This environment has changed drastically in the early 2020s.[114] Emerging challenges to space norms in place since the late 1950s, as well as the general lack of credible space-based weapons until recently means that we are caught attempting to analyze a new militarized space problem that we do not completely understand and have little experience to work

---

[111] (Downes-Martin, Adjudication: The Diabolus in Machina of War Gaming 2013), (Downes-Martin, Speakers Notes: Your Boss, Players, and Sponsor: the Three Witches of Wargaming 2012), and especially McGrady, "Should we identify bad games? Of course. And most experienced game designers will almost unanimously point to the discussion game, or BOGSAT ("Bunch of Guys Sitting Around a Table"), as the worst offender amongst games. And that is true. It's a meeting with a fancy name." (McGrady 2019).

[112] (Raymond 2020), xiii.

[113] "This early concept of cooperation is the foundation that many spacefaring nations rely on at present." (Poole and Bettinger 2021), 13.

[114] "The reemergence of great power competition and a rapid expansion of allied, partner, and commercial activities in space in recent years have drastically changed the character of the space domain. The actions, intentions, and military strategies of potential adversaries have transformed space into a warfighting domain. In parallel, growth in allied, partner, and commercial space capabilities has added complexity to the space operating environment while creating an unprecedented level of collaborative opportunities." (Esper 2020), 3.

with. Because of this, the Design Considerations detailed here were selected with discovery wargames in mind. These are not offered as the
"be all, end all," of space wargame design, but as a "jumping off point"
for designers and wargamers to use and expand upon.

**CONSIDERATION: RESOURCE MOVEMENT AND THE COMMERCIAL SPACE
FACTOR**

Privately owned commercial space flight has perhaps finally begun
to come into its own, with the 30 May 2020 launch of the SpaceX Crew
Dragon crewed capsule aboard a Falcon 9 rocket to the International
Space Station.[115] Not only did this signal the return of manned space
launch from the territorial United States since the sunset of the space
shuttle program in 2011, but it also signaled the arrival of a major new
factor in the role of space in national prosperity and security in the form
of a commercial operator launching and carrying astronauts into orbit.[116]
Instead of a more traditional government program, in which private
contractors produce capabilities and end-items for a lead government
agency, SpaceX operated within the contexts of a new public-private
partnership established with NASA in 2010.[117] This is increasingly a feature of the modern era, in that it is not unusual to see private commercial
entities grabbing the baton from formerly government or military-only
technological advances. Furthermore, former president Donald Trump's
April 6, 2020, *Executive Order on Encouraging International Support for the
Recovery and Use of Space Resources* opened a path forward for the

---

[115] (Luscombe and Sample 2020)

[116] Ibid.

[117] "Equally significant, it heralded a new direction for crewed spaceflight, entrepre-
neur Elon Musk's company SpaceX becoming the first commercial operator to carry
astronauts into space under a public-private partnership set up by Nasa, the American space agency, in 2010." Ibid.

economic exploitation of space, which could take the form of asteroid or other celestial body mining.[118]

The center of gravity for the successful growth of commercial space enterprises is in resource movement, especially the ability to reduce the cost of launch and expand payload capacity. The *Harvard Business Review* highlights this as the move from a "space-for-Earth" economic model and the growth into a "space-for-space" emergent economy.[119] This goes beyond rocketry and includes other capabilities and services "that leverage commoditized, off-the-shelf technologies and lower barriers for market entry." This growth and expansion present an opportunity for the Space Force and other components of the Department of Defense, to acquire and field capabilities at a much cheaper cost and at speed and scale that defense acquisition timetables cannot achieve. The same is also true of American adversaries who can leverage the same and use them a means to rapidly counter or even threaten to overtake US power and influence with a much lower investment of national treasure than they might otherwise have to commit.[120]

The role of commercial space enterprises, spacecraft, and infrastructure could present an interesting design element for space wargaming not readily seen in military wargames, given the dependency of military space on commercial resource for its very existence. While the need for commercial transport resources, such as rail, shipping, and the Civil Reserve Air Fleet (CRAF) is highlighted and factored into large-scale Title 10 wargames that depict mobilization and execution of major theater wars, this form of commercial reliance is not comparable to the private-military relationship described for space, at least not until rapid launch and recovery and on-orbit fueling become true realities.

---

[118] (Poole and Bettinger 2021), 5.
[119] (Weinzierl and Sarang 2021).
[120] (Esper 2020), 5.

Instead, the commercial aspect starts with the realization that privately owned and operated satellites now far outnumber their military and government counterparts.[121] Furthermore, is the sharing of data collected by privately owned and operated satellites with military customers, the purchase and sharing of uplink and downlink nodes and the bandwidth to communicate and transport massive amounts of data. If these resources are shared between the private and public space as such, they become targetable and in need of defending. Conflicts of interest, competition for prized orbits as space continues to get more and more crowded, competition for bandwidth and station time, and the relationship between military space capabilities which cannot operate without commercial infrastructure which is not necessarily hardened against threats are ripe gaming topics that can generate new gameplay mechanics, player briefs for roleplay, and specialized objectives for win/loss criteria.

Transitioning thinking wargaming from the present environment to the potential future means considering the rapidly advancing developments in rocketry, as these have the potential greatest and game-changing application for military use. Some point the to the Boeing X-37B spaceplane, first glimpsed by the American public in 2012, as the forerunner of this change.[122] As commercial rocketry rapidly advances, the "US military may be able to reach orbit cheaply, refuel in orbit at low cost, and use this fuel to maneuver extensively once there."[123] As of this writing, all eyes are on whether the SpaceX Starship rocket and its

---

[121] Ibid., 13.

[122] "The X-37B spacecraft — the first true military spaceplane — foreshadows the "end of the beginning" for military space as satellites, tiny spaceplanes, and single-use orbital boosters give way to massive fleets of very large, maneuverable, and reusable spacefaring vehicles." (Becker 2021).

[123] Ibid.

Superheavy booster succeeds or fails.[124] Changing the cost / weight / frequency ratio of launch to orbit changes the space game itself, and this is not lost on either the commercial space industry or the national defense enterprise. "With its 100-ton payload capacity and $2 million-per-launch operating cost, Starship promises to drop the cost of putting payloads in orbit -- any payload, be it satellites, astronauts, or rocket fuel -- from $2,500 per pound currently to as low as $10 per pound."[125]

If Starship, and other rockets like it, bring about the ability to refuel on orbit, than the name of the military game begins to switch from a satellite-focused architecture to one in which maneuvering vessels, potentially the equivalent of today's major weapons systems platforms.[126] The expansion and normalization of frequent orbital and deep space maneuvering, enabled by the availability of refueling for manned or unmanned space assets in addition to satellites of all kinds and sizes makes the space domain more dynamic and dangerous as a military environment. It also will put a premium on fuel storage, protection, and on tanker-like spacecraft themselves.

This could put rocket manufacturers and operators in the same class as the major aircraft producers, shipbuilders, and armored vehicle producers of the previous century. How this effects military space options, capabilities, and requirements becomes a ready-made discovery wargame question. This means, from a military context, the need to think and wargame a "a true space-going US Space Force," that can "conduct both intelligence, surveillance, and reconnaissance and combat missions anywhere from [Low Earth Orbit], to Geostationary or Geosynchronous Orbit, to cislunar (between Earth and Moon) orbit and

---

[124] In the interest of full disclosure, the author discloses he owns a small amount of Tesla micro-stock.

[125] (R. Smith 2021)

[126] (Berger 2021)

beyond.".[127] As many analysts are now pointing out, this operationalizes the space environment well beyond terrestrial-focused "blue space," into "black space" beyond Earth. This means that wargaming space power will require scenarios and in-game events in cislunar space and perhaps even deeper into the Solar System should Mars and the asteroid belt come in to use.[128] This sort of speculatory and exploratory proceeding matches the discovery game discussion; a concept or event about which we have little experience, and little data to guide us.

Simply put, while commercial space could come to eclipse and vastly outnumber military space, codependence will always be a feature of their relationship. The *SCP* encapsulates this in the form of "national spacepower," or the "totality of a nation's ability to exploit the space domain in pursuit of prosperity and security.".[129] The relationship is circular: commercial space enables more effective and lethal space military capabilities while creating requirements for military space to defend and protect. As such, the space domain for warfighting comes to resemble the high seas, with military actors alongside and dependent on private concerns, who both enable their operations and present a need for their existence.[130] This is an area where professional wargaming may once again draw upon the commercial gaming sector for inspiration. Two popular commercial games, *High Frontier 4 All*[131] and *SpaceCorp:*

---

[127] (R. Smith 2021)

[128] See (Poole and Bettinger 2021) for the full explanation of their terms "blue space" and "black space."

[129] (Raymond 2020), 13.

[130] (Poole and Bettinger 2021), 5, 9-15.

[131] Eklund's *High Frontier 4 All* is the fourth edition of his signature game. "This is the 4th edition of Phil Eklund's signature game High Frontier. It all started with Rocket Flight. This game had the ambition to let 'Each player start as a space faring company in the year 2020 trying to make a profit in trade and technology development.'" Adding in a military space component, such as the need for defense and commercial-

2025-2300 A.D.[132] present well-developed models exploring how to build a successful private space company in the present (2021), near future and beyond, and are worth exploring for applicable concepts and systems useful to wargaming the commercial/military space intersection.

CONSIDERATION: SPACE POWER DOCTRINE AND INTEGRATING THE JOINT FORCE

Chief among these new concepts is the emergence of an independent concept of "space power," in both national and military forms. A quick look at what the SPC says, and how to either portray or depart from what it says: "Independent theory of space power ... Military space power has deterrent and coercive capacities — it provides independent options for National and Joint leadership but achieves its greatest potential when integrated with other forms of military power." The focus on joint force integration is intriguing. Nowhere does the SCP suggest that space power is a war-winning factor in and of itself. In a marked departure from early airpower advocates, while the theory of space power and the Space Force itself may be independent, zero pretense is made that either are independently decisive in conflict. The implications for space wargaming are clear: wargames should portray interdependence and jointness. They should also feature the friction between legacy decentralized space capabilities development, treating space as an element supporting the traditional services and warfighting domains, and the emergent push for centralization under the rubric of space power, "as a distinct formulation of military power on par with land power, sea power, airpower, and cyber power."[133] Any game depicting how the United States

---

military mutual support agreements and contracting make this a contender for an adaptable, preexisting space wargame design. (Eklund n.d.)

[132] (Butterfield 2018).

[133] Ibid., xi.

can fight in or through space must take the roles of the Combatant Commands into account, especially with respect to authorities.

CONSIDERATION: ADVERSARIES, THREATS, WEAPONS AND CAPABILITIES

The dependency of America's military considerable advantages on space-based satellites and other technologies is well documented and needs no further explanation. This discussion could readily be alternatively titled "to classify or not?" "Not only are space operations global, but they are also multi-domain. A successful attack against any one segment (or combination of segments), whether terrestrial, link, or space, of the space architecture can neutralize a space capability; therefore, space domain access, maneuver, and exploitation require deliberate and synchronized defensive operations across all three segments."

This section talks about the situation taken from the recently released ODNI Annual Threat Assessment – Russia, China, DRPK, Iran and others.

CONCLUSION

This chapter is nothing like a final answer or sole source presentation on wargaming but is intended to pique the interest of space military professionals, as well as those of other services, the intelligence community and throughout the national security enterprise to deliberately think about wargaming space power. It is certainly not intended as the authoritative or definition work on the subject, but to introduce wargaming concepts, ideas, and lexicon, and connect them to the emerging military space milieu. This brief discussion of history, theory, and utility of wargames intends to lay a foundation to think creatively about how space power can be wargamed and named three specific "umbrella" ideas to do so successfully. The three design considerations outlined here are deliberately broad, to encourage all wargamers, whether professional, amateur, and hobbyist to start thinking critically about what warfare to, within, and from space really means in the rapidly changing twenty-first century. The three design considerations can readily support their own specific lines of research, wargame development, testing, and playing to get at the emerging space warfare environment.

BIBLIOGRAPHY

Air Force Space Command. 2013. *Resiliency and Disaggregated Space Architectures.* White Paper, Colorado Springs: United States Air Force Space Command.

Anderson, Collin, and Karim Sadjadpour. 2018. *Iran's Cyber Threat.* Washington DC: Carnegie Endowment for International Peace.

Andrewes, A. 1962. "The Mytilene Debate: Thucydides 3.36-49." *Phoenix* (Classical Association of Canada) 16 (2): 64-85. Accessed December 5, 2018. www.jstor.org/stable/1086942.

Babb, Robin, David DellaVolpe, Nick Miller, and Gordon Muir. 2014. *War Gamers' Handbook.* Edited by Shawn Burns. Newport, RI: War Gaming Department, U. S. Naval War College.

Barbosa, Rui C. 2018. "Haiyang-1C launched by China's Long March 2C." *NASAspaceflight.com*, 6 September. Accessed February 18, 2019. https://www.nasaspaceflight.com/2018/09/haiyang-1-launched-by-chinas-long-march-2c/.

Barlow, John P. 1996. "A Declaration of the Independence of Cyberspace." Accessed March 5, 2019. http://editions-hache.com/essais/pdf/barlow1.pdf.

Barros, Andrew. 2009. "Bombing and Restraint in 'Total War', 1915-1918." *The Historical Journal* (Cambridge University Press) 52 (2): 413-431. https://www.jstor.org/stable/40264177.

Becker, Jeff. 2021. *A STARCRUISER FOR SPACE FORCE: THINKING THROUGH THE IMMINENT TRANSFORMATION OF SPACEPOWER.* Texas National Security Review. 19 May. Accessed May 19, 2021. https://warontherocks.com/2021/05/a-starcruiser-for-space-force-thinking-through-the-imminent-transformation-of-spacepower/.

Berger, Eric. 2021. "The US military is starting to get really interested in Starship." *ars technica.* 1 June. Accessed June 1, 2021.

https://arstechnica.com/science/2021/06/the-us-military-is-starting-to-get-really-interested-in-starship/.

Blair, Dennis C., and Jon M. Huntsman. 2013. *The Report of the Commission on the Theft of American Intellectual Property.* National Bureau of Asian Research.

Bodner, Matthew. 2017. "60 years after Sputnik, Russia is lost in space." *SpaceNews*, 4 October. Accessed February 23, 2019. https://spacenews.com/60-years-after-sputnik-russia-is-lost-in-space/.

Bolger-Cortez, Philip S. 2018. "Principles of Game Design." *Military Operations Research Society.* Washington, District of Columbia: MORS, 23 July.

Brodie, Bernard. 1958. *"The Anatomy of Deterrence".* U. S. Air Force Project Rand Research Memorandum, RAND Corporation.

Brodie, Bernard. 1957. "More About Limited War." *World Politics* 10 (1): 112-122. Accessed October 25, 2018. https://www.jstor.org/stable/2009228.

Brown, Chris. 2018. "Russian space program in 'crisis' as David Saint-Jacques set to balst off." *CBC News*, 28 November. Accessed February 23, 2019. https://www.cbc.ca/news/world/russian-space-program-in-crisis-as-david-saint-jacques-set-to-blast-off-1.4922114.

Bullough, Vern L. 1963. "The Roman Empire vs. Persia: A Study of Successful Deterrence." *The Journal of Conflict Resolution* (Sage Publications, Inc) 7 (1): 55-68. ttps://www.jstor.org/stable/172830.

Bury, John Bagnell. 1889. *A History of the Later Roman Empire: From Arcadius to Irene (395 A.D. to 800 A.D.).* London: MacMillian and Company.

Butterfield, John H. 2018. "SpaceCorp: 2025-2300 A.D." GMT Games. https://www.gmtgames.com/p-904-spacecorp-2nd-printing.aspx.

Caffrey, Matthew B. Jr. 2019. *On Wargaming: How Wargames Have Shaped History and How They May Shape the Future.* Newport: Naval War College Press.

Capaccio, Anthony. 2019. "China's Space Debris Cleanup May Be Cover Story, Pentagon Says." *Bloomberg*, 11 February. Accessed February 18, 2019. https://www.bloomberg.com/news/articles/2019-02-11/china-s-space-debris-cleanup-may-be-cover-story-pentagon-says.

Cenciotti, David. 2016. "Russia has completed ground tests of its high-energy airborne combat laser system." *The Aviationist*, 5 October. Accessed February 27, 2019. https://theaviationist.com/2016/10/05/russia-has-completed-ground-tests-of-its-high-energy-airborne-combat-laser-system/.

Chickering, Roger, and Stig Förster. 2005. "A World at Total War: Global Conflict and the Politics of Destruction 1937-1945." Edited by Roger Chickering, Stig Forster and Bernd Greiner. Cambridge: Cambridge University Press.

—. 2003. *Shadows of Total War.* Cambridge: Cambridge University Press.

Clausewitz, Carl von. 1984. *On War.* Princeton: Princeton University Press.

Coats, Daniel R. 2018. *Worldwide Threat Assessment of the US Intelligence Community.* Statement for the Record, Washington DC: Office of the Director of National Intelligence.

Compton, Jon. n.d. "Toward an Epistemology of Wargaming: A Drunkard's Walk."

Conn, Stetson. 1968. "Examples of Total War." Memorandum. https://history.army.mil/documents/misc/ocmh26.htm.

Connell, Michael, and Sarah Vogler. 2017. *Russia's Approach to Cyber Warfare.* Washington DC: CNA.

Curry, John. 2012. *The History of Wargaming Project.* Accessed April 4, 2021. http://www.wargaming.co/index.htm.

Curtis E. LeMay Center. 2018. *Annex 3-14 Counterspace Operations.* Maxwell Air Force Base, Alabama. Accessed February 25, 2019.

https://www.doctrine.af.mil/Portals/61/documents/Annex_3-14/3-14-D04-SPACE-SSA.pdf.

Defense Intelligence Agency. 2019. *Challenges to Security in Space.* Washington DC: Defense Intelligence Agency. Accessed February 18, 2019. https://media.defense.gov/2019/Feb/11/2002088710/-1/-1/1/SPACE-SECURITY-CHALLENGES.PDF.

Defense Science Board. 2016. *Summer Study on Autonomy.* Washington DC: DOD.

2018. *Dictionary.com.* December. Accessed December 5, 2018. https://www.dictionary.com/browse/trireme.

DiNote, Christopher R. 2017. "Operation AZURE OSPREY: Wargaming Intelligence, Surveillance, and Reconnaissance." *Vigilance Horizons: ISR Research Task Force.* Maxwell AFB, AL: Air University, 29 August. https://www.airuniversity.af.edu/Portals/10/ISR/student-papers/AY16-17/Operation_AZURE_OSPREY--Wargaming_ISR.pdf.

DoD. 2018. "Interim Report on Organizational and Management Structure for the National Security Space Components of the Department of Defense." Accessed February 15, 2019. https://media.defense.gov/2018/Mar/07/2001887047/-1/-1/1/Interim-Report-on-Organizational-and-Management-Structure-for-the-National-Security-Space-Components-of-the-Department-of-Defense.PDF.

DOD. 2017. *Military Securiy Developments involving the Democratic People's Republic of Korea.* Report to Congress, Washington DC: Department of Defense (DOD).

DOD. 2018. *Summary of the 2018 National Defense Strategy of the United States of AMerica.* Washington DC: Department of Defense.

—. 2018. *Summary: Department of Defense Cyber Strategy.* Washington DC: Department of Defense.

Douhet, Giulio. 1942. *The Command of the Air.* Translated by Dino Ferrari. New York: Coward-McCann.

Downes-Martin, Stephen. 2013. "Adjudication: The Diabolus in Machina of War Gaming." *Naval War College Review* 66 (3): 67-81.

—. 2012. "Speakers Notes: Your Boss, Players, and Sponsor: the Three Witches of Wargaming." *Connections 2012 Conference, Panel: Wargaming in Support of Defense Decision Making.* Washington, District of Columbia: National Defense University. 1-10.

Drake, Nadia. 2018. "Where, exactly, is the edge of space? It depends on who you ask." *National Geographic.* 20 December. Accessed February 16, 2019. https://www.nationalgeographic.com/science/2018/12/where-is-the-edge-of-space-and-what-is-the-karman-line/.

Dunnigan, James F. 2000. *Wargames Handbook, Third Edition: How to Play and Design Commercial and Professional Wargames.* Lincoln: Writers Club Press.

Edwards, Jane. 2021. *Gen. John Raymond: Space Force Seeks to 'Move at Speed' Through Partnerships.* ExecutiveMosaic. 10 May. Accessed May 10, 2021. https://www.executivegov.com/2021/05/gen-john-raymond-space-force-seeks-to-move-at-speed-through-partnerships/.

Eklund, Phil. n.d. "High Frontier 4 All." ION Game Design/Sierra Madre Games. https://ionsmg.com/products/high-frontier-4-all.

Elbert, Bruce R. 2014. *The Satellite Communications Ground Segment and Earth Station Handbook.* Second Edition. Boston: Artech House.

Erwin, Sandra. 2019. *Trump formally reestablishes US Space Command at White House ceremony.* 29 August. Accessed December 11, 2020. https://spacenews.com/usspacecom-officially-re-established-with-a-focus-on-defending-satellites-and-deterring-conflict/.

Esper, Mark T. 2020. *Defense Space Strategy Summary (Unclassified).* Unclassified Summary Report of Classified Strategy, Department of Defense, Office of the Secretary of Defense, Pentagon: Department of Defense. Accessed April 3, 2021. https://media.defense.gov/2020/Jun/17/2002317391/-1/-1/1/2020_DEFENSE_SPACE_STRATEGY_SUMMARY.PDF?source=email.

Evans, Stephen. 2016. "North Korea 'jamming GPS signals' near South border." *BBC News*, 01 April. Accessed February 17, 2019. https://www.bbc.com/news/world-asia-35940542.

Everts, Sarah. 2015. "A Brief History of Chemical War." *Distillations*, Spring. Accessed December 16, 2018. https://www.sciencehistory.org/distillations/magazine/a-brief-history-of-chemical-war.

FARS News Agency. 2018. *MSN Middle East.* 19 December. Accessed February 18, 2019. https://www.msn.com/en-xl/middleeast/top-stories/minister-iran-to-launch-1st-operational-satellite/ar-BBRaHx9.

Federal Research Division. 2012. *Iran's Ministry of Intelligence and Security: A Profile.* Washington DC: The Library of Congress.

Fielder, James "Pigeon". 2020. "Reflections on Teaching Wargame Design." *War on the Rocks.* 1 January. Accessed January 4, 2020. https://warontherocks.com/2020/01/reflections-on-teaching-wargame-design/.

—. 2020. *Start on Day 3: Liminality in High-Stress Wargames.* 5 November. Accessed January 4, 2021. https://www.ludogogy.co.uk/article/start-on-day-3-liminality-in-high-stress-wargames/.

Fixler, Annie, and Frank Cilluffo. 2018. *Evolving Menace: Iran's Use of Cyber-Enabled Economic Warfare.* Washington DC: Foundation for Defense of Democracies. Accessed February 28, 2019. https://www.fdd.org/wp-content/uploads/2018/11/REPORT_IranCEEW.pdf.

Floridi, Luciano. 2014. *The 4th Revolution: How the Infoshere is Reshaping Human Reality.* Oxford: Oxford University Press.

Fowlkes-Childs, Blair. 2003. *The MET: The Sasanian Empire (224–651 A.D.).* October. Accessed December 3, 2018. https://www.metmuseum.org/toah/hd/sass/hd_sass.htm.

Friedman, George. 2009. *The Next 100 Years: A Forecast for the 21st Century.* New York: Anchor Books.

Garamone, Jim. 2017. "Selva Discusses Nature of Nuclear Deterrence at Mitchell Institute Forum." *DoD News, Defense Media Activity.* 3 August. Accessed December 4, 2018. https://www.jcs.mil/Media/News/News-Display/Article/1266853/selva-discusses-nature-of-nuclear-deterrence-at-mitchell-institute-forum/.

Gertz, Bill. 2021. "Space Force general: Chinese lasers, jammers threaten GPS satellites." *The Washington Times.* Washington, District of Columbia, 10 May. Accessed May 10, 2021. https://www.washingtontimes.com/news/2021/may/10/air-force-gen-john-w-raymond-chinese-lasers-jammer/.

Ghoshal, Debalina. 2018. "North Korea's Toxic Space Program." *Gatestone Institute*, 22 October. Accessed February 17, 2019. https://www.gatestoneinstitute.org/13157/north-korea-space-program.

Gibson, William. 2000. *Neurmancer.* New York: ACE.

GlobalSecurity.org. n.d. *Chinese Space Facilities.* Accessed February 18, 2019. https://www.globalsecurity.org/space/world/china/facility.htm.

—. n.d. *Yuan Wang tracking ship.* Accessed February 18, 2019. https://www.globalsecurity.org/military/world/china/yuan-wang.htm.

Goswami, Namrata. 2018. "Waking Up to China's Space Dream." *The Diplomat*, 15 October. Accessed February 18, 2019. https://thediplomat.com/2018/10/waking-up-to-chinas-space-dream/.

Gov.UK. 2018. *Gov.UK.* 4 October. Accessed March 14, 2019. https://www.gov.uk/government/news/uk-exposes-russian-cyber-attacks.

Haines, Avril. 2021. *2021 Annual Threat Assessment of the US Intelligence Community.* Unclassified Analysis Report, April, Office of the Director of National Intelligence, Washington: Director of National Intelligence. Accessed April 13, 2021.

https://www.dni.gov/files/ODNI/documents/assessments/ATA-2021-Unclassified-Report.pdf.

Harrison, Todd, Kaitlyn Johnson, and Thomas G. Roberts. 2018. *Space Threat Assessment 2018.* Assessment, Washington DC: Center for Strategic and International Studies.

Herman, Mark, Mark Frost, and Robert Kurtz. 2009. *Wargaming for Leaders.* New York: McGraw-Hill.

Hilgers, Philipp von. 2012. *War Games: A History of War on Paper.* Translated by Ross Benjamin. Cambridge, MA: The MIT Press.

Hobbes, Thomas. 1660, first digital edition 2017. *The Leviathan.* Edited by Anna Ruggieri. Kindle Edition.

House of Representatives. 1999. *Report of the Select Committee on U. S. National Security and Military/Commercial Concerns with the People's Republic of China.* 105-851, Washington DC: Government Printing Office (GPO).

Howell, Elizabeth. 2018. "Roscosmos: Russia's Space Agency." *Space.com*, 30 January. Accessed February 23, 2019. https://www.space.com/22724-roscosmos.html.

Huth, Paul K. 1999. "Deterrence and International Conflict: Empiracle Findings and Theoretical Debates." *Annual Review of Political Science,* June: 25-48. https://www.annualreviews.org/doi/pdf/10.1146/annurev.polisci.2.1.25.

ICJ. 1996. "Legality of the Threat or use of Nuclear Weapons." *International Court of Justice.* 8 July. Accessed April 2, 2018. http://www.icj-cij.org/files/case-related/95/095-19960708-ADV-01-00-EN.pdf.

ICRC. 2010. *Protocols Additional to the Geneva Conventions of 12 August 1949.* Geneva: International Committee of the Red Cross (ICRC).

Jabbari, Cyrus. 2018. *UNODA.* 25 October. Accessed March 6, 2019. https://www.un.org/disarmament/update/the-application-of-international-law-in-cyberspace-state-of-play/.

Jakhar, Pratik. 2018. "How China's GPS 'rival' Beidou is plotting to go global." *BBC News*, 20 September. Accessed February 18, 2019. https://www.bbc.com/news/technology-45471959.

Johnson-Freese, Joan. 2019. "China launched more rockets into orbit in 2018 than any other country." *MIT Technology Review*, 19 December. Accessed February 18, 2019. https://www.technologyreview.com/s/612595/china-launched-more-rockets-into-orbit-in-2018-than-any-other-country/.

2017. *Joint Publication 1-0: Doctrine for the Armed Forces of the United States*. Washington DC: Department of Defense.

Joint Staff. 2018. *Joint Publication 3-0: Joint Operations*. Washington District of Columbia: Department of Defense.

—. 2018. *Joint Publication 3-12: Cyberspace Operations*. Washington DC: Department of Defense.

—. 2018. *Joint Publication 3-14 Space Operations*. Washington DC: Department of Defense.

—. 2017, Change 1 2018. *Joint Publication-1: Joint Operations*. Washington DC: Department of Defense.

Jones, Morris. 2017. "North Korea's space program aims higher." *The Interpreter*, 31 October. Accessed February 17, 2019. https://www.lowyinstitute.org/the-interpreter/north-korea-space-program-aims-higher.

Jun, Jenny, Scott LaFoy, and Ethan Sohn. 2015. *North Korea's Cyber Operations: Strategy and Responses*. Lanham: Rowman and Littlefield.

Kahn, Herman. 2017. *On Escalation: Metaphors and Scenarios*. New York: Routledge.

Kahn, Herman. 1960. *The Nature and Feasibility of War and Deterrence*. Santa Monica : The Rand Corporation.

Karash, Yuri. 2016. "Russian Space Program: financil state, current plans, ambitions and cooperation with the United States." The Space Congress Proceedings. Accessed February 26, 2019.

https://commons.erau.edu/cgi/viewcontent.cgi?article=3648&cont
ext=space-congress-proceedings.

Kimball, Darryl, and Kingston Reif. 2012. *Arms Control Association.* 1
August. Accessed January 20, 2019.
https://www.armscontrol.org/factsheets/abmtreaty.

Kissinger, Henry. 1969. *Nuclear Weapons and Foreign Policy.* New York:
W. W. Norton & Company, Inc.

Koblentz, Gregory D. 2014. *Strategic Stability in the Second Nuclear Age.*
Council Special Report, Council on Foreign Relations.

Kramer, Andrew E. 2019. "Russian General Pitches 'Inofrmation'
Operations as a Form of War." *The New York Times,* 02 March.
Accessed March 4, 2019.
https://www.nytimes.com/2019/03/02/world/europe/russia-
hybrid-war-gerasimov.html.

Krauthammer, Charles. 1990. "The Unipolar Moment." *Foreign Affairs*
70 (1): 23-33. http://www.jstor.org/stable/20044692.

Kyle, Ed. 2018. *Space Launch Report.* 29 December. Accessed February
25, 2019. http://www.spacelaunchreport.com/log2018.html#site.

Langham, Gary. 2013. *Threat vs Risk.* IMSL.
http://intelmsl.com/insights/other/threat-vs-risk/.

Launius, Roger D. 1995. "Prelude to the Space Age." In *Exploring the
Unknown: Selected Documents in the History of the US Civil Space
Program, Volume I,* by John M. Logsdon, Linda J. Lear, Jannell
Warren-Findley, Ray A. Williamson and Dwayne A. Day.
Washington DC: NASA.

—. 2019. *Sputnik and the Origins of the Space Age.* Accessed February 09,
2019. https://history.nasa.gov/sputnik/sputorig.html.

LBS Consultancy. n.d. *Professional Wargaming Explains: What is
Wargaming?* http://lbsconsultancy.co.uk/our-approach/what-is-it.

Lebow, Richard Ned. 2007. "Thucydides and Deterrence." *Security
Studies* 163-188. Accessed December 5, 2018.
doi:10.1080/09636410701399440.

Lebow, Richard Ned, and Janice Gross Stein. 1995. "Deterrence and the Cold War." *Political Science Quarterly* (The Academy of Political Science) 110 (2): 157-181. doi:10.2307/2152358.

Lee, Connie, and Jon Harper. 2020. *BREAKING: Pentagon Unveils New Defense Space Strategy.* 17 June. Accessed May 2, 2021. https://www.nationaldefensemagazine.org/articles/2020/6/17/pen tagon-unveils-new-defense-space-strategy.

Leiner, Barry M., Vinton G. Cerf, David D. Clark, Robert E. Kahn, Leonard Kleinrock, Daniel C. Lynch, Jon Postel, Larry G. Roberts, and Stepher Wolff. 1997. "Brief History of the Internet." *Internet Society.* Accessed March 3, 2019. https://www.internetsociety.org/internet/history-internet/brief-history-internet/?gclid=CjOKCQiAk-7jBRD9ARIsAEy8mh7jDjUh1dLUlb1xEw0-hf58A4FOFCjoWFZavExENbweTvthobRTvOkaAirPEALw_wcB.

LeMay Center for Doctrine. 2017. *Annex 3-70 Strategic Attack.* Maxwell Air Force Base: United States Air Force.

Levy, Jack S. 1985. "Theories of General War." *World Politics* (Cambridge University Press) 37 (3): 344-374. https://www.jstor.org/stable/2010247.

Lillard, John M. 2016. *Playing War: Wargaming and US Navy Preparations for World War II.* Lincoln: Potomac Books.

Luscombe, Richard, and Ian Sample. 2020. "SpaceX successfully launches Nasa astronauts into orbit." *The Guardian.* 30 May. Accessed November 11, 2020. https://www.theguardian.com/science/2020/may/30/spacex-nasa-crewed-spaceflight-launch-dragon-capsule-elon-musk-trump.

Magnuson, Stew. 2014. *US Military Stepping Up Space Cooperation with Japan, Australia.* 18 July. Accessed May 10, 2021. https://www.nationaldefensemagazine.org/articles/2014/7/18/us-military-stepping-up-space-cooperation-with-japan-australia.

Mattis, James N. 2018. *Nuclear Posture Review.* Washington DC: Department of Defense.

Mattis, JIm. 2018. *Summary of the 2018 National Defense Strategy of the United States of America.* Washington District of Columbia: Department of Defense.

McDougall, Walter A. 1985.....*The Heavens and the Earth: A Political History of the Space Age.* New York: Basic Books.

McGrady, E.D. 2019. "GETTING THE STORY RIGHT ABOUT WARGAMING." *War on the Rocks.* 8 November. Accessed January 4, 2020. https://warontherocks.com/2019/11/getting-the-story-right-about-wargaming/.

MessageToEagle.com. 2017. "What is the Karman Line?" *MessageToEagle.* 16 February. Accessed February 16, 2019. http://www.messagetoeagle.com/what-is-the-karman-line/.

Mitchell, William "Billy". 1925. *Winged Defense: The Development of Modern Air Power--Economic and Military.* Tuscaloosa: University of Alabama.

Morag, Nadav. 2014. "Cybercrime, Cyberespionage, and Cybersabotage: Understanding Emerging Threats." College of Security Studies, Colorado Technical University. Accessed March 9, 2019. https://www.coloradotech.edu/media/default/CTU/documents/resources/cybercrime-white-paper.pdf.

Mukhatzhanova, G. 2017. "The Nuclear Weapons Prohibition Treaty: Negoiations and Beyond." *Arms Control Today* 47. https://www.armscontrol.org/act/2017-09/features/nuclear-weapons-prohibition-treaty-negotiations-beyond.

Murphy, Julia, and Max Roser. 2019. ""Internet"." *Published online at OurWorldInData.org.* Accessed March 2, 2019. https://ourworldindata.org/uploads/2018/09/Internet-users-by-world-region.png.

Murray, Andrew. 2012. "Uses and Abuses of Cyberspace: Coming to Grips with the Present Dangers." In *Realizing Utopia: The Future of International Law*, by Antonio Cassese, 496-507. Oxford: Oxford University Press.

N2YO.com. 2019. *Chuang Xin.* 18 February. Accessed February 18, 2019. https://www.n2yo.com/satellite/?s=40137.

NASA. 2005. "International Geophysical Year (IGY)." *NASA.* 02 February. Accessed February 15, 2019. https://history.nasa.gov/sputnik/usannounce.html.

—. 2013. *NASA.* 26 September. Accessed February 09, 2019. https://www.nasa.gov/mission_pages/station/news/orbital_debris.html.

—. 2007. *Sputnik adn the Dawn of the Space Age.* 10 October. Accessed February 15, 2019. https://history.nasa.gov/sputnik/.

NCSC. 2018. *Foreign Economic Espionage in Cyberspace.* Washington DC: National CounterIntelligence and Security Center.

Nebehay, Stephanie. 2008. "China, Russia to offer treaty to ban arms in space." *Reuters*, 25 January. Accessed February 27, 2019. https://www.reuters.com/article/us-arms-space/china-russia-to-offer-treaty-to-ban-arms-in-space-idUSL2578979020080125.

—. 2018. "Reuters World News." *Reuters.* 14 August. Accessed December 18, 2018. https://www.reuters.com/article/us-russia-usa-space/u-s-warns-on-russias-new-space-weapons-idUSKBN1KZ0T1.

NOAA. 2016. *National Oceanic and Atmospheric Administration (NOAA).* 22 February. Accessed February 10, 2019. https://www.nesdis.noaa.gov/content/where-space.

North, Robert C., Howard E. Koch, and Dina Z. Zinnes. 1960. "The Integrative Functions of Conflict." *The Journal of Conflict Resolution* 3: 355-74.

Norton. 2019. *Symantec Corporation.* Accessed March 11, 2019. https://us.norton.com/internetsecurity-malware-what-is-a-botnet.html.

Office of the Secretary of Defense. 2015. *Annual Report to Congress: Military and Security Developments Involving the People's Republic of China 2015.* Annual Report, Washington DC: Department of Defense.

Accessed February 18, 2019.
https://dod.defense.gov/Portals/1/Documents/pubs/2015_China_M
ility_Power_Report.pdf.

Ohlin, Jens David, Kevin Govern, and Claire Finkelstein. 2015. "Cyber
War: Law and Ethics for Virtual Conflicts." *Oxford Scholarship Online*.
doi:10.1093/acprof:oso/9780198717492.003.0008.

ORF. 2014. *Observer Research Foundation (ORF)*. 01 February. Accessed
March 6, 2019. https://www.orfonline.org/article/the-un-and-
cyberspace-governance/.

Overy, R. J. 1992. "Air Power and the Origins of Deterrence Theory
before 1939." *The Journal of Strategic Studies* 15 (1): 73-101.
doi:10.1080/01402399208437474.

Panda, Ankit. 2018. "Russia Conducts New Test of 'Nudol' Anti-Satellite
System." *The Diplomat*, 02 April. Accessed February 27, 2019.
https://thediplomat.com/2018/04/russia-conducts-new-test-of-
nudol-anti-satellite-system/.

Perla, Peter P. 1990. *Peter Perla's The Art of Wargaming: A Guide For
Professional's and Hobbyists*. 2011. Edited by John Curry. Middletown,
DE: The History of Wargaming Project.

Perla, Peter P., and E. D. McGrady. 2011. "Why Wargaming Works."
Naval War College Review 64 (3): 111-130.

Persio, Sofia Lotto. 2017. "Star Wars: North Korea Unveils Five Year
Plan to Conques Space." *Newsweek*, 30 October. Accessed February
17, 2019. https://www.newsweek.com/star-wars-north-koreas-
unveils-5-year-plan-conquer-space-695896.

Peterson, Jon. 2016. "A Game Out of All Proportions: How a Hobby
Miniaturized War." In *Zones of Control: Perspectives on Wargaming*,
edited by Pat Harrigan and Matthew G. Kirschenbaum, 3-31.
Cambridge, MA: The MIT Press.

Pifer, Steven, Richard C Bush, Vanda Felbab-Brown, Martin S. Indyk,
Michael O'Hanlon, and Kenneth M. Pollack. 2010. *US Nuclear and
Extended Deterrence: Considerations and Challenges*. Brookings.

Poole, Carl A., and Robert A. Bettinger. 2021. "Black Space versus Blue Space: A Proposed Dichotomy of Future Space Operations." Edited by Richard T. Harrison. *Air and Space Power Journal* (Air University) 35 (1): 4-18. Accessed April 11, 2021. https://www.airuniversity.af.edu/Portals/10/ASPJ/journals/Volume-35_Issue-1/F-Poole.pdf.

Popescu, Nicu. 2018. "Russia cyber sins and storms." European Council on Foreign Relations. Accessed March 4, 2019. https://www.ecfr.eu/article/commentary_russian_cyber_sins_and_storms.

Protalinski, Emil. 2012. "NSA: Cybercrime is 'the greatest Transfer of Wealth in History'." *ZDNet*, 10 July. http://www.zdnet.com/article/nsa-cybercrime-is-the-greatest-transfer-of-wealth-in-history/.

Putin, Vladimir. 2011; amended 2015. "Priority Directions Decree Number 899: Development of Science, Technologies and Technology in the Russian Federation." Moscow. Accessed February 23, 2019. https://policy.asiapacificenergy.org/node/2238.

Putin, Vladimir V. 2014. *The Miltary Doctrine of the Russian Federation.* Moscow: Russian Federation.

Putin, Vladimr. 2015. "Russian National Security Strategy." Moscow. Accessed February 2019, 2015. http://www.ieee.es/Galerias/fichero/OtrasPublicaciones/Internacional/2016/Russian-National-Security-Strategy-31Dec2015.pdf.

RAND. n.d. *Paul Baran and the Origins of the Internet.* Accessed March 3, 2019. https://www.rand.org/about/history/baran.html.

Raymond, John W. 2020. *Space Capstone Publication, Space Power: Doctrine for Space Forces.* Doctrine, Department of the Air Force, Pentagon: United States Space Force. https://www.peterson.spaceforce.mil/Portals/15/Space%20Capstone%20Publication_10%20Aug%202020.pdf.

Recorded Future. 2017. *North Korea Cyber Activity.* Recorded Future.

Reed, John. 2019. "Chinese hackers target Cambodia opposition ahead of elections." *Financial Times*, 10 July. Accessed March 14, 2019. https://www.ft.com/content/4d4482e6-84a0-11e8-96dd-fa565ec55929.

ROSCOSMOS. 2019. *ROSCOCMOS*. Accessed February 23, 2019. http://en.roscosmos.ru/119/.

—. 2019. *ROSCOSMOS Space Centers*. Accessed February 26, 2019. http://en.roscosmos.ru/30/.

Sabin, Philip. 2015. *Simulating War: Studying Conflict Through Simultion Games*. New York: Bloomsbury Academic.

Scardera, Michael P., and B T Cesul. 2021. "Media Interaction Warfare Theory." Edited by Richard T. Harrison. *Air and Space Power Journal* (Air University) 35 (1): 37-59. Accessed April 11, 2021. https://www.airuniversity.af.edu/Portals/10/ASPJ/journals/Volume-35_Issue-1/F-Scardera.pdf.

Schelling, Thomas C. 1981. *The Strategy of Conflict*. Cambridge: Harvard University Press.

Schelling, Thomas C., and Morton H. Halperin. 1961. *Strategy and Arms Control*. New York: The Twentieth Century Fund.

Schultz, George P., and Eduard A. Shevardnadze. 1988. *Agreement Between the United States of America and the UNion of the Soviet Socialist Republics on Notifications of Launches of Intercontinental Ballistic Missiles and Submarine-Launched Ballistic Missiles (Ballistic Missile Launch Notification Agreement)*. Treaty, Moscow: US Governemnt. https://www.state.gov/t/isn/4714.htm.

SCIO. 2015. *China's Military Strategy*. The State Council Information Office of the People's Republic of China (SCIO).

Secure World Foundation. 2018. *Global Counterspace Capabilities: An Open Source Assessment*. Assessment, Secure World Foundation.

Segal, Adam. 2017. "The Development of Cyber Norms at the United Nations Ends in Deadlock. Now What?" *Council on Foreign Affairs*. Accessed March 6, 2019. https://www.cfr.org/blog/development-cyber-norms-united-nations-ends-deadlock-now-what.

Siddiqi, Asif A. 2010. "Competing Technologies, National(ist) Narratives, and Universal Claims: Toward A Global History of Space Exploration." *Technology and Culture* 51 (2): 425-443. Accessed February 23, 2019. https://www.jstor.org/stable/pdf/40647107.pdf?refreqid=excelsior %3A1f79f65913fb46c7eaf31f711f4ed6ad.

Siddiqi, Asif. 2017. "Russia's Space Program is Struggling Mightily." *Slate*, 21 March. Accessed February 25, 2019. https://slate.com/technology/2017/03/russias-space-program-is-in-trouble.html.

Simpson, William L., Jr. 2017. "A Compendium of Wargaming Terms." *US Naval War College, Research and Wargaming, Publications and Journals.* 20 September. Accessed April 24, 2021. https://dnnlgwick.blob.core.windows.net/portals/0/NWCDepartm ents/Wargaming%20Department/A%20Compendium%20of%20Wa rgaming%20Terms%2020%20Sept%202017.pdf?sr=b&si=DNNFileM anagerPolicy&sig=BEh3XmMzUbqnHm2SIms6QAWn5YWCMWBW nU8Ira1Oud8%3D.

Smith, Malcolm. 1980. "A Matter of Faith: British Strategic Air Doctrine Before 1939." *Journal of Contemporary History* (Sage Publications, Ltd) 15 (3): 423-442. https://www.jstor.org/stable/260412.

Smith, Rich. 2021. "How SpaceX Could Become Space Force's No. 1 Defense Contractor." *The Motley Fool.* 1 June. Accessed June 1, 2021. https://www.fool.com/investing/2021/06/01/how-spacex-could-become-space-forces-no-1-defense/.

Soldatov, Andrei, and Irina Borogan. 2015. *The Red Web: The Struggle Between Russia's Digital Dictators and the New Online Revolutionaries.* New York: Pubic Affairs.

Space.com Staff. 2005. "Space.com." *Making History: China's First Human Spaceflight.* 28 September. Accessed February 16, 2019. https://www.space.com/1616-making-history-china-human-spaceflight.html.

Speller, Elizabeth. 2003. *Following Hadrian: A Second Century Journey through the Roman Empire.* Oxford: Oxford University Press.

sputniknews.com. 2015. "Russia Establishes Satellite Ground Station on US Doorstep-German Media." *sputniknews.com,* 5 February. Accessed February 25, 2019. https://sputniknews.com/latam/201505021021637618/.

Staff of Strategy and Tactics Magazine. 1977. *Wargame Design: The History, Production, and Use of Conflict Simulation Games.* New York: Simulations Publications, Inc.

Stevens, Jon. 2018. *Internet Stats & Facts for 2019.* 17 December. Accessed March 02, 2019. https://hostingfacts.com/internet-facts-stats/.

2013. *Strategic Stability: Contending Interpretations.* Strategic Studies Institute and the U. S. Army War College Press.

Sunstein, Cass R. 2001. *Probability Neglect: Emotions, Worst Cases, and.* Working Papers, Chicago: University of Chicago Law School. https://chicagounbound.uchicago.edu/law_and_economics?utm_source=chicagounbound.uchicago.edu%2Flaw_and_economics%2F385&utm_medium=PDF&utm_campaign=PDFCoverPages.

Tabansky, Lior. 2011. "Basic Concepts of Cyber Warfare." *Military and Strategic Affairs* 3 (1): 75-92.

The State Council Information Office of the People's Republic of China. 2015. "China's Military Strategy." Strategy. https://jamestown.org/wp-content/uploads/2016/07/China%E2%80%99s-Military-Strategy-2015.pdf.

Theohary, Catherine A., and Anne I. Harrington. 2015. *Cyber Operations in DOD Policy and Plans: Issues for Congress.* Washington DC: Congressional Research Service.

Thucydides. 1954. *The History of the Peloponnesian War.* Translated by Rex Warner. London: Penguin Classics.

Trenchard, Hugh M. 1928. "Note by the First Sea Lord." London (PRO), AIR 9/8 COS 156,: Public Record Office.

2019. *Trend Micro.* March. Accessed March 11, 2019. https://www.trendmicro.com/vinfo/us/security/definition/distrib uted-denial-of-service-temp.

Trump, Donald J. 2020. *Establishment of United States Space Command as a Unified Combatant Command: Memorandum to the Secretary of Defense.* Presidential Document - Memorandum, Executive Office of the President, Executive Branch of the U.S Federal Government, Washington: Federal Register. Accessed May 30, 2021. doi:83 FR 65483.

—. 2018. *National Cyber Strategy of the United States of America.* Washington DC: White House.

Trump, Donald J. 2017. *National Security Strategy of the United States of America.* Washington DC: US Government.

Trump, Donald J. 2018. *Space Policy Directive-3, National Space Traffic Management Policy.* Presidential Memoranda, Washington DC: White House.

U. S. Department of State. 2018. "Outlaw regime: A Chronicle of Iran's Destructive Activities." U. S. Department of State, 31. https://www.state.gov/documents/organization/286410.pdf.

Union of Concerned Scientists. 2018. *UCS Satellite Database.* 30 November. Accessed February 09, 2019. https://www.ucsusa.org/nuclear-weapons/space-weapons/satellite-database#.XF8X_lxKiUk.

Union of Concerned Scientists. 2017. "Whose Finger Is on the Button? Nuclear Launch Authority in the United States and Other Nations." Accessed March 4, 2019. https://www.ucsusa.org/nuclear-weapons/us-nuclear-weapons-policy/sole-authority.

United Nations. 1945. *Charter of the United Nations and Statute of the International Court of Justice.* San Francisco: United Nations.

United Nations. 1945. *Charter of the United Nations and Statute of the International Court of Justice.* Charter, San Francisco: United Nations.

United Nations Office of Outer Space Affairs. 2019. *United Nations Office of Outer Space Affairs Space Law.* Accessed February 18, 2019. http://www.unoosa.org/oosa/en/ourwork/spacelaw/index.html.

United Nations. 1967. "United Nations Office of Outer Space Affairs." *Treaties and Principles.* 10 October. Accessed February 10, 2019. http://www.unoosa.org/oosa/en/ourwork/spacelaw/treaties/intro outerspacetreaty.html.

—. 1986. "United Nations Office of Outer Space Affairs." *Treaties and Principles.* Accessed February 10, 2019. http://www.unoosa.org/oosa/oosadoc/data/resolutions/1986/gener al_assembly_41st_session/res_4165.html.

United States Space Force. 2019. *About the United States Space Force.* 20 December. Accessed November 11, 2020. https://www.spaceforce.mil/About-Us/About-Space-Force/.

n.d. "UNOOSA." *United Nations.* Accessed December 14, 2018. http://www.unoosa.org/oosa/en/ourwork/spacelaw/nationalspacel aw/russian_federation/decree_5663-1_E.html.

US Department of Defense. 2010. *Nuclear Posture Review Report.* Washington DC: US Governemnt.

Vasani, Harsh. 2017. "How China is Weaponizing Outer Space." *The Diplomat*, 19 January. Accessed February 18, 2019. https://thediplomat.com/2017/01/how-china-is-weaponizing-outer-space/.

Verizon. 2013. *2013 Data Breach Investigation Report.* Verizon.

Wall, Mike. 2019. *Space.com.* 03 January. Accessed February 16, 2019. https://www.space.com/42883-china-first-landing-moon-far-side.html.

—. 2018. "Spaceflight." *Space.com.* 16 August. Accessed December 14, 2018. https://www.space.com/41511-weird-russian-satellite-not-so-abnormal.html.

Walter, Phil. 2016. "What is an Existential Threat." *Real Clear Defense.* 09 February. Accessed January 26, 2019.

https://www.realcleardefense.com/articles/2016/02/10/what_is_a
n_existential_threat_109009.html.

Walton, C. Dale. 2007. *Geopolitics and the Great Powers in the Twenty-first Century.* Abingdon: Taylor & Francis.

Waltz, Kenneth N. 1979 reissued 2010. *Theory of International Politics.* Long Grove: Waveland.

Weinzierl, Matt, and Mehak Sarang. 2021. "The Commercial Space Age Is Here." *Harvard Business Review.* 12 February. Accessed February 12, 2021. https://hbr.org/2021/02/the-commercial-space-age-is-here.

Wells, H. G. 1911/1913. *Floor Games and Little Wars.* 2016. Springfield, IL: Monroe St. Press.

Wells, Herbert George. 1908. *The War in the Air and Particularly how Mr. Bert Smallways Fared While It Lasted.* London: George Bell and Sons.

Welsh, Mark A. III. 2015. *Volume 1: Basic Doctrine of the United States Air Force.* Curtis E. LeMay Center. https://www.doctrine.af.mil/Portals/61/documents/Volume_1/Volume-1-Basic-Doctrine.pdf.

Werrell, Kenneth P. 1986. "The Strategic Bombing of Germany in World War II: Costs and Accomplishments." *The Journal of American History* (Oxford University Press on Behalf of Organization of American Historians) 73 (3): 702-713. https://www.jstor.org/stable/1902984.

Weuve, Christopher A., Peter P. Perla, Michael C. Markowitz, Robert Rubel, Stephen Downes-Martin, Michael Martin, and Paul V. Vebber. 2004. *Wargame Pathologies.* Analysis Paper, War Gaming Department, US Naval War College, Alexandria: The CNA Corporation. Accessed November 6, 2016. doi:CRM D0010866.A1/Final.

White House. 2015. *The White House President Barack Obama.* 25 September. Accessed March 17, 2019. https://obamawhitehouse.archives.gov/the-press-office/2015/09/25/fact-sheet-president-xi-jinpings-state-visit-united-states.

Wilson, Heather A., David L. Goldfein, John W. Raymond, and Samuel A. Greaves. 2017. "Department of the Air Force Presentation to the Subcommittee on Strategic Forces." *Military Space Policy.* Washington, District of Columbia: House of Representatives Armed Services Committee, 17 May. Accessed April 30, 2021. https://armedservices.house.gov/_cache/files/a/6/a64b0c4d-bf42-4ca7-862c-e67efdbe9412/2FC8F8210148E95EF3115A6C82AA9CDD.hmtg-116-as00-wstate-goldfeind-20190402.pdf.

Wolfgang, Ben. 2018. "US official raises alarm on Russia's satellites." *The Washington Times*, 14 August. Accessed February 27, 2019. https://www.washingtontimes.com/news/2018/aug/14/yleem-ds-poblete-raises-alarm-on-russias-satellite/.

Wright, David, Laura Grego, and Lisbeth Gronlund. 2005. *The Physics of Space Security: A Reference Manual.* Cambridge: American Academy of Arts and Sciences.

Wright, Gordon. 1968. *The Ordeal of Total War: 1939-1945.* New York: Harper & Row.

Xinhua. 2017. *New China.* 17 October. Accessed March 14, 2019. http://www.xinhuanet.com//english/2017-10/17/c_136686770.htm.

Yu, Jess Macy. 2018. "Chinese cyber-attacks on Taiwan government becoming harder to detect: source." *Reuters*, 15 June. Accessed March 14, 2019. https://www.reuters.com/article/us-taiwan-china-cybersecurity/chinese-cyber-attacks-on-taiwan-government-becoming-harder-to-detect-source-idUSKBN1JB17L.

Zagare, Frank C. 1985. "Toward a Reformation of the Theory of Mutual Deterrence." *International Studies Quarterly* 29 (2): 155-169. https://www.jstor.org/stable/2600504?seq=1#metadata_info_tab_contents.

Zak, Anatoly. 2018. *RussianSpaceWeb.com.* 20 February. Accessed February 25, 2019. http://www.russianspaceweb.com/kik.html.

Zhang, Laney. 2018. "China: New Regulation on Police Cybersecurity Supervision and Inspection Powers Issued." *Library of Congress.* 13

November. Accessed March 14, 2019.
http://www.loc.gov/law/foreign-news/article/china-new-regulation-on-police-cybersecurity-supervision-and-inspection-powers-issued/.

CHAPTER 5: POLARIS — STRATEGIC THEORY AS THE GUIDING LIGHT FOR SPACE WARFARE

BY COLONEL RYAN SANFORD

INTRODUCTION

The space domain cannot escape strategy's gravitational pull. "Man made [strategy] in his own image."[134] Where humankind goes, so too follows the logic and grammar of strategy. In a book addressing space warfare, it bears repeating the truth articulated by the Prussian military theorist, Carl von Clausewitz. That is, the characteristics of each war transform, chameleon-like, to fit the unique context within which such a war occurs; yet, an enduring nature remains.[135] As Colin Gray noted, "strategy rules!"[136] The "why" and "what" of space warfare—to achieve specific political aims—require foremost consideration to ensure the "how" of space warfare achieves the ends for which such an instrument was selected. While the answers to the above inquiries are context-dependent, strategic theory illuminates the general framework upon

---

[134] H. P. Willmott, *When Men Lost Faith in Reason: Reflections on War and Society in the 20th Century* (Westport, CT: Praeger, 2002), 14. Like war, as Willmott noted, strategy is inherently a human endeavor, reflective of the qualities and characteristics of the culture it serves.

[135] Carl von Clausewitz, *On War* ed. Michael Howard and Peter Paret, trans. Michael Howard and Peter Paret (Princeton, NJ: Princeton University Press, 1989), 85-89.

[136] Colin S. Gray, *Airpower for Strategic Effect* (Maxwell AFB, AL: Air University Press, 2012), 176.

which such strategies are laid. In other words, to contemplate space warfare properly, the strategist and practitioner alike must first understand how warfare fits within the broader auspice of strategy. Theory, and, in particular, strategic theory, aids such contemplation. Yet, theory is not suited for formulaic problem-solving or laying out the exact path to follow.[137] Instead, theory guides and illuminates such that the strategist may "avoid pitfalls" that lay before her.[138] Moreover, theory "studies the nature of ends and means," which is ultimately the very purpose of strategic behavior.[139]

Of course, recognizing the guiding light of theory is not novel. Moreover, this chapter is by no means the first to examine space power theory. This chapter, however, suggests that current thinking about space power is inadequate for the context within which practitioners must operate. That is not to suggest existing theory is bad. As Dr. Harold R. Winton articulated in "An Imperfect Jewel: Military Theory and the Military Profession," if a theory is to be the Clausewitzian "inner light" that lights the way, then the theory should be able to: define, categorize, explain, connect, and anticipate.[140] Existing theory, however, falls short of meeting Winton's criteria, especially in its power to explain and connect.

Space power theory carries an aroma of salty, sea air betraying its heavy reliance on sea power theory.[141] Scholars sought to explain

---

[137] Clausewitz, *On War*, 141.

[138] Ibid.

[139] Ibid., 142.

[140] Harold R. Winton, "An Imperfect Jewel: Military Theory and the Military Profession," *Journal of Strategic Studies* 34, no. 6 (2011): \854-858.

[141] This work uses the term sea power theory to incorporate both maritime and naval theory and to avoid categorical confusion. Sir Julian Corbett delineated between maritime strategy, or those "principles which govern a war in which sea is a substantial factor," and naval strategy, "which determines the movements of the fleet when maritime strategy has determined what part the fleet must play in relation to the action of the land forces." Thus, naval theory nests within maritime theory,

strategic behavior in space using analogs from better-understood domains—namely the sea—because the domains share apparent physical
and theoretical traits. John J. Klein's *Space Warfare* is one example
wherein a scholar adapted sea power theory for the space environment.[142] Some sea power concepts, however, as currently applied, do not
sufficiently address the strategic environment in space. Additionally,
few scholars tested the applicability of airpower theory to space power
theory.[143] When scholars evaluated airpower theory, their treatment

---

which falls under sea power theory. See Julian Corbett, *Some Principles of Maritime Strategy* (Annapolis, MD: Naval Institute Press, 1988), 15.

[142] John Klein built his theory following the maritime theory of Sir Julian Corbett in *Some Principles of Maritime Strategy*. Specifically, Klein adapted Corbett's writings on lines of communication, blockades, offensive and defensive strategies, concentration and dispersal, strategic positions, and command of the sea for celestial purposes to develop thinking that is "relevant and appropriate" for understanding how space power theory can inform space strategy to enhance national power. See John J. Klein, *Space Warfare: Strategy, Principles and Policy* (Hoboken, NJ: Routledge, 2006).

Brent L. Ziarnick adapted Alfred Thayer Mahan's naval theory and meshed it with James Holmes and Toshi Yoshihara's interpretation of Mahan's theory, and Joseph Schumpeter's economic theory to develop his general space power theory. See Brent Ziarnick, *Developing National Power in Space: A Theoretical Model* (Jefferson City, NC: McFarland, 2015), 3, 39-61.

Conversely, Bleddyn Bowen offered the final and most recent space power theory whose theoretical apogee lay well-beyond debating weaponization. Upon a Clause-witzian foundation, Bowen attempted to develop a comprehensive theory through the careful exposition of seven propositions, however, despite such an aim, Bowen's theory is fundamentally a maritime theory clothed in a spacesuit that attempted to address strategy at the grandest level. Still, Bowen's theory is unique in its correc-tion to what Bowen averred are misapplications of Corbett and Mahan and by his weaving of Charles Callwell's and Raoul Castex's strategic concepts into his narra-tive. See Bleddyn E. Bowen, "Spacepower and Space Warfare: The Continuation of Terran Politics By Other Means" (PhD diss., Aberystwyth University, 2015), 1-8, 127-128, esp. chap. 4 & 5.

[143] See Everett C. Dolman, "Geostrategy in the Space Age," in *Geopolitics: Geography and Strategy*, ed. Colin S. Gray and Geoffrey Sloan (London: Frank Cass, 1999). Dolman's theory parallels Halford MacKinder's "Heartland" geopolitical theory wherein Dol-man argued that in space, whoever controls the orbital high ground, could control

was superficial, based on an incomplete understanding and examination of airpower thought. Such oversight hampers thinking about space. While airpower concepts have no isomorphic equivalents in space, airpower theory can inform space power theory, especially as the space domain matures into a warfighting domain. Still, this work does not advocate throwing sea power theory's conceptual offspring out with the bathwater.

In 1996, Dr. Colin S. Gray asked, "Where is the theory of space power? Where is the Mahan for the final frontier?".[144] Since then, many have answered and advanced the conversation on space power. This chapter aims to spur further incisive and vigorous thinking about space power.[145] It does not, however, "pretend to give the power of conduct in [orbit]; it claims no more than to increase the effective power" of strategic thinking in space.[146] While acknowledging that space is the most technology-dependent domain, the reader "must remember that the basic element of strength in any nation is not in its machines but in its [people]."[147] To that end, this chapter offers nine propositions—six based on airpower theory and three adapted from sea power thought—

---

near-Earth space, and consequently, the Earth itself. Dolman's conceptual framework included adaptations of airpower theorists Alexander P. de Seversky's great-circle mapping concepts and William Mitchell's and Giulio Douhet's thoughts regarding vital centers and their targeting. Yet, aside from these inclusions, at its core, Dolman's theory is a sea power theory adapted for space. In particular, like Mahan a century before, Dolman specifically addressed how the application of his theory could benefit the United States through the exercise of astropolitical tenets in the same vein as Mahan's geopolitical considerations. See especially, pg. 26-45.

[144] Colin S. Gray, "The Influence of Space Power Upon History," *Comparative Strategy* 15, no. 4 (1996): 307.

[145] Bernard Brodie, *A Guide to Naval Strategy* (Princeton, NJ: Princeton University Press, 1944), 292.

[146] Raoul Castex, *Strategic Theories* ed. Eugenia C. Kiesling, trans. Eugenia C. Kiesling (Annapolis, MD: Naval Institute Press, 1994), 23.

[147] Brodie, *Naval Strategy*, 293.

that as prisms and lenses, cast space power theory in various hues before focusing the light to illuminate the path of the strategist.

INTO THE WILD BLUE: SPACE POWER TAKES FLIGHT

Space power theorist Dr. John Klein claimed that airpower theory's main shortfall in informing strategic theory for space was its sole focus on its military characteristics.[148] Klein averred that "a maritime inspired framework most fully embraces the strategic issue of space operations."[149] Klein's conclusion, however, lacked an in-depth evaluation of airpower theory. In other words, the strategic environment in space demands a theory that considers all instruments of national power, not merely the "light, handy rapier" found in the military instrument.[150] The discounting of airpower theory because of an alleged spotlight-like focus on the use of armed force, however, has dispersed the very light space power theory should cast for the practicing strategist, thereby weakening theory's illuminative qualities. "Strategy for airpower is not all about targeting."[151] As Colin Gray noted, "Doucet was wrong."[152] So, too, was Klein. Moreover, airpower is not all about air superiority. Nevertheless, John Sheldon, in his analysis of air and sea as strategic analogies for space, focuses solely on one aspect of airpower, air superiority.[153]

Klein's—and to a lesser extent, Sheldon's—evaluation of airpower theory's applicability to space power theory are superficial. By conflating the existing body of airpower thought with targeting and air superiority concepts, both claimed that airpower theory inadequately

---

[148] Klein, *Space Warfare*, 18.

[149] Ibid., 19.

[150] Clausewitz, *On War*, 606; Klein, *Space Warfare*, 18-19.

[151] Gray, *Airpower for Strategic Effect*, 294-295.

[152] Ibid.

[153] John B. Sheldon, "Reasoning By Strategic Analogy: Classical Strategic Thought and the Foundations of a Theory of Space Power" (PhD diss., University of Reading, 2005), 258.

addressed the strategic environment. Their claims, however, ignored other airpower theorists—like oft-overlooked General of the Air Force Henry H. Arnold—who, like Mahan for naval theory, advanced broader theories to launch airpower into the heavens than is accorded them. Notably, "air power is not composed alone of the war-making components of aviation. It is the total aviation activity — civilian and military, commercial and private, potential as well as existing."[154] Airpower is not solely about bombs; neither is its theory. While few airmen have "been accused of being thinkers" or recorded their ideas on airpower, airpower theory has ascendancy in space power thought.[155]

Furthermore, airpower's theoretical contributions to strategic thinking go beyond the adaptations employed by Bleddyn E. Bowen and Everett C. Dolman.[156] Put simply, their treatment of airpower theory concepts overlooked ideas that also have an inheritance in space power thinking. Accordingly, the following section examines airpower concepts and offers six propositions that apply to strategy in a grander sense.

Proposition One: Space power is the ability to do something strategically useful.

Brigadier General William Mitchell averred that "air power is the ability to do something in or through the air."[157] Building upon Mitchell's concept, Dr. Brent Ziarnick suggested that "space power is simply

---

[154] US Army Air Forces, *Third Report of the Commanding General of the Army Air Forces to the Secretary of War.* (Baltimore: Schneidereith & Sons, 1945), 61.

[155] Phillip S. Meilinger, *Airmen and Air Theory* (Maxwell AFB, AL: Air University Press, 2001), 97.

[156] See Note 10 above for a brief overview of Bowen's and Dolman's space power theories.

[157] William Mitchell, *Winged Defense* (1925; repr., Tuscaloosa: University of Alabama Press, 2009), 3-4.

the ability to do something in space."[158] The ability to do something, however, is not in and of itself evocative of power—at least not in the realm of strategy. Strategy is inherently a practical subject.[159] Any use of power which does not avail itself to achieving an end that policy requires is arguably an exercise in vanity[160] Noting such a disconnect between that which is useful to policy versus that which is merely a display of power, Colin Gray modified Mitchell's definition of airpower by adding the adjectives "strategically useful" to that which airpower does in the air.[161]

After simplifying and adapting these definitions, it follows that space power is the ability to do something strategically useful in or through space.[162] Moreover, space is not the sole venue for space power. A space actor who achieves strategically useful aims via aspects of its terrestrial space capabilities wields space power. Space launch sites present such an example.[163] Land-based missile-warning systems present another.[164] A simple definition of space power runs counter to previous scholars' nuanced definitions. David E. Lupton defined space power as the "ability of a nation to exploit the space environment in pursuit of national goals and purposes and includes the entire astronautical capabilities of the nation."[165] M. V. Smith suggested that since space is not solely the domain

---

[158] Ziarnick, *Developing Space Power*, 13.

[159] Colin S. Gray, *Categorical Confusion? The Strategic Implications of Recognizing Challenges Either as Irregular or Traditional* (Carlisle Barracks, PA: Strategic Studies Institute, 2012), ix.

[160] Colin S. Gray, "Why Strategy is Difficult," *Joint Force Quarterly*, no. 22 (3rd Quarter 1999): \7.

[161] Gray, *Airpower for Strategic Effect*, 8-10.

[162] Gray stated that space power "must always be useful" in Gray, "The Influence of Space Power Upon History," 302.

[163] Air Command and Staff College (ACSC) Space Research Electives Seminars, ACSC, *AU-18 Space Primer* (Maxwell AFB, AL: Air University Press, 2009), 108-109.

[164] Ibid., 227-232.

[165] David E. Lupton, *On Space Warfare* (Maxwell AFB, AL: Air University Press, 1998), 4.

of states, neither is space power wielded only by state actors; thus, space power achieves ends "through the exploitation of the space environment.".[166] Finally, even though this work built on Gray's definition of airpower, Gray's 1996 definition of space power was equally narrow as he wrote that "space power may be defined as the ability to use space while denying reliable use to any foe.".[167]

Scholars' additional qualifications concerning the exploitation of space, however, obfuscated a fundamental truth of strategy—that strategy is "a plan for attaining continuing advantage" to which actors wield power without concern over by whom and upon whom such an instrument is wielded.[168]. Conversely, Ziarnick's straightforward but prosaic modification begged the strategist's question, "So what?".[169] Thus, space power must be defined broadly enough to avail itself of strategic considerations beyond just military means while being simultaneously narrow in its focus toward achieving strategically useful ends. The definition offered here achieves both aims.

Proposition Two: Space covers all the Earth; its effects are global.

In attempting to define airpower, Mitchell noted that since "air covers the whole world, aircraft are able to go anywhere on the planet," implying airpower's effects were global.[170] Likewise, Giulio Douhet reasoned that, in the air, the restrictions manifested by terrain or by coastlines, no longer hindered freedom of navigation—to him, the airplane

---

[166] M. V. Smith, *Ten Propositions Regarding Spacepower* (Maxwell AFB, AL: Air University Press, 2002), 5.
[167] Gray, "The Influence of Space Power Upon History," 293.
[168] Everett C. Dolman, *Pure Strategy* (New York: Frank Cass, 2005), 6.
[169] Gray, *Airpower for Strategic Effect*, 11.
[170] Mitchell, "Winged Defense," 3-14.

had "complete freedom of action."[171] While the analogy is imperfect—
the realities of orbital mechanics gravitate toward limits on space maneuvers—the proposition that space covers the Earth, and hence space
power is global, is both prosaic yet significant. Unlike any other domain,
no nation is wholly inoculated to space power's effects.[172] Beyond the
ready example whereby humanity receives solar energy daily, there exist myriad other examples of space power's penetrating effects into all
parts of the globe. Whether transiting space parabolically in the vein of
an intercontinental ballistic missile or monitoring tropical storms via
weather-tracking satellites, space power can affect the entire planet.[173]
Burgeoning efforts to explore outer space for rare resources suggests
that future space power will continue to influence the whole Earth
through economic endeavors.[174]

It is important for the student of strategy to appreciate space power's
ubiquity. As noted above, power projected through space can reach anywhere in the world with a speed that is only matched by the near-light-
speed quality of cyber power. Space power exhibits a "strategic ubiquity" as "a critical strategic enabler for land, sea, air power, as well as for
cyber power and for nuclear operations, across the entire spectrum of
conflict."[175] Today, a nation can wield significant influence across the

---

[171] Giulio Douhet, *The Command of the Air* (Tuscaloosa: University Alabama Press, 2009),
8-9.

[172] Compare space power's global nature to cyberpower. Cyberpower has global reach
only in so far as there exists network connectivity.

[173] ACSC, "Space Primer," 201-212.

[174] John S. Lewis, *Mining the Sky: Untold Riches From the Asteroids, Comets, and Planets*
(Reading, MA: Helix Books, 1996); *U.S. Commercial Space Launch Competitiveness Act*,
114th Cong., 1st sess., 2015; "Helium-3 Mining on the Lunar Surface / Energy," *European Space Agency*, 2016, accessed 22 February 2016, http://www.esa.int/Our_Activi-
ties/Preparing_for_the_Future/Space_for_Earth/Energy/Helium-3_min-
ing_on_the_lunar_surface; "Space Solar Power," National Space Society, accessed
November 4, 2019, https://space.nss.org/?s=space+solar+power.

[175] Sheldon, "Strategic Analogy," 303.

entire diplomatic, information, military, and economic instruments of power by disrupting position, navigation, and timing systems in space. These systems not only guide terrestrial military systems, but provide key timing signals for electronic financial transactions, enable strategic information flow, and support arms control monitoring capabilities.[176]

Certainly, space power's far-reaching effects do not mean it will necessarily be decisive.[177] Nevertheless, such interconnectedness between space-based systems and terrestrial activity merits the strategist's consideration. Space power's global nature extends beyond the capability to reach anywhere on the Earth. Namely, exercises of an actor's space power, in space especially, can have long-lasting, deleterious effects on all nations. One needs only to examine the extent of orbital debris to see this truism.[178] To launch an anti-satellite missile or detonate a nuclear weapon on-orbit not only affects other space actors and creates environmental hazards in space, but these actions invariably "junk up" one's own "front yard.".[179]

Nations may bring their "political-social baggage" to space, but to date, humanity has created plenty of new baggage in the space environment.[180] Proposition Two reminds the strategist and leader that actions taken in the name of space strategy must abide by what Dr. Edward N. Luttwak called the "logic of strategy" that is pervaded by paradox and nonlinearity.[181] Space power is not just far-reaching in its global quality;

---

[176] ACSC, "Space Primer," 163-257; Linda Dawson, *War in Space: The Science and Technology Behind Our Next Theater of Conflict* (Chichester, England: Praxis, 2018), 131-156.

[177] Gray, "The Influence of Space Power Upon History," 303-304.

[178] Dawson, *War in Space*, 46-60; "Debris Modeling," Orbital Debris Program Office, accessed November 5, 2019, https://orbitaldebris.jsc.nasa.gov/modeling/.

[179] James C. Moltz, *The Politics of Space Security: Strategic Restraint and the Pursuit of National Interests*, 2nd ed. (Stanford, CA: Stanford Security Studies, 2011), 64, 227.

[180] Bowen, "Spacepower and Space Warfare," 151-157.

[181] Edward N. Luttwak, *Strategy: The Logic of War and Peace* (Cambridge, MA: Belknap Press, 2001), 1-31, 258.

it has an enduring nature. As nations act in ways that damage the global commons of space, they potentially do so to their detriment. Indeed, the chances are high that any victory in space, purchased with kinetic means, will be Pyrrhic in nature. Debris and other by-products of war in space, much like unexploded ordinance on land, exist well after conflict subsides, perhaps even more so given the persistent nature of the space environment.[182] Thus, exercising space power provides both an opportunity for enduring global influence, but also risk if one ignores the potential nonlinear effects of actions made in the pursuit of expedience.

Proposition Three: Space power has currency only on Earth, for now.

Proposition One defined space power as the ability to do something strategically useful while Proposition Two espoused the global nature of space using Mitchell's and Douhet's concepts for airpower. From these two propositions, a third materializes as a corollary. That is, space power at present has currency only on Earth. In other words, even in the face of space power's global qualities and pervasive nature, it must be evaluated for its effects on Earth.[183]

Colin Gray's airpower theory is instructive in this regard. "Airpower is a strategic instrument in that it is a servant of politics" and thus must have "strategic and political meaning on land.".[184] In a similar vein, space

---

[182] Bruce M. DeBlois, ed. *Beyond the Paths of Heaven* (Maxwell AFB, AL: Air University Press, 1999), ix; Bruce M. DeBlois, "Ascendant Realms: Characteristics of Airpower and Space Power," in *The Paths of Heaven: The Evolution of Airpower Theory,* ed. Phillip S. Meilinger (Maxwell AFB, AL: Air University Press, 1997), 558; Moltz, *Politics of Space Security,* 343; Robert E. Larned, *1994 Air and Space Doctrine Symposium* (Maxwell AFB, AL: Air University Press, 1994), 8-9.

[183] Clausewitz, *On War,* 605.

[184] Colin S. Gray, *Always Strategic: Jointly Essential Landpower* (Carlisle Barracks, PA: Strategic Studies Institute, 2015), 8-9; Gray, *Airpower for Strategic Effect,* 278.

power, to be strategically useful, must exhibit "important territorial definition" since *terra firma* is currently the only domain for humanity.[185] To that end, Proposition Three allows for thinking of space power in its full global breadth but enjoins the strategist to remember that strategically useful space power must—at least until humans find the ability to live permanently beyond Earth—refer to the strategic and political gravitational fields emanating from Earth. Although potentially wielded from or through celestial means, space power's influence is still tellurian.

Proposition Four: Space power has strategic effect, but it is not inherently strategic.

The preceding propositions frame how to contemplate space power properly. Namely, space power, acting globally, is the ability to do something strategically useful toward ends as conceived for terrestrial purposes. Caution, though, is warranted. A careless reading may intimate that space power is inherently strategic. It is not. Rather, space power exhibits strategic effect, which follows naturally from this work's definition of space power. Exhibiting strategic effect, however, does not imply the presence of an inherently strategic nature.

In his 2009 *Understanding Airpower: Bonfire of the Fallacies*, Colin Gray wrote that airpower is not inherently strategic.[186] Strategists must evaluate airpower for its strategic meaning, that is, for "consequences of (tactical) actual military behavior for the course and outcome of a

---

[185] Gray, *Airpower for Strategic Effect*, 72.
[186] Colin S. Gray, *Understanding Airpower: Bonfire of the Fallacies* (Maxwell AFB, AL: Air University Press, 2009), 17-21.

conflict."[187] Similarly, space power's tools help adjoin all building blocks necessary for bridging the present to future political ends deemed desirable for enduring statecraft. While the carpenter's plane smooths the wood to fit together the framework of a structure, it does not build the structure alone.

Such caveats, however, do not comport with airpower (or space power) as traditionally conceived. Indeed, USAF doctrine defined airpower as "the ability to project military power or influence through the control and exploitation of air, space, and cyberspace to achieve strategic, operational, or tactical objectives."[188] Moreover, the same doctrine claimed, "airpower is an inherently strategic force."[189] It is beyond the scope of this monograph to address the fallacy as stated literally; Gray skillfully addressed the waywardness of such thinking.[190] The logical deduction from the above doctrinal claims, however, are salient to space power thought. Taking the claims at face value—and ignoring the theoretical and operational confusion which tends to result from a remiss wording—one concludes that space power is inherently strategic.[191]

To think of space power as being inherently strategic, however, besmirches the tool doctrine hopes to praise. Namely, such labeling forces "strategists to seek independent decision through [space power] because of their assertion of the uniquely strategic quality of their

---

[187] Ibid., 19.

[188] US Department of the Air Force, USAF, *Basic Doctrine* (Maxwell AFB, AL: Air University Press, February 27, 2015), 25.

[189] Ibid., 34.

[190] See Colin S. Gray, *Weapons Don't Make War: Policy, Strategy, and Military Technology* (Lawrence, KS: University Press of Kansas, 1993); Colin S. Gray, *Weapons for Strategic Effect: How Important is Technology?* (Maxwell AFB, AL: Air University Press, 2001); Gray, *Airpower for Strategic Effect*; Gray, *Understanding Airpower*.

[191] See DeBlois, "Ascendant Realms,". DeBlois' evaluated the claim that space power is merely a theoretical and operational extension of airpower. He concludes quite convincingly that they are not the same and should be treated within their proper contexts.

instrument," which creates an undue burden on space strategists due to a higher propensity for "demonstrable failure."[192] The propensity for failure manifests from the expectation that if the space power instrument is uniquely and inherently strategic, then uses thereof will necessarily deliver decisive results independent of other forms of national power. Rare is the occasion, however, where such success is possible because of the "complexity and variety" found in the "dialectic of wills" that is strategy.[193] Consequently, disappointment in the space instrument's efficacy follows when its use fails to meet such lofty claims of an inherently strategic and decisive nature. Therefore, one should avoid overstating and overpromising on space power's capabilities lest space advocates discredit the contributions space power can make.

Lacking an inherent, strategic nature, however, does not blunt the space implement. Instead, understanding that space power exhibits strategic effect but not an inherently strategic quality makes clear the prism through which the strategist must view space power. For example, the Corona satellite system enabled the United States to see that visions of a Soviet nuclear missile advantage were apparitional, which buttressed a changing American foreign policy toward the Soviets.[194] Satellites, or any space capability, are not inherently strategic, no matter their label.[195] Additionally, the American Apollo space program sought to increase American prestige abroad, and by doing so, garnered

---

[192] Gray, *Understanding Airpower*, 20.

[193] Gray, *Understanding Airpower*, 20; John J. Klein, *Understanding Space Strategy: The Art of War in Space* (London: Routledge, 2019), 24; Beatrice Heuser, *The Evolution of Strategy: Thinking War From Antiquity to the Present* (Cambridge: Cambridge University Press, 2010), 27-28.

[194] Dino A. Brugioni, *Eyes in the Sky: Eisenhower, the CIA and Cold War Aerial Espionage* (Annapolis, MD: Naval Institute Press, 2010), 387-391; Martin Van Creveld, *The Age of Airpower* (New York: PublicAffairs, 2011), 221-222.

[195] For examples wherein "strategic" is included in a system's name, see Dawson, *War in Space*, 148-150.

significant international influence to challenge Soviet aspirations on-orbit and on Earth.[196] Here, space power had a lasting strategic effect. It is arguable, though, that sending humans to the Moon was inherently strategic.

A more recent example of space power's strategic effect is worth noting. During Operations *Odyssey Dawn* and *Unified Protector*, the United Nations coalition utilized sixty-three various satellite systems to pinpoint Libyan forces and employ 2,844 satellite-guided weapons to help achieve the strategic aims of protecting Libyan civilians and toppling Muymar Quaddafi's regime.[197] Space power aided tactical victories on the battlefield that ultimately paved the way for strategic success, but space power was not decisive. Instead, space power—and arguably even airpower—was an "indispensable adjunct."[198] Nevertheless, operations in Libya addressed Gray's question from 1996 concerning whether space power would someday become a "leading edge" military capability as the "most potent source of military effectiveness."[199] Space power answered Gray affirmatively while postponing an answer to his additional inquiry concerning space power's ability to be an independent war winner.[200]

---

[196] James E. Webb and Robert S. McNamara, Jr., *Recommendations for Our National Space Program: Changes, Policies, and Goals* (Washington, DC: White House, May 8, 1961), 1-12.; Joan Johnson-Freese, *Space as a Strategic Asset* (New York: Columbia University Press, 2007), 8-11, 56.

[197] Karl P. Mueller, "Examining the Air Campaign in Libya," in *Precision and Purpose: Airpower in the Libyan Civil War*, ed. Karl P. Mueller (Santa Monica, CA: RAND Corporation, 2015), 4; Robert C. Owen, "The US Experience: National Strategy and Campaign Support," in *Precision and Purpose: Airpower in the Libyan Civil War*, ed. Karl P. Mueller (Santa Monica, CA: RAND Corporation, 2015), 72-74, 97-98.

[198] Gray, "The Influence of Space Power Upon History," 294-295. Gray, using historical analogy, explained how space power after Desert Storm was much like airpower was following World War I. At each point, these military tools were indispensable in accomplishing strategic aims.

[199] Ibid., 303-304.

[200] Ibid., 295, 299.

Modifying Gray's notion of "leading edge" for broader application beyond the military realm, one can see that space power has not yet achieved "leading edge" status. Space power has not yet "decided the course or outcome" of grand strategy.[201] Such status, though, is immaterial. Strategy is about the harnessing of all forms of power to influence actors and attain an enduring advantage. Whether as an adjunct, "leading edge," or sole guarantor of strategic success, space power's gravity is felt in the effects it achieves. Space power is not strategic because its perspective is global or because of its geographic-specific qualities; an instrument is only strategic in its consequences.[202] Space power possesses such consequences.

Proposition Five: Space power should be used as a general strategy

The previous four propositions situate this space power theory within strategic theory proper. Space power is subordinate to general strategy.[203] While covering, quite literally, the entirety of Earth—and having global effects with currency yet felt only on Earth—space power is not inherently strategic. Space power, however, wielded within a broad, holistic framework can yield the results intended by its political masters. In other words, as part of a general strategy, space power is powerful.

As before, early airpower thinking informs this proposition. Richard J. Overy wrote in *The Air War: 1939-1945* that "before 1939 a dichotomy was developing between air forces favoring limited, tactical air power

---

[201] Ibid., 303.
[202] Gray, *Understanding Airpower*, 19.
[203] Gray, *Airpower for Strategic Effect*, 275.

and those favoring a more general air power."[204] A limited air strategy comprised those methods wherein the air force supported service "to the practical exclusion of other alternative uses of air power."[205] Conversely, a general strategy entailed the use of "all areas of air power...simultaneously and in an inter-related way."[206] Specifically, Overy asserted that during World War II, Japan and Germany subordinated airpower solely to the role of supporting other services, namely the Japanese navy and German army. Conversely, Britain and the US "practiced a general air strategy" that involved all facets of airpower while resourcing the instrument to "meet the demands of such a policy."[207] The general air strategy the Allies employed upheld the sanctity of airpower as an indivisible instrument and aided victory while contrasting with the piecemeal approach used by the Axis powers.[208] More generally, "air strategy should be indivisible," in part, because of the easily verifiable "geophysical unity" of the sky.[209] No physical barrier

---

[204] Richard J. Overy, *The Air War: 1939-1945* (Washington, DC: Potomac Books, 2005), 45.

[205] Ibid., 17.

[206] Ibid.

[207] Ibid., 203.

[208] Overy, *The Air War*, 204-205; Luttwak, *Strategy*, 177-178. Airpower was not necessarily decisive during World War II, but for the student of strategy, such designation is immaterial. Airpower was a necessary, but not sufficient, cause for allied victory in the European and Pacific theaters. See Richard J. Overy, *Why the Allies Won* (New York: W. W. Norton & Company, 1997); Phillips Payson O'Brien, *How the War was Won: Air-Sea Power and Allied Victory in World II* (Cambridge: Cambridge University Press, 2015). That strategic bombing did not force enemy capitulation in the case of Germany is not dispositive of the strategic usefulness of airpower employed in a general strategy. The combination of strategic bombing, interdiction, air transport, and ground support, opened a second front for the Nazi regime, sustained allied war-making efforts, and virtually guaranteed a continental Europe beachhead devoid of enemy aircraft. See Tami Davis Biddle, *Rhetoric and Reality in Air Warfare: The Evolution of British and American Ideas About Strategic Bombing, 1914-1945* (Princeton, NJ: Princeton University Press, 2004), chap. 5.

[209] Gray, *Airpower for Strategic Effect*, 286-287.

prevents traversing the globe via the air. Therefore, Gray insisted "without equivocation that the essential unity and distinctiveness of the aerial domain and the nature of aircraft imply that airpower should be employed in ways that exploit its nature rather than contradict it."[210]

Applying the logic used to protect the unity of airpower and its employ, it readily follows that space power is similarly indivisible. Moreover, space power, because of its indivisible nature, should be used as part of a general vice limited strategy. The reasons for protecting the unity of space power follow from strategic theory's logic.

This logic, however, does not require centralizing control of space assets in the hands of a space operator. Just as Gray noted for airpower, the idea that "[space] is one and so is [space]power" does not require that space power "of whatever character, ought to be commanded and controlled centrally."[211] This assertion stands in contrast to theorists like Smith.[212] Parceling out aspects of space power to support single services or single theaters to the neglect of a broader strategy, as sometimes happened for airpower in World War II, negates the geographic nature of space.[213] In many cases, centralizing command is preferred. Yet, context matters. As Klein and Bowen noted, concentration and dispersal factor significantly in space strategy.[214] Usually, centralization and

---

[210] Ibid., 286.

[211] Ibid., 287. For examples wherein theory is manipulated to justify centralizing space power under a single commander, see Mark E. Harter, "Ten Propositions Regarding Space Power: The Dawn of a Space Force," *Air & Space Power Journal* 20, no. 2 (Summer 2006): \64-78; Michael R. Mantz, *The New Sword: A Theory of Space Combat Power* (Maxwell AFB, AL: Air University Press, 1995); Smith, *10 Propositions of Spacepower*.

[212] Smith, *10 Propositions of Spacepower*, 53-56. With the advent of the US Space Force, the idea that an airman would control space assets is likely no longer a real concern.

[213] Arthur W. Tedder, *Air Power in War* (1947; repr., Tuscaloosa: University of Alabama Press, 2010), 126; Robert S. Ehlers, Jr., *The Mediterranean Air War: Airpower and Allied Victory in World War II* (Lawrence, KS: University Press of Kansas, 2015), 259-280.

[214] Bowen, "Spacepower and Space Warfare," 260-284; Klein, *Space Warfare*, 107-115; Klein, *Understanding Space Strategy*, 34-36.

concentration are simpatico. Dispersing forces amid the vastness of space, however, may necessitate decentralization of command and control.

The enjoinder to wield space power in general, rather than limited, ways follows from the indivisibility of space, the interconnectedness of its capabilities, and its global presence. The urging, however, is not for centralized command and control regardless of context. Space power can operate at all levels of war simultaneously, without being confined to military uses, and covers the spectrum of competition and conflict.[215] Indeed, service or theater-specific challenges will solicit support from the space instrument. However, the strategist must be wary of the luminance cast from enthralling but perhaps not strategically compelling conflagrations. These blazes can drown out the stars necessary for navigating strategy. Like celestial navigation, the strategist must orient to an inertial frame of reference, the maxims of theory, and wield space power holistically, amid a general strategy.

Proposition Six: Space-mindedness — a key to space power — is the mental lens through which to view space.

Proper ordering and placement of theoretical ideas and concepts are essential. As Carl von Clausewitz noted, "the function of theory is to put [things] in systematic order, clearly and comprehensively."[216] However, "theory cannot equip the mind with formulas for solving problems, nor can it mark the narrow path on which the sole solution is supposed to lie by planting a hedge of principles either side."[217] Therefore, while the

---

[215] Harter, "Ten Propositions," 68-70.
[216] Clausewitz, *On War*, 578.
[217] Ibid.

previous propositions provide a framework for thinking about space power, they are not panaceas. They can, however, act as palliatives for the symptoms of astrategic thought and action. Indeed, to think correctly about space power, to appreciate its capabilities, and to champion its development, evokes a mindedness deemed space-mindedness. Space-mindedness is foundational to space power.

Correct thinking about space power evidences a lineage in airpower theory. In other words, the air-mindedness of yesteryear provides the airfoil for space-mindedness to take flight today. The first powered flight trumpeted in grandiose ideas of humankind's future technologic triumphs and adventures in the cosmos. Despite many figments of imagination, ideations of what aviation could be indicated a budding mental framework and enthusiasm amid those who believed in airpower's promise and future. Moreover, this framework and enthusiasm, in part, helped forge airpower for the nations who allowed the heavens to captivate their imaginations.[218]

Oddly, modern USAF doctrine ignored the enthusiastic quality of air-mindedness. Indeed, USAF doctrine described air-mindedness as the province of those imbued with an airman's perspective.[219] Furthermore, doctrine suggested air-mindedness "entails thinking beyond two dimensions" and enables airmen to think at all levels of war

---

[218] See especially Peter Fritzsche, *A Nation of Fliers: German Aviation and the Popular Imagination* (Cambridge: Harvard University Press, 1992); Robert Wohl, *A Passion for Wings: Aviation and the Western Imagination, 1908-1918* (New Haven: Yale University Press, 1994)

[219] USAF, "Basic Doctrine," 33. USAF doctrine incorrectly ascribed the term to General of the Air Force Henry H. Arnold. The term existed at least as early as 1927 when it was first documented in *The Oxford English Dictionary*. Brigadier-General Christopher J. Coates, Royal Canadian Air Force, offered evidence that attribution to Gen. Arnold fit well the idea of tying doctrinal concepts to one of airpower's early founders. See Christopher J. Coates, "Airmindedness: An Essential Element of Air Power," *The Royal Canadian Air Force Journal* 3, no. 1 (Winter 2014): \70-84.

simultaneously to empower the "flexibility and utility of airpower.".[220] Dr. Dale J. Hayden suggested that air-mindedness is a global, strategic mindset through which airmen perceive war and the battlespace.[221]

While Hayden asserted that air-mindedness has a protean nature, his definition and USAF doctrine missed that air-mindedness and airpower as originally conceived entailed more than military might. Air-mindedness connoted an appreciation, especially among those who had "slipped the surly bonds of Earth" for all that aviation could achieve, not just on the battlefield, but for all humankind, even when the promise was not yet evident to the greater public.[222] Of course, from these various definitions of air-mindedness, one senses that air-mindedness has often escaped definition because of the "chicken-and-the-egg" problem of grasping what airpower "does" versus what airpower "is," and thus how one contemplates airpower. As recently as 2019, Dr. Jason M. Trew updated the definition to address contemporary influences. For Trew, air-mindedness constituted a blend of "passion for cultivating airpower" with the proper "strategic perspective" to employ airpower proficiently.[223] Early airpower theorists understood that a unique perspective and mindset, coupled with a zest for airpower, was required to champion aviation if it were to take off.

In *The Command of the Air*, Italian airpower theorist Giulio Douhet responded to the horrific loss of life from the Great War by suggesting that any future war would require the command of the air, both to ensure victory and to counter any enemy.[224] Accordingly, Douhet argued that to secure a nation's command of the air, it would have to combine and

---

[220] USAF, "Basic Doctrine," 33.

[221] Dale L. Hayden, "Air-Mindedness," *Air & Space Power Journal* 22, no. 4 (2008): 44-45.

[222] John Gillespie Magee, Jr., "High Flight," line, 1., (1941); Wohl, *Passion for Wings*.

[223] Jason M. Trew, "Rescuing Icarus," *Air & Space Power Journal* 33, no. 2 (Summer 2019): \48-60.

[224] Douhet, *The Command of the Air*, 7-23.

synchronize military and civilian aviation development.[225] Further-more, to ensure that efforts remained focused upon the goal of develop-ing airpower, "air-minded" individuals needed to lead the develop-ment.[226] Disappointingly, Douhet failed to define what such a term meant. Yet, within context, Douhet's concept suggested that air-mind-edness constituted an understanding of airpower's present and future utility coupled with an enthusiasm for its development.[227]

In America, enlisted infantryman turned pilot and eventual Army Air Corps Chief, Major General Benjamin D. Foulois, foresaw the promise of airpower and championed air-mindedness to ensure the US maintained strategic advantage.[228] Foulois' contemporary, William Mitchell, also carried the torch for airpower and "made Americans an air-minded peo-ple.".[229] In writing about "air-going people," Mitchell observed that those who danced upon the clouds thought differently about aviation and ap-preciated what airpower meant for the future of the nation.[230] Although Mitchell did not use the term air-mindedness, he recognized that ad-vancing airpower required a different mindset. Indeed, Mitchell, like Douhet, argued that developing airpower required a whole-nation ap-proach driven by a vision "of at least seven years ahead."[231] Mitchell's purpose was, as General Arnold later summarized, about convincing the

---

[225] Ibid., 87.

[226] Ibid., 88.

[227] Douhet, *The Command of the Air*, 71, 101-103, 175-177; Phillip S. Meilinger, "Giulio Douhet and the Origins of Airpower Theory," in *The Paths of Heaven: The Evolution of Airpower Theory*, ed. Phillip S. Meilinger (Maxwell AFB, AL: Air University Press, 1997), 17.

[228] Benjamin D. Foulois and C.V. Glines, *From the Wright Brothers to the Astronauts: The Memoirs of Major General Benjamin D. Foulois* (New York: McGraw Hill, 1968), 1-6, 42-59.

[229] Robert S. Ehlers, Jr. quoted in \Mitchell, "Winged Defense," vi.

[230] Ibid., 6.

[231] Ibid., 198.

nation that airpower was more than airplanes or even an air force.[232] Air-mindedness was about taking a whole-of-nation viewpoint regarding airpower, especially in light of its potential applications. Major Alexander P. de Seversky captured such a frame of mind when he tried to spark air-minded thinking in the American populace.

> *A nation content to imitate and "catch up" must in the nature of the case remain backward... As far as the aircraft of tomorrow is concerned, all nations are starting from scratch. America is more richly endowed with the resources of brains, materials, personnel, and industrial efficiency than any other country...Whether it utilizes these potentialities, or once more allows itself to trail along imitatively, depends on how quickly and thoroughly we comprehend the nature of the new weapon—and on how quickly and thoroughly we cleanse our air power from the accretions of conservatism, timidity, and astigmatic leadership...Above all, I hope to convey the sense of air power as a dynamic, expanding force, the growth of which must be anticipated by courageous minds.[233]*

De Seversky's air-mindedness reverberated within the US Congress, where his enthusiasm engendered debate on the need to get out of "rut mind" to prepare America's airpower.[234] Despite congressional attention, advocates felt compelled to renew public pleas centered upon building a hopeful enthusiasm for the development of airpower. As General Arnold noted:

> *Since military air power depends for its existence upon the aviation industry and the air-mindedness of the Nation, the Air Forces must promote the development of American civil air power in all of its forms, both commercial and private...No activity having to do*

---

[232] Henry H. Arnold, *Global Mission* (New York: Harper, 1949), 100.

[233] Alexander P. de Seversky, *Victory Through Air Power* (New York: Simon and Schuster, 1942), 4-6.

[234] *Congressional Record*, 77th Cong., 2nd sess., 1942, vol. 88, pt. 3 : \3745-3748.

with aviation in any form can be considered as being completely in-
dependent of national security. Civil aviation must be encouaged,
both internally and internationally.[235]

Both de Seversky's and Arnold's thoughts conveyed the realization that civil, commercial, and military aviation development were symbiotic processes. One could not advance airpower by simply cultivating just one aspect of it. To truly foster growth, all three areas required tending as developments in one tended to sprout new growth in the other legs of the trinity. Such a realization manifested for more than just the so-called prophets of airpower. The lay airman recognized the intertwining of threads that constituted the very mantle demanded of a truly ascendant airpower—airpower that would satisfy the "Jules Verne imagination" that would cross any frontier, to include space.[236] Being airminded was more than merely advocating for airpower or understanding its proper use in strategy. Perhaps most importantly, being airminded entailed displaying a vision for what airpower can be. Air-mindedness was practical. It was also aspirational.

It is the juxtaposition of these concepts, or the amalgamation thereof, that offers a useful definition of space-mindedness. Combining Trew's updated definition with original conceptions is useful for space power theory. Space-mindedness "is a lens [through] which the mind's eye views the vast potential of space, and in recognizing this potential, advocates for the 'constant development and experimentation' of space-going capabilities to harness the latent power of space in the continuing

---

[235] Henry H. Arnold, "Air Power for Peace," *National Geographic Magazine*, February 1946, 193.

[236] Cy Caldwell, *Air Power and Total War* (New York: Coward-McCann Inc., 1943), ix, 242.

pursuit of national power."[237] Moreover, in contemplating space war-fare, space-mindedness is the "lens through which [space operators] perceive warfare and view the battlespace," in space.[238] Being space-minded means possessing equal doses of a mind rooted in reality—that is, one that remains cognizant of the present's requirements for practi-cality—admixed with a spark of imagination and thoughts that aspire to see space power reach its full potential. Space-mindedness is the dutiful Daedalus and the imaginative Icarus.[239] It is the prism through which one views space power. This prism focuses the eye not only on space power's present use but also on the promise of space power's future use-fulness.[240] Similarly, space-mindedness epitomizes both a passion for the cultivation of space power and the sober-minded consideration of how such power, available now, can influence other actors for the achievement of political aims deemed necessary in the present.

Of course, it is easy to define the state of mind that is space-minded-ness. It is altogether a separate task to cultivate it. Indeed, Wendy Whit-mann Cobb noted in 2011 that "those supporting space activities must broaden the appeal of space, making it more accessible and understand-able for those with whom the issue does not have much saliency."[241] In other words, support for space activity follows from an enthusiasm for space, which comes through making it more relevant and understanda-ble.[242] Without such broad support, space activity remains a niche

---

[237] Ryan A. Sanford, "Space-Mindedness: The Application of Space Power," The Sir Richard Williams Foundation - The Central Blue, July 22, 2018, accessed December 4, 2019, http://centralblue.williamsfoundation.org.au/space-mindedness-the-applica-tion-of-space-power-ryan-sandford/.

[238] Dale L. Hayden, "Air-Mindedness," *Air & Space Power Journal* 22, no. 4 (2008), 44-45.

[239] Trew, "Rescuing Icarus," 48-49.

[240] Ibid., 55-56.

[241] Wendy N. Whitman Cobb, "Who's Supporting Space Activities? An 'Issue Public' for US Space Policy," *Space Policy* 27, no. 4 (2011): \234.

[242] Ibid., 238.

hobby. A whole-of-nation approach is required to develop space power founded on enthusiasm for space.

How, then, may space-minded thinking be grown? Bleddyn Bowen suggested that military and strategic cultures influence such growth as both illuminate—and even clarify or blur—how each actor viewed space power.[243] Space power theory must recognize this truism.[244] Even so, Bowen's recognition of the formative power of culture upon space power does not prepare the ground for cultivating the space-minded. Klein and Ziarnick both advocated for higher-learning institutions to stimulate proper thinking about space.[245] For both scholars, though, their recommended solution to hewing the framework for space-mindedness entailed only one of the three pillars of space power. Namely, they recommended establishing a space war college focused solely on viewing space as a warfighting domain. While any formal educational institution is arguably better than its complete absence, such a war college will address only the former of the Daedalus-Icarus duality that is space-mindedness. In other words, a space war college curriculum may well hone the space power instrument in preparation for warfare by establishing "wise and sound" thinking about space to help wade through "extraordinary outpouring of feeling" and "utopian hopes and gnawing fears.".[246] Yet, such education will not necessarily imbue or even excite a passion for space power—one that appreciates the potential of space and seeks to bring to fruition such potential. It is not enough to understand the principles and applications of space power; development requires both practicality and passion.

---

[243] Bowen, "Spacepower and Space Warfare," 254-259.
[244] Ibid., 259.
[245] Klein, *Space Warfare*, 151-152; Ziarnick, *Developing Space Power*, 235-237.
[246] Wohl, *Passion for Wings*, 1.

What enflames such passion? Peter Fritzsche evaluated German aviation development by examining the accompanying popular ideas and public imaginations regarding airpower. In *A Nation of Fliers: German Aviation and the Popular Imagination*, Fritzsche explained how public interest in aviation evolved in Germany under different governments and zeitgeists. In particular, Fritzsche recorded Nazi efforts to engender a passion for aviation through formal educational programs.[247] Despite the deficiencies of Nazi ideology, the pragmatism behind such education did not spark the imagination as hoped.[248] As may be the case for space war colleges, formal schooling can husband practical thinkers—many of whose minds' eyes twinkle for space—but it cannot occasion imagination. Creativity abhors formality.

Therefore, perhaps the only way to truly ignite a passion for space is to parallel the flight path of the likes of generals Henry H. Arnold and Ira C. Eaker. The two coauthored three books meant to explain airpower to the public, while Arnold tried to instill "aeromania" in the US' youth through six children's books that championed the adventure of aviation.[249] Arnold and his ilk recognized that a nation's people needed to embrace airpower to ensure its development.

> *Air Power will always be the business of every American citizen. The Army Air Forces recognizes its duty in formulating intelligent*

---

[247] Ibid., 200-203.

[248] Ibid., 215-219.

[249] Dik A. Daso, *Hap Arnold and the Evolution of American Airpower* (Washington, DC: Smithsonian Institution Press, 2000), 297; Henry H. Arnold and Ira C. Eaker, *Army Flyer*, 3rd ed. (New York: Harper & Brothers, 1942); Henry H. Arnold and Ira C. Eaker, *This Flying Game*, 3rd ed. (New York: Funk & Wagnalls Company, 1943); Henry H. Arnold and Ira C. Eaker, *Winged Warfare*, 3rd ed. (New York: Funk & Wagnalls Company, 1941); Peter R. Faber, "Interwar US Army Aviation and the Air Corps Tactical School: Incubators of American Airpower," in *The Paths of Heaven: The Evolution of Airpower Theory*, ed. Phillip S. Meilinger (Maxwell AFB, AL: Air University Press, 1997), 188-189.

*programs of education to the end that the public will understand
aviation in all of its forms as well as realize the danger of unprepar-
edness in the air. Propaganda has no place in this program. Public
relations must give the public a thorough understanding of...Air
Power.*[250]

For Arnold, air-mindedness derived from public awareness events,
education programs, and other outreach efforts.[251] These efforts set to
inspire in the hearts and minds of the American public the belief that
airpower was necessary and worthwhile. Perchance, today's Elon
Musks and Richard Bransons can inspire similar feelings for space
power. As Bowen noted, though, space-mindedness will form according
to the strategic culture of the public it serves.[252] Moreover, it is unlikely
that "an upsurge in public support for [a] space program could serve as
a panacea.".[253] Space-mindedness will spur space power on for the nations who contemplate such things.

Consequently, this section recalls the coda written by Arnold and
Eaker in *Winged Warfare*. The coda, with the score's key adjusted for
space, resonates today. "Popular support [for space] cannot be maintained over the long period of time" for a "superior [space power]" unless there is a demonstrated "national will" and "universal public deter-
mination to have one. [Space power] in reality is a national state of
mind.".[254]

The beguiling nature of analogy caused many theorists to overlook an
ancestral theory found in airpower—whose hereditary traits partially

---

[250] *Commanding General Report*, 71-72.
[251] David K. Vaughan, "Hap Arnold's Bill Bruce Books: Promoting Air Service Awareness
in America," *Air Power History* 40, no. 4 (1993): \43, 49; Faber, "Incubators of American Airpower," 228n25.
[252] Bowen, "Spacepower and Space Warfare," 254-259.
[253] Cobb, "Who's Supporting Space?", 238.
[254] Arnold and Eaker, *Winged Warfare*, 260.

manifest in the physical realm of aerospace operations—because of the apparent kinship between the open ocean and outer space. On the other hand, other space power theories treated airpower only superficially by viewing theory and targeting concepts as synonymous.

Wholesale adoption of airpower thinking, however, is not wise. Bruce M. DeBlois argued that the characteristics of air and space power are different enough to prevent such a bijection between their respective theories.[255] Yet, he admitted, and this section has shown, that there exists an injection from airpower to space power thought. The physical geographies are distinct, but there is harmony between air-minded and space-minded thinking, especially if both schools of thought remain subordinate to the logic of strategic theory writ large. Some ideas map from one domain to the other.[256] "Correct thinking is the basis of all successful strategy.".[257] The propositions contained herein will not help derive answers formulaically, but they will suggest in which direction those making and executing strategy should go.

ANCHORS AWEIGH: SPACE POWER SETS SAIL

"Space is an ocean," according to Samuel J. Tangredi.[258] Tangredi was not speaking metaphorically. Instead, Tangredi argued it was more appropriate to view space as a vast body like the ocean—rather than viewing space as an extension of the air—whose very geophysical characteristics warranted a navalist mindset to address the future strategic challenges of space.[259] If space and the sea are homeomorphic, strategic

---

[255] DeBlois, "Ascendant Realms," 563-565.

[256] One should note the abuse of mathematical language and excuse the author, who, as a mathematician, knows better but desires for simplicity to avoid a tangent on the use of set theory terminology.

[257] Arnold and Eaker, *Winged Warfare*, 141.

[258] Sam J. Tangredi, "Space is an Ocean," *Proceedings* 125, no. 1 (January 1999), 52.

[259] Ibid., 53.

environments—Sheldon would beg to differ—then such sea power ideas as competing for the command of the sea, through manipulation and control of sea lines of communication, would apply equally as well in space.[260] Jeremy Straub, however, believed the analogy is appropriate but incomplete. His 2015 article, "Application of a Maritime Framework to Space: Deep Space Conflict and Warfare Scenario," espoused the view that maritime models apply equally well to deep space, not just near-Earth.[261] Ziarnick's theory also addressed space strategy beyond Earth's orbit.[262] Thus, scholars addressed near and deep space, and it seems maritime concepts, as currently applied, cover the entirety of space or require correction. Space, however, is practically infinite. The sea is not. From a mathematical perspective, a finite domain cannot cover an infinite range and still be well-defined. Furthermore, scholars failed to map a few maritime concepts to the space domain. Consequently, this section evaluates sea power thinking and offers propositions that hopefully further the conversation concerning space power theory.

Proposition Seven: There is strength in weakness: a fleet in being approach is not merely for inferior forces.

Admiral Philip Colomb of the British Royal Navy, in his 1690 exposition of the Nine Years' War, coined the term and concept of a fleet in being.[263] The term generally conveyed a concept of pursuing a defensive

---

[260] Sheldon, "Strategic Analogy," 146, 206, 295-299.

[261] Jeremy Straub, "Application of a Maritime Framework to Space: Deep Space Conflict and Warfare Scenario," *Astropolitics* 13, no. 1 (2015): \65-77.

[262] See Ziarnick, *Developing Space Power*

[263] John B. Hattendorf, "The Idea of a 'Fleet in Being' in Historical Perspective," *Naval War College Review* 67, no. 1 (Winter 2014): \44.

strategy without sacrificing opportunities to contest for command of the sea actively through: "raiding campaigns, intended to wear away the enemy;" attacking enemy commerce; denying the decisive battle through avoidance; and seeking merely to survive against a stronger fleet.[264] British Army Major General and military theorist, Charles E. Callwell, added that a fleet in being must be "a perpetual menace to... the enemy, who cannot tell when a blow may fall, and who is...compelled to retard his operations until that fleet can be... neutralised."[265] Sir Julian Corbett, in his exposition of a defensive strategy, fleshed out the concept of a fleet in being, and it was Corbett's concept that John Klein adapted for space with his term "force in being."[266]

Overall, Klein's force-in-being concept accounted well for the strategic environment in space. Namely, he observed the critical fact that, in space, forces in being could influence other actors through physical and nonphysical means.[267] While Klein did not explicitly limit a force-in-being approach to a "medium space power," his theory intimated that a superior space force need not employ such a concept.[268] This implicit limitation to lesser-matched space powers missed an essential adaptation of sea power's fleet in being analogy. Geoffrey Till noted that the fleet in being approach "is of particular value for a fleet that knows it is inferior", yet "it is by no means restricted to [inferior forces]."[269] A stronger fleet could resort to such an approach in some instances, such as a local "limited defensive."[270] Corbett, after whom Klein modeled his theory,

---

[264] Geoffrey Till, *Seapower: A Guide for the Twenty-First Century* (New York: Routledge, 2012), 173.

[265] Charles E. Callwell, *Military Operations and Maritime Preponderance: Their Relations and Interdependence* (Edinburgh: William Blackwood and Sons, 1905), 203.

[266] Corbett, *Some Principles*, 209-227; Klein, *Space Warfare*, 122-123.

[267] Klein, *Space Warfare*, 122-123.

[268] Klein, *Space Warfare*, 28, 122-123; Klein, *Understanding Space Strategy*, 124-142.

[269] Till, *Seapower*, 173.

[270] Till, *Seapower*, 173. See also Corbett, *Some Principles*, 106.

argued that keeping a fleet in being is primarily for "avoiding decisive action" until the situation turns favorable and an opportunity for counterattack materializes.[271] Corbett, notably, did not exclude such use to inferior forces only.

On the seas and in space, however, opportunity does not come to those who wait. Instead, a fleet in being must be "active and vigorous," or as French Navy admiral and theorist, Raoul Castex, noted, a fleet in being "must give proof of life" and "act to impose its will to the extent that its means allow. It must take as much initiative as possible, even if nothing decisive results."[272] Note the lack of restrictions concerning relative strength in either theorist's statements. At the risk of banality, fleet in being approaches present viable options for superior forces, especially in space. On the seas, if an inferior force decides to retire completely, it allows the enemy to secure "the ulterior object, which is the control of sea communications."[273] Thus, the superior force retains command of the sea without effort. If, however, the inferior force decides to avail itself of a decisive battle, the superior force is unlikely to resort to a fleet in being approach since it should attain victory in battle—at least in theory.

In space, force size and strength does not automatically convey superiority. "Intrinsic strength does not give importance, if the position has not strategic value."[274] In a medium wherein "warfare is about the command of space," and "the command of space is about manipulating celestial lines of communication," positioning and the ability to control mission-essential orbits, orbital transition points, and choke points enable—if not general and persistent command—temporary, localized

---

[271] Ibid., 211.

[272] Till, *Seapower*, 212; Castex, *Strategic Theories*, 344.

[273] Corbett, *Some Principles*, 212.

[274] Alfred T. Mahan, *The Influence of Sea Power Upon History, 1660-1783*, 5th ed. (Mineola, NY: Dover Publications, 1987), 373.

command of "celestial lines of communication."[275] In other words, greater numbers may enable the ability to simultaneously disperse over a broader area and allow concentration at critical nodes. However, as M. V. Smith noted, "a state that has overwhelming space power may successfully dissuade another actor from competing militarily in space."[276] Sun Tzu's reminder, however, is appropriate: "Numbers alone confer no advantage. Do not advance relying on sheer military power."[277] Quite significantly, experience shows that overwhelming space power has not deterred aggression in space.[278]

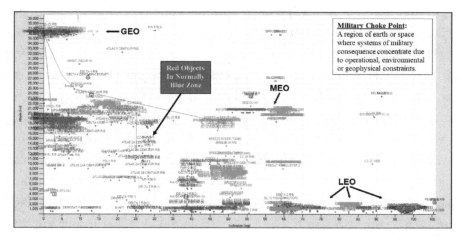

Figure 1 – Illustration of Space Choke Points. Colors: blue are US & allies; red are likely adversaries; green are neutrals. The lines show

---

[275] Bowen, "Spacepower and Space Warfare," 135-150, 171-180; Klein, *Understanding Space Strategy*, 23-24.

[276] M. V. Smith, "Spacepower and the Strategist," in *Strategy: Context and Adaptation From Archidamus to Airpower,* ed. Richard J. Bailey, James W. Forsyth, and Mark O. Yeisley (Annapolis, MD: Naval Institute Press, 2016), 168.

[277] Sun Tzu, *The Illustrated Art of War,* trans. Samuel B. Griffith (Oxford, England: Oxford University Press, 2005), 192.

[278] Todd Harrison, Kaitlyn Johnson, and Thomas G. Roberts, *Space Threat Assessment 2018* (Washington, DC: Center for Strategic & International Studies, 2018), 1-25.

movements of satellites over time. The labels with arrows refer to certain regions of space with official names such as "LEO" for Low Earth Orbit.

How can such a power compete? Smith suggests that a superior space power could either resort to asymmetric or violent means to dissuade aggression and recommends the latter as a force-in-being approach. While space is contested and competitive—a fact the strategist ignores to their peril—using violent means against uninhabited satellites, even if consistent with "the spirit and intent of the law of armed conflict," would be escalatory.[279] Moreover, depending on the weapon and target type, such actions run antipodal to an actor's aims considering space debris that results from kinetic attacks. Instead, this work suggests choosing the former of Smith's two options, the asymmetric response, which can include terrestrial-based means against non-space targets, although such responses could be considered escalatory as well. In effect, if overwhelming space power cannot dissuade competitors' aggressive actions, perchance using nonphysical, asymmetric means can without being overtly escalatory. Interestingly, a fleet in being approach need not use space assets at all. Indeed, a superior power could use cyberspace means to affect a competitor's space network or interfere with overhead image and signal collection processing to deny an adversary's aim of satellite overflight. Moreover, nations may choose to respond using terrestrial-based means against non-space targets. Undoubtedly, such actions have the potential to incite responses, but just as there appears to be a threshold below which aggression is considered "acceptable" in the cyber domain, the same seemingly applies in space, especially if such means employ covert, low probability of attribution, non-kinetic space weapon systems that would not be observable to the general public.

---

[279] Smith, "Spacepower and the Strategist," 168.

Absent active responses to competitors' aggression, the only other potential recourse is to rely on the international community to impose political costs upon aggressors. Arms control and long-awaited international legal regimes and norms, however, have not dissuaded aggressors yet.[280] Nevertheless, open, physical hostility is untenable too. Therefore, a fleet in being approach that travails the middle ground may be most appropriate.

As in maritime theory, the space actor who retires into harbor, who does not react to aggression, effectively cedes command of celestial lines of communication to its competitor. A space actor employing a fleet in being approach must compete actively since "the mere existence of such a fleet" may not impress "those who [choose] to act in spite of the fleet in being."[281] In other words, a superior space power cannot rely on size and strength alone. It must give "proof of life" by disputing command, through asymmetric means, knowing that command is rarely absolute.[282] "[I]t is as a threat, that the fleet in being is chiefly formidable," but it is only through vigorous action that the fleet can "potentially serve as a temporary deterrent in one area, if for a very limited time."[283] Without such vigor, adversaries learn that within the shadows of such a threat, there exists no substance to incur upon them costs or induce in them caution.[284] In addition, fear of political or diplomatic repercussions

---

[280] The *Outer Space Treaty* provides the sole, internationally recognized and agreed-to legal framework for space behavior. Since its inception, however, many have advocated for a better, more detailed framework only to find hopes left unfulfilled. See Elbridge Colby, *From Sanctuary to Battlefield: A Framework for a U.S. Defense and Deterrence Strategy in Space* (Washington, DC: Center for a New American Strategy, 2016), 15-16.

[281] Castex, *Strategic Theories*, 343.

[282] Castex, *Strategic Theories*, 344; Corbett, *Some Principles*, 103-105, 166, 224.

[283] Alfred Thayer Mahan quoted inCallwell, *Maritime Preponderance*, 219; Hattendorf, "Fleet in Being," 57.

[284] Brodie, *Naval Strategy*, 116; Callwell, *Maritime Preponderance*, 219.

for employment of space weapons may lead to strategic paralysis and self-deterrence, no matter how technologically superior a nation's space weapons systems may be.

Proposition Eight: The concept of space blocking, for now, is geocentric and may be less relevant in the future.

Like the previous proposition, this eighth proposition corrects existing space power thought. Theorist John Klein offered significant contributions to the body of space power theory with his adaptation of the maritime concept of blocking. As noted above, command of space is about control of celestial lines of communication, and one such way to dispute command is through blocking key positions and communications.[285] However, as Bleddyn Bowen noted, "the strategic analogy of blockade can be taken too far."[286] To wit, in space, blocking celestial lines of communication is inherently geocentric—not solely in effect, which follows from this work's third proposition, but in theoretical conception as well. Moreover, a geocentric conception may be less relevant in the future.

In *Space Warfare*, Klein discussed the various considerations for space blockades, determining that while the naval analogy is imperfect, "the strategic concept of blocking is fundamentally different from the strategy of the naval blockade."[287] That is, his theory admits the intricacies of a naval blockade are inherently different from blocking celestial lines of communication. What is noteworthy, however, is that blocking—at least in theory—is a strategic concept worth considering amid the

---

[285] Klein, *Space Warfare*, 91-99.
[286] Bowen, "Spacepower and Space Warfare," 177.
[287] Klein, *Space Warfare*, 98.

strategist's tool chest. In the Corbettian fashion, Klein distinguished between close and distant blocking, where "close blocking is obstructing or interfering with space communications within the proximity of up-links, downlinks, crosslinks, launching facilities, or any hubs of activity.".[288] "Distant blocking is the denial or disruption of space communications far away from the hubs of distribution, but still along celestial lines of communication.".[289] Bowen noted, however, "celestial lines of communication may move or change their composition, so an analogy of a... blockade may not be particularly apt.".[290]

To wit, Klein's space blocking concept revolves around the space systems situated on Earth or on-orbit and how blocking affects terrestrial activity. In other words, blocking is geocentric. On the sea, however, close versus distant blocking relates to the proximity to the enemy—it is enemy-centric.[291] Notably, Klein overlooked that many space systems today are distributed and redundant, thus obviating the ability to block by negating a single hub as can be done in the maritime domain. Notwithstanding such an admission, Bernard Brodie observed that distant naval blockades offer no "blockade at all.".[292] At best, the blockade threatens the enemy with punishment and interception, and it can only protect in so far as intercepting the enemy is possible.[293] Finally, Klein's concept involved the physical measure of distance from the Earth. In space, however, the meaning of distance becomes murky. If space blocking includes blocking enemy lines of communication, and such communications rely exclusively on information transmissions at light speed, distance is irrelevant in Klein's geocentric scenario. Moreover, the

---

[288] Ibid., 94.
[289] Ibid., 95.
[290] Bowen, "Spacepower and Space Warfare," 175.
[291] Brodie, *Naval Strategy*, 98.
[292] Ibid., 96.
[293] Ibid., 96-97.

combination of hubless space systems and the tyranny of orbital mechanics and the time and fuel restrictions they impose suggest that the adaptation of maritime blocking is not appropriate as explicated.

Even if future technology helps make small the vastness of space, Klein's description still fails. In that case, geocentrism would no longer be appropriate since, with such technology, one could posit that humankind has expanded beyond the Terran. Consequently, close or distant blocking even more closely parallels the maritime analog as being enemy-centric than it does now because a space power could harness technology to impose an enduring close blockade, or travel at sufficient speed to respond as part of a distant cover.

Klein's work is helpful; "'space blockade' thinking in terms of denying lines of communication at points of convergence or highly valuable celestial lines of communications is still useful."[294] However, analysis of Klein's conception of celestial blocking shows the direct mapping of maritime terminology to space invites confusion over what constitutes close versus distant. Moreover, the conceptual adaptation for space is still Earth-centric. For the practitioner of strategy, clarity is paramount. "Much of what appears to be wise and indeed is prudent as high theory is unhelpful to the poor warrior who actually has to do strategy."[295] Importantly, future space conflict may require denying an ability to use lines of communication, whether close or distant to the enemy or near or far from the Earth.

Proposition Nine: Space power strategy is sequential and cumulative.

Whereas the previous proposition offered a correction to Klein's concept of space blocking, this proposition builds on a corollary to

---

[294] Bowen, "Spacepower and Space Warfare," 177.
[295] Gray, "Why Strategy is Difficult," 7.

Proposition Five and Klein's adaptation of Rear Admiral J. C. Wylie's cumulative strategy approach. To that end, Wylie, a US Navy officer and military theorist, developed two methods of executing strategy: a sequential and cumulative approach. Wylie offered that in a sequential strategy, the overarching design contained a "series of discrete steps," foreknown to the strategist, whose results were predictable.[296] However, "there is another way to prosecute a war.".[297] This other way entails an "entire pattern...made up of a collection of lesser actions" that are not sequentially interdependent.[298] Despite the distinction between sequential and cumulative strategies, they are not mutually exclusive but are "usually interdependent in their strategic result.".[299]

Wylie recognized that cumulative strategy was a characteristic of sea power, and because of the similarities between sea and space domains, Klein applied the concept to space power.[300] Klein suggests that while the idea of a cumulative strategy applies to all space actors, he considered the concept to be a likely "centerpiece" for emerging space powers, mainly because emerging powers often cannot employ a sequential strategy at the outset.[301] Still, both Wylie and Klein noted that the "strength of the cumulative strategy" factored considerably into the success of its sequential sibling.[302]

The above assertion leads to this work's ninth proposition. Put simply, it is the accumulation of space power, through cumulative strategy—that is, "the less perceptible minute accumulation of little items piling" up that reach critical mass—that enables a sequential strategy to

---

[296] Joseph C. Wylie, *Military Strategy: A General Theory of Power Control* (Annapolis, MD: Naval Institute Press, 1989), 22-23.

[297] Ibid., 23.

[298] Ibid.

[299] Ibid., 24-25.

[300] Klein, *Understanding Space Strategy*, 155-160.

[301] Ibid., 155, 159.

[302] Klein, *Understanding Space Strategy*, 156; Wylie, *Military Strategy*, 25.

succeed.[303] With perspective, one sees the dyad of sequential and cumulative strategies nest in the conception of a general strategy as exposited in Proposition Five. That is, the combination of cumulative and sequential aspects of space strategy wields all forms of space power, as demanded by general strategy. Space power is indivisible and thus should be wielded as part of a general strategy, wherein space power in all its forms aid accomplishing policy's aims. Thus, it is a false dilemma to choose cumulative or sequential strategies within a space strategy. The student of strategy employs both.

Furthermore, both cumulative and sequential strategies look outward, to adjudge the environment and adversaries; however, cumulative strategy exhibits an inward-tending quality as well. Cumulative space strategies cultivate the capability for future sequential strategies. Such cultivation requires forethought and forbearing care. Mahan exhorted the US to take sea power seriously over a century ago. He claimed, "in such anticipation, such forethought...lies the best hope of the best solution.".[304] Space power is grown, as Klein noted, by "instilling national pride" and developing a "technically educated workforce.".[305] Additionally, a nation must "'strike down roots' deep into the heart of its country...to lay the foundation...to build" space power, and make space "part of its national character.".[306] In other words, space power accretes gradually, through careful cultivation of space capability founded upon a nation's space-mindedness as delineated in Proposition Six.

---

[303] Wylie, *Military Strategy*, 24.

[304] Alfred T. Mahan, *The Interest of America in Sea Power, Present and Future* (1897; repr., Boston: Little, Brown, and Company, 1918), 177.

[305] Klein, *Understanding Space Strategy*, 160-161.

[306] Trevor Brown, "Space and the Sea: Strategic Considerations for the Commons," *Astropolitics* 10, no. 3 (2012): \239-240. See the maritime analog in Mahan, *Influence of Sea Power*, 50-58.

Certainly, an actor may wield space power within a sequential strat-egy. One need only look at discrete events like the Chinese anti-satellite test in 2007. The power reserve from which sequential strategy draws, however, is fashioned by an inward-looking, cumulative strategy that seeks to grow an enduring space power. Conversely, successful sequen-tial strategies provide opportunities—new pastures—to harvest space power. Cumulative and sequential space strategies are, much like space power, essentially indivisible, nested under the general employ of a broad, holistic strategy.

CONCLUSION

Is it appropriate to apply sea power analogies—or airpower for that matter—to space? In 2005, John B. Sheldon asserted that the uncritical application of strategic analogies could lead the student and practitioner of strategy from the correct path.[307] Sheldon evaluated existing analo-gies and concluded that "adaptation [was] not possible."[308] Instead, Sheldon argued that only an inductive, creative development of space power theory could produce the correct path.[309]

Whereas Sheldon argued against analogical reasoning using strategic theory itself, Elizabeth Mendenhall extended the argument using scien-tific rationale. In her 2018 article, "Treating Outer Space Like a Place: A Case for Rejecting Other Domain Analogies," Mendenhall contended that "using direct scientific evidence to construct a representation of the outer space environment [was] superior" to the use of analogical "plan-etary domains."[310] She recommended viewing space through a lens that casts gravity, distance, inhospitable conditions, technological reliance,

---

[307] Sheldon, "Strategic Analogy," 284-329.
[308] Ibid., 295.
[309] Ibid.
[310] Elizabeth Mendenhall, "Treating Outer Space Like a Place: A Case for Rejecting Other Domain Analogies," *Astropolitics* 16, no. 2 (2018): \114-115.

and the size of celestial bodies in stark relief against all other considerations.[311] Only then can governments develop "sober and informed understanding about consequences for the space environment."[312]

Such a reminder is necessary. Strategic analogies "must in the end diverge."[313] However, as Colin Gray noted, "Geography is inescapable."[314] If "all strategy is geostrategy" that "cannot be evaded by... orbital overflight," and if human politics will continue to spread to the heavens just as they pervade the Earth, then viewing space as a place comports well with Gray's exhortation that "strategy and politics must be done within geography."[315]

Nevertheless, Sheldon's and Mendenhall's words help avoid oversimplifying space's strategic environment while attempting to explain strategic behavior therein. Undoubtedly, the propositions offered here rely on simplification and analogy. Such is the essence of strategic theory. Space power theorists, however, leaned too far toward caution in avoiding apparently ill-fitting analogies and overlooked useful concepts to explain spacefaring activity. Indeed, previous scholars committed the very error they hoped to avoid when they eschewed airpower thought while adopting alternative analogies in toto because some concepts of the former did not translate well into space. That some airpower concepts do not translate well to space while seemingly many sea power concepts do, is not dispositive of sea power theory's primacy for building space power theory. Indeed, as Sheldon noted, "the making of a theory

---

[311] Ibid., 110-114.

[312] Ibid., 115.

[313] Klein, *Space Warfare*, 151.

[314] Colin S. Gray, "Inescapable Geography," in *Geopolitics: Geography and Strategy*, ed. Colin S. Gray and Geoffrey Sloan (London: Frank Cass, 1999), 175.

[315] Gray, "Inescapable Geography," 164-165, 175; Robert C. Harding, *Space Policy in Developing Countries: The Search for Security and Development on the Final Frontier* (New York: Routledge, 2012), 19.

of space power... is one that will take place over a long period of time involving many people... for this reason alone, the development of a theory of space power will always be a team effort that builds on and corrects that which has gone before.".[316] No previous body of strategic thought should or even can hold pride of place in developing theory for space power. Consequently, Sheldon concluded that "there can be no Mahan for the final frontier.".[317]

For different reasons, Bruce DeBlois reached a similar conclusion:

> That is, one cannot build space power theory and doctrine in general upon airpower theory and doctrine...space power clearly requires fundamental, bottom-up, theoretical and doctrinal development. The most conducive environment for such development remains a separate space corps or service [and practical historical experience in space conflicts].[318]

Perhaps having a comprehensive theory for space in the vein of Mahan is not required. In the twenty years since DeBlois' words, many theorists have provided helpful and insightful thoughts on space power, its meaning, and its use. Still, analogical reasoning is imperfect. The absence of a comprehensive, bottom-up theory, however, hints at the implausibility of the task to build one, especially if theory-building occurs in humanity's near-vacuum of space warfare experience.

Nevertheless, as terrestrial "political-cultural baggage" accompanies human presence in celestial areas, one cannot help but conclude that until humanity makes space a permanent home, strategic theory's terrestrial vestiges will always be present.[319] People may tend to forget the

---

[316] Sheldon, "Strategic Analogy," 328-329.
[317] Ibid.
[318] DeBlois, "Ascendant Realms," 564-565.
[319] Bowen, "Spacepower and Space Warfare," 157, 181, 239.

past, but strategy continues as part of the human condition.[320] Even if space power theory requires a clean slate, adept thinking need not be restricted to a separate military service, especially if, as this chapter claims, space power entails the full complement of instruments of power. Thus, Edward Luttwak's words are still appropriate when he stated, "the way of strategy is not given to all--and certainly not to those who would approach its truths from the perspective of a narrow-minded bureaucratic interest.".[321]

To that end, this chapter has approached the truths of space power while looking beyond bureaucratic or even military interests. Perhaps it is ironic, that in this reevaluation of airpower and sea power theories, seven of the above propositions speak to space power under a broader strategic banner. Furthermore, all six airpower-based precepts exhibit panoramas more extensive than mere military vantages. Additionally, this work uncovered two maritime-based propositions whose application rests solely within the military domain, namely the concepts of space fleets in being and blocking celestial lines of communication. Recall that previous theorists asserted that airpower theory's shortcoming "is that it primarily has a military focus.".[322] Despite this juxtaposition of broader versus military-focused strategic concepts, previous theoretical concepts still prove useful. The propositions contained above hopefully build upon such concepts and place in proper orbital position, new ideas that revolve around the central truths of strategic theory by defining what space power is; categorizing characteristics of space power; explaining space power's effects on humanity's experience; connecting it

---

[320] B. H. Liddell Hart, *Why Don't We Learn From History?*, Revised ed. (New York: Hawthorn Books Inc., 1971); Colin S. Gray, *The Future of Strategy* (Cambridge, England: Polity, 2015), 11-14, 22.

[321] Edward N. Luttwak, *On the Meaning of Victory: Essays on Strategy* (New York: Simon & Schuster, 1986), 103.

[322] Klein, *Space Warfare*, 18.

to other fields of strategic thought; and anticipating the future of human space activity.[323] While the ideas contained herein are not exhaustive nor comprehensive, the reevaluation of strategic antecedents of space power has hopefully advanced theory by acting similar to a rocket booster, gathering velocity for a future, celestial rendezvous with the next space power theorist.

---

[323] Winton, "An Imperfect Jewel: Military Theory and the Military Profession," 854-858.

CHAPTER 6: THE REMOTE SENSING REVOLUTION

BY LTC(R) BRAD TOWNSEND

COUNTERING SPACE-BASED RECONNAISSANCE

Early on the morning of January 8, 2020, as many as ten Iranian missiles struck Al-Assad Airbase in Iraq, a major hub of US military activity in the region.[324] That same day news outlets around the world were commenting on the apparent effectiveness of the Iranian missiles and the implications of the damage caused by the strikes. This commentary and analysis were made possible by high-quality satellite imagery taken hours after the attack. Using this imagery—provided by US-based and licensed company Planet—the American public could see the extent of the damage and judge the relative accuracy of the strikes.[325] Commentary centered on these images provided the media with a day or two of sensational news coverage on rising tensions in the Middle-East before other topics captured the news cycle. What was missed is that a watershed event in the history of space had just occurred—a US-based

---

[324] "Satellite Photos Reveal Extent Of Damage From Iranian Strike On Air Base In Iraq," NPR.org, accessed January 18, 2020, https://www.npr.org/2020/01/08/794517031/satellite-photos-reveal-extent-of-damage-at-al-assad-air-base.

[325] Diana Stancy Correll Mehta Aaron, "See the Damage at Al-Asad Airbase Following Iranian Missile Strike," Military Times, January 8, 2020, https://www.militarytimes.com/news/your-military/2020/01/08/see-the-damage-at-al-asad-air-base-following-iranian-missile-strike/.

commercial remote sensing company had just released detailed same-day satellite images of the effects of war between the US and a foreign power.

Planet's publicly available imagery did far more than inform the domestic news cycle. It provided Iran with vital information that they would otherwise not have had access to on the effectiveness of their strikes and targeting. Using this imagery, Iran could conduct post-strike analysis allowing them to refine their targeting for future strikes, presenting a real risk to US and Iraqi forces. Without the satellite data provided by Planet, Iran would have only had access to fragmented and unconfirmed reports from eye-witnesses on the ground. Neither Iraq nor the US would have allowed Iranian aircraft or drones to overfly Al-Assad Airbase uncontested to obtain an overhead view of the damage, and it is highly unlikely that any attempt to do so would have succeeded. Ultimately, Iran declined to conduct follow-up strikes and further escalate the conflict, mitigating any potential damage that Planet's imagery release could have caused. However, the rapid public release of high-quality satellite imagery of an attack on US forces signaled the beginning of a new era in warfare, one that brings significant challenges, risks, and opportunities to future warfighting.

This chapter will look at the challenges and opportunities presented by the proliferation of high-quality, high-revisit rate, space-based remote sensing data in modern warfare and propose a multi-part solution to managing the threat. While the opportunities inherent in having access to real-time imagery are easy to grasp, addressing the threat is more complicated and will require a tailored approach with military, regulatory, and diplomatic aspects. This chapter will address each aspect of the threat mitigation approach in turn. First, it will discuss how remote sensing developed as well as trends in the rapidly evolving remote sensing market and how they will impact future warfighting. Second, it will look at military approaches to addressing the threat from remote sensing using both passive and active measures. Third, it will look at existing regulatory controls that can help mitigate the risk from domestic and allied commercial satellite imagery providers while balancing industry needs and national security. Finally, this chapter will outline the challenges of controlling third-party remote sensing through diplomatic means and propose an approach to managing the third-party threat when diplomacy is too slow or fails.

REVOLUTIONARY CHANGE

Prior to the advent of satellites, obtaining post-strike data required risky overflights of enemy targets or the use of ground-based reconnaissance to judge effectiveness and to determine the need for subsequent strikes or to simply gather additional intelligence. Outside of conflict, overhead imagery of other nations for intelligence purposes is even more difficult to obtain without satellites as nations jealously guard their sovereign airspace. That satellites can pass over countries without interference today is not just a function of the physics of maintaining Earth orbit, but a norm set by the Soviet Union. With the launch of Sputnik, the Soviets established the precedent that satellites are not subject to the same overflight restrictions as aircraft. The Eisenhower administration was quick to realize the implications of this and turn that precedent into the first real international norm that would make satellite imaging possible.[326] The race was now on to develop a way to take images of the Earth's surface and effectively return them to Earth, a truly daunting technical challenge at the dawn of the Space Age.

In 1956, even before the launch of Sputnik, the US started early work on what would eventually be called the Corona project, which aimed to develop the first satellite capable of imaging inside the Soviet Union.

---

[326] Andrew Goodpaster, "Memorandum of Conference with the President," October 9, 1957, 2, Eisenhower Library, https://www.eisenhowerlibrary.gov/sites/default/files/research/online-documents/sputnik/10-16-57.pdf.

With spaceflight still an unproven concept, the ambitious and highly secretive Corona project quickly ran into technical and budgetary problems that were overcome only due to pressing need and strong presidential support.[327] After numerous failures, the US succeeded in launching
an imagery satellite and recovering the film from it in August 1960.[328]
Corona's success was timely as just a few months prior the Soviet Union
had shot down Gary Power's U-2, effectively removing aerial imagery as
an option for monitoring Soviet actions. Despite its success, Corona was
nothing like today's highly capable satellites. The first generation of Corona satellites were crude and inefficient due to technical limitations.
Since digital photography was years in the future, the satellite needed to
eject its film payload and have it recovered after it de-orbited. This limited the lifespan of these satellites to just a couple of days before the satellite ejected the film payload and became useless. The resulting imagery
from these early satellites was also of significantly lower quality than
imagery previously provided by the U-2 (see Figure 1). The first Corona
satellites had a roughly 12 meters ground sample distance (GSD), which
was only good enough to discern large structures, but this quickly improved to a much more useful 1.8 meters by 1963.[329] Even with these limitations, satellites did have one major advantage; the first Discoverer

---

[327] Kevin C. Ruffner, ed., Corona: America's First Satellite Program, CIA Cold War Rec-
ords (CIA History Staff, Center for the Study of Intelligence, 1995), 6.

[328] Ibid., 22.

[329] Ground Sample distance in modern terms is the distance between two adjacent pixel
centers as measured on the ground, it is the most common method of measuring the
resolution of satellite images. "USGS EROS Archive-Declassified Data-Declassified
Satellite Imagery-1" (USGS), accessed April 16, 2020, https://www.usgs.gov/cen-
ters/eros/science/usgs-eros-archive-declassified-data-declassified-satellite-im-
agery-1?qt-science_center_objects=0#qt-science_center_objects.

payload alone returned more imagery than all previous U-2 flights combined.[330]

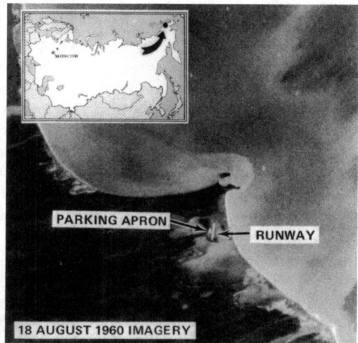

Figure 3. First Corona Satellite Image. Imagery from the first successful return of Corona imagery in 1960. "Discoverer 12 Imagery" (National Reconnaissance Office, August 18, 1960).[331]

With the advent of remote sensing, satellites could now largely replace aircraft overflights for intelligence gathering purposes, but not without limitations. While a satellite can pass freely overhead in its orbit, it cannot reasonably change its orbits to pass over a specific target

---

[330] Ruffner, Corona: America's First Satellite Program, 23.

[331] https://www.nro.gov/Portals/65/images/corona/¬highres/cor1h.jpg?ver=2018-04-30-144015-230.

sooner. This places time limitations (temporal resolution) on space-based intelligence's usefulness that is exacerbated by cost and target resolution limitations (spatial resolution). Once digital return was possible and imagery satellites were no longer single use, a balance needed to be struck between resolution and on-orbit lifetime. Imagery satellites are, or at least were, ruinously expensive which meant that they needed to be high enough in their orbits to ensure that they did not suffer from significant atmospheric drag that would limit their on-orbit lifetime. Higher altitudes drove the need for larger and more exquisite optics to ensure that spatial resolution remained relevant, further increasing cost. These high costs made space-based intelligence a privilege limited to the handful of nations that could afford to build, launch, and operate remote sensing satellites. It was not until 2001 with the advent of fully commercial remote sensing satellites beginning with the launch of QuickBird 2, that relatively high-resolution imagery became readily available for purchase by third parties. Despite this paradigm shift, space-based imagery remained expensive, and the number of commercial platforms remained relatively small, limiting their operational impact as satellite imagery remained largely a strategic intelligence tool.

Dramatic decreases in the cost of reaching orbit over the last decade combined with the miniaturization of satellite technology have altered the economics of satellite construction and led to a revolution in satellite imagery. Previously, market forces encouraged the development of large, highly capable, and therefore expensive satellites. Until very recently, the commercial remote sensing industry followed this model of producing costly and exquisite platforms. High costs meant that the number of commercial remote sensing satellites on-orbit was relatively small and that the number of those capable of taking imagery at better than 0.5-meter resolution was limited. The first commercial satellite to break the 0.5-meter resolution barrier was US-based DigitalGlobe's World-View 1 launched in 2007. World-View 1's capabilities were exceeded by World-View 3 in 2014. World-View 3 was capable of 0.3-meter panchromatic resolution imagery but cost nearly $600 million and had a best-case revisit rate to anywhere in the world of just over one day.[332] The most recent commercial satellite to follow this model was World-View 4 which launched in 2016 and failed on orbit in early 2019 only two years into an expected ten-year lifespan.[333] These satellites provided exquisite high-resolution imagery but were limited by a variety of technical factors to imaging 680,000 km^2 per day, an area roughly equivalent to the size of Texas.[334] With high spatial resolution but low temporal resolution, these satellites were valuable intelligence tools but remained a relatively small operational risk to military forces in the field.

Increasing temporal resolution requires launching more satellites, but the technical limitations discussed above made this cost-prohibitive as long as launch costs remained high. Only since 2015 have launch costs begun to fall in real terms as true commercial companies, most notably SpaceX, entered a market previously dominated by near national monopolies. These national monopolies primarily relied on domestic government contracts for funding and had no real competition, so they had little incentive to attempt revolutionary innovation. Beginning with NASA's Commercial Orbital Transportation Services (COTS) contract that essentially provided seed funding for SpaceX, real commercial competition entered the launch market for the first time leading to dramatic technological leaps that have opened up new market opportunities.

---

[332] "WorldView-4's Long Road to Launch about to Pay off for DigitalGlobe | SpaceNews Magazine," accessed January 19, 2020, http://www.spacenewsmag.com/feature/worldview-4s-long-road-to-launch-%E2%80%A8about-to-pay-off-for-digital-globe/.

[333] "DigitalGlobe Loses WorldView-4 Satellite to Gyro Failure - SpaceNews.Com," accessed January 19, 2020, https://spacenews.com/digitalglobe-loses-worldview-4-satellite-to-gyro-failure/.

[334] "WorldView-3 Satellite Sensor | Satellite Imaging Corp," accessed January 19, 2020, https://www.satimagingcorp.com/satellite-sensors/worldview-3/.

The drop in launch costs coincided with a rapid shift toward satellite miniaturization. Smaller satellites are cheaper, and dozens can be launched at once into a single orbital plane where careful manipulation of the space environment can then place them in useful configurations and significantly decrease temporal resolution. The tradeoff is that the remote sensing satellites launched in this way are individually much less capable of hosting large optical payloads, reducing their spatial resolution. Small remote sensing satellites compensate for this by launching into much lower orbital altitudes—250km versus 600km or more for Digital Globe's more traditional World-View satellites. Of course, this means that these small satellites have a greatly reduced lifetime as atmospheric drag is much more significant, necessitating frequent replenishment to maintain a constellation. A benefit to this approach is that it drives demand for more launches and the construction of more satellites, reducing unit cost and allowing for iterative improvements of both, further reinforcing the economic incentives associated with this approach.

A race is on to achieve the best spatial and temporal resolution possible. In late 2017, the US-based company Planet attained the goal of imaging the entire Earth's surface at a 3-5-meter resolution in a single day.[335] This was a paradigm-shifting achievement that most would have considered impossible just a few years earlier, and it was one of these relatively cheap satellites that provided the initial imagery of Al-Assad. Planet is not alone in introducing disruptive approaches to remote sensing. Dozens of new imagery providers have begun to enter the market, offering a variety of capabilities from Synthetic Aperture Radar (SAR) to hyperspectral imaging capabilities. As of 2020, many of these systems

---

[335] "Planet Launches Satellite Constellation to Image the Whole Planet Daily," February 14, 2017, https://www.planet.com/pulse/planet-launches-satellite-constellation-to-image-the-whole-planet-daily/.

are already present on orbit in small numbers as the first tranche of future constellations of similar satellites. The end-state of this race between commercial companies and nations leveraging commercial technology is ubiquitous high-resolution coverage of the entire globe at all times. This event, a resolution convergence, will undoubtedly occur before 2030. However, the impact of this shift is already a major concern for military operations as evidenced by the timely release of imagery of the attack on Al-Asaad Airbase.

The effect of a resolution convergence on military operations will become impossible to ignore over the next decade. Space-based remote sensing platforms are rapidly transitioning from primarily an intelligence risk to a real-time operational risk to military forces. Satellites will observe nearly every action by military forces in real-time; only fast-moving aircraft are likely to have any real chance of avoiding accurate tracking by remote sensing satellites. For naval and land forces, both the threats and opportunities will be enormous. Surface ships and land forces will be continuously tracked and observed, greatly increasing the risk associated with entering an opponent's engagement range. The threat might seem intuitive, but the magnitude of it is difficult to grasp, as are the challenges associated with effective mitigation.

MILITARY MEASURES OF CONTROL

The challenges associated with mitigation measures for space-based remote sensing are daunting and frequently lead to the conclusion that there is no way to control these capabilities; instead, we must simply learn to live with them. This argument is bolstered by the sheer potential number of space systems that could be present in remote sensing constellations and the inability to manage the threat with existing capabilities except through difficult to implement passive deception measures. However, the potential for these systems to tilt the battlefield calculus is too great for passive-only measures as a solution; a comprehensive approach to solving this problem is necessary. A strategy that emphasizes increased deception measures but also includes active measures since effective passive deception will be extremely burdensome, relatively easy to defeat, and very limited in its effectiveness when an opponent has near real-time observation capabilities. This section will demonstrate the need for aggressive active measures as a complement to passive measures to manage this rapidly emerging threat.

Demonstrating the linkage between increased ability to observe a target from Remote Sensing platforms and the increased threat to forces can be highlighted using the OODA loop concept developed by Air Force Colonel John Boyd. The OODA loop, observe—orient—decide—act, is a useful model for understanding the operational impact of constant space-based observation.[336] In this context, *observe* is the ability to see a target, encompassing the ability of ground, air, and space assets to collectively observe a target. Space systems are the new and dominant variable in this formulation. *Orient* is the ability to process the data observed and separate the target from the background noise. Orient has historically been a limiting factor for space systems that generate large quantities of data. These images once required a careful and time-consuming review by experienced imagery analysts, limiting the operational utility of satellite imagery. This process is rapidly evolving, aided by optical recognition algorithms designed to identify and prioritize targets that will largely automate this process.[337] The next variable in the OODA loop—*decide*—is, in this context, the conscious allocation of

---

[336] John Boyd, *A Discourse on Winning and Losing*, ed. Grant Hammond (Maxwell Air Force Base, Alabama: Air University, 2018), 2.

[337] Karsten Schulz, Ronny Hansch, and Uwe Sorgel, "Machine Learning Methods for Remote Sensing Applications: An Overview," *Proceedings of the Society of Photo-Optical Instrumentation Engineers* 10790 (2018): 1–2, https://www.spiedigitallibrary.org/conference-proceedings-of-spie/10790/2503653/Machine-learning-methods-for-remote-sensing-applications-an-overview/10.1117/12.2503653.short?SSO=1.

resources capable of ranging and striking the target. The final variable—*act*—is the ability of a weapons system to strike a target. Act is mitigated both by the availability of a weapons system to strike a target, but also by the target's ability to defend against the strike.

Table 1. Operational targeting OODA Loop

Observe	The ability of ground, air, and space assets to collectively observe a target.
Orient	The ability to process the large quantities of observational data and separate the target from the background noise.
Decide	The conscious allocation of resources capable of ranging and striking the target.
Act	The ability of an attacker to strike a target balanced by the defender's ability to prevent the strike.

Looking at each variable in turn from the perspective of the defender, it becomes apparent that the ability to influence some variables is more limited than others. A defender has little influence on an attacker's ability to orient as this factor will progress and develop independently of any practical ability to disrupt it, although some deception measures may be undertaken to influence any known weaknesses in detection algorithms and sensors. A defender has some ability to influence the decide factor as they can attrite an opponent's resources and reduce his capability to strike targets within limits. Leaving aside any ability to affect the observe variable, a defender's primary focus on interfering with the OODA loop and preventing an adversary from striking their target lies within the act variable. Stopping an opponent from striking an objective is the logical and seemingly obvious focus of this problem set, but it leaves the defender in a purely reactive mode. Measuring the impact of variations in each of these variables is difficult, though the necessity of applying resources to as many aspects of the targeting OODA loop can be easily illustrated mathematically.

Applying a numerical value between 0 and 1, where one represents a perfect ability to observe, orient, decide, or act by the attacker to each of these values demonstrates why the observe variable, in particular, cannot be ignored and requires intense active mitigation. Ubiquitous all-weather space-based remote sensing will create a near-perfect ability to identify and observe a target that passive deception measures, such as camouflage netting or decoys, will find extremely difficult to defeat, as will be discussed later. Passive defense measures are also extremely difficult to maintain for operational forces maneuvering for advantage as even a slight slip in deception or protection measures will be catastrophic under these circumstances. Therefore, passive-only measures against remote sensing systems will only be moderately effective, placing this variable at or near 0.8 for illustrative purposes. The value for orient is at or approaching one since, as discussed previously, capable opponents will have the ability to use machine learning to process bulk data into meaningful targeting information with minimal capacity for a defender to influence the result directly. Since long-range precision strike systems will likely be placed deep in an adversary's homeland within a layered air defense architecture, the defender will also have difficulty attriting these systems before they are employed, meaning that the adversary enjoys a high degree of freedom to decide to use them. The act variable is then limited to a contest between an opponent's long-range precision strike capabilities and a defender's defenses against these systems. Assuming that this contest is intense and reasonably balanced as these systems are relatively mature means that this variable can be placed at 0.5, the values for this scenario are on the left of Table 2 below.

It quickly becomes apparent that the variable most open to manipulation is observe. Using only passive measures to mitigate this variable in line with current approaches leaves the attacker unmolested. Here the defender has an advantage, a system designed to actively defeat an opponent's remote sensing satellites does not necessarily need to be positioned near the battlefield. A defender can influence the attackers' remote sensing satellites at any point in their orbit using approaches detailed later. This flexibility in engagement method and zone makes it extremely difficult for a defender to actively protect individual remote sensing platforms from interference, potentially creating windows where a defender is unobserved. If even a semi-effective active approach to denying an opponent their ability to observe friendly forces is taken, we can assume that the orient value is reduced by roughly half, or to 0.4. Multiplying the values assigned to each variable in the OODA loop together to find a product returns a value that can be interpreted as the probability of an attacker effectively striking a target, see the right-hand side of Table 1 below. Since, in this case, no complex equation is used, the relative impact of each variable is equal, halving the possibility of observation by taking active measures halves the probability of striking the target. This simple exercise highlights the importance of moving beyond passive means for mitigating observation used today toward a much more active approach.

Table 2. Applying the OODA loop. This analysis demonstrates the need for active mitigation of opponent's ability to observe targets. Probability of successfully striking a defended high value target is halved.

No active countermeasures against remote sensing satellites		Active and passive countermeasures against remote sensing satellites	
Observe	0.8	Observe	0.4
Orient	1.0	Orient	1.0
Decide	0.8	Decide	0.8
Act	0.5	Act	0.5
PROBABILITY OF SUCCESSFUL STRIKE	**32%**	PROBABILITY OF SUCCESSFUL STRIKE	**16%**

Before discussing active military measures for mitigating remote sensing systems, the challenges associated with passive measures require discussion. Passive measures can be broken into two categories, measures of denial and measures of deception. Measures of denial include conducting testing, training, and preparation under overhead cover or during windows when no satellites are overhead. As we approach the resolution convergence, the already small opportunity windows for unobserved movement and preparation will disappear. These windows are already primarily limited to darkness or periods of heavy cloud-cover where traditional visible wavelength electro-optical sensors are incapable of gathering functional imagery. The presence of constellations of space-based SAR will close these windows as these systems are unaffected by cloud-cover or lighting conditions. Another threat to denial approaches is the increase in high-resolution systems capable of capturing non-visible wavelengths such as short-wave infrared (SWIR), which can penetrate smoke screens, dust storms, and other visibility limiting situations.[338] Even so, darkness or inclement weather will still decrease observation opportunities as all non-SAR remote sensing systems will be hampered by conditions that create windows of reduced observation.

Unlike measures of denial, measures of deception are intended to be observed, and if executed successfully, can be extremely effective, though modern sensors are making this much more difficult than in the past. Allied efforts to deceive the German military intelligence before the D-day landings in WW2 best epitomize military deception measures against overhead imagery. In a coordinated operation involving misleading signals intelligence and false media stories, the Allies also produced hundreds of decoy tanks, airplanes, and landing craft that were convincing enough to fool German intelligence officers reviewing aerial reconnaissance photos.[339] These same deception measures would have little chance of success against modern remote sensing systems. Even if all other aspects of the D-day deception plan could be replicated successfully against a modern opponent, it would be impossible to trick multi and hyperspectral sensors using decoys. These satellites operate in dozens or hundreds of spectral bands that can easily differentiate between objects which are otherwise visually very similar, such as live grass versus artificial turf or camouflaged vehicles hidden under vegetation.[340] The inflatable tanks and aircraft used in WW2 would be easily

---

[338] "WorldView-3 Datasheet" (Digital Globe, n.d.), https://www.spaceimagingme.com/downloads/sensors/datasheets/DG_WorldView3_DS_2014.pdf.

[339] Danielle Lupton, "Analysis | D-Day Would Be Nearly Impossible to Pull off Today. Here's Why.," Washington Post, accessed April 2, 2020, https://www.washingtonpost.com/politics/2019/06/06/d-day-would-be-nearly-impossible-pull-off-to-day-heres-why/.

[340] Xavier Briottet et al., "Military Applications of Hyperspectral Imagery," in *Proceedings*, vol. 6239 (Defense and Security Symposium, Orlando, Florida: SPIE, 2006), https://doi.org/10.1117/12.672030.

differentiated from the real thing today, nothing short of actual tanks and aircraft would fool modern sensors.

Despite the shortcomings of passive measures alone for mitigating the threat from remote sensing platforms, there is very little action being taken to pursue active measures, at least by Western militaries. The 2014 Quadrennial Defense Review (QDR), in its discussion on space called for accelerated "initiatives to counter adversary space capabilities including adversary ISR and space-enabled precision strike."[341] This mention of a need for active measures stands in isolation despite a recent shift in tone within the US military space community toward a more aggressive warfighting stance in its space activities. The closest official mention is in a recent Aerospace Corporation publication discussing a future geospatial intelligence singularity which calls for a combination of active and passive measures for managing space systems. The active measures mentioned in this report include lasing and jamming adversary sensors as well as interfering with communications links.[342] The report does not cite any other categories of space control systems as mitigation measures such as anti-satellite weapons (ASATs) or co-orbital threats despite the very public and active development by both China and Russia of these space control systems.[343] Each of these major categories of space control systems—ASATs, laser weapons, and co-orbital threats—can be used to actively target remote sensing systems to deny observation, though their usefulness varies.

Anti-satellite missiles are a relatively common space control system that have existed in one form or another for decades, and that could be moderately useful against remote sensing constellations. Several

---

[341] "Quadrennial Defense Review 2014" (Department of Defense, 2014), 37.

[342] Josef S. Koller, "The Future of Ubiquitous, Realtime Intelligence: A GEOINT Singularity" (The Aerospace Corporation, 2019), 11.

[343] "Challenges to Security in Space" (Defense Intelligence Agency, January 2019), III.

countries have conducted high-profile tests of ASATs in the last few decades, including the US, Russia, China, and India. The US first tested an ASAT launched from a F-15 fighter aircraft in 1985 and later used a modified standard missile-3 (SM-3) fired from an Aegis cruiser in 2008 to destroy a malfunctioning satellite.[344] The Chinese and Indian launches relied on land-based interceptor missiles, which struck targets at 865 and 262 kilometers, respectively.[345] The variety of launch platforms in these test launches demonstrate that ASATs are relatively flexible systems capable of striking most satellites in low Earth orbit where remote sensing satellites are typically located. The challenge with ASATs as a mechanism for active denial is that by their nature, each missile is only capable of destroying a single target. In an era where only a handful of exquisite remote sensing platforms exist, ASATs make attractive weapons for denying adversary remote sensing systems. However, we are already in an era where remote sensing satellite constellations numbering dozens and hundreds of satellites exist. The cost of an individual satellite in these constellations can be as little as $7,000, with an additional $50,000 in launch costs. These numbers stand in stark contrast to the hundreds of millions in total costs for large legacy remote sensing platforms like World-View 4.[346] Assuming that the publicized SM-3-unit cost of approximately $10 million is accurate, the cost-benefit of using

---

[344] John A. Tirpak, "Operation Burnt Frost 'Historic,'" *Air Force Magazine*, February 22, 2008, http://www.airforcemag.com/Features/security/Pages/box022208shootdown.aspx.

[345] Ashley J. Tellis and Ashley J. Tellis, "India's ASAT Test: An Incomplete Success," Carnegie Endowment for International Peace, accessed April 19, 2020, https://carnegieendowment.org/2019/04/15/india-s-asat-test-incomplete-success-pub-78884.

[346] Jon Markman, "This Maker Of Tiny Satellites Is Disrupting The Space-Industrial Complex," Forbes, accessed April 19, 2020, https://www.forbes.com/sites/jonmarkman/2018/05/28/this-maker-of-tiny-satellites-is-disrupting-the-space-industrial-complex/.

ASATs as weapons to target constellations does not favor the attacker.[347] This disparity in satellite versus missile cost allows a defender to overcome the affordable magazine depth of the attacker easily.

An alternative option to ASATs is to use some type of co-orbital kinetic weapon system that follows a target satellite during times of peace and strikes on command. Russia demonstrated behavior consistent with a potential pre-positioned weapon system in 2020 when it was publicly criticized by General John Raymond, then commander of US Space Command, for maneuvering two satellites to follow a US spy satellite closely.[348] It is not clear what the intended purpose of the Russian satellites were; however, they were positioned close enough to a US satellite that they could have quickly collided or otherwise interfered with it. Such a system represents a threat of great enough concern to the US that the US government decided to chastise Russia over it publicly. Despite the usefulness of having a co-orbital system pre-positioned near your opponent, it does have several drawbacks. First, while a co-orbital system would be an ever-present threat to the target, informing the defender about which systems were at risk allows them time to develop mitigation measures for the expected loss of those satellites. Second, the cost of co-orbital threat systems would likely be at least equal to the cost of the target satellite if not much more expensive. An attacker would have to consider the tradeoff between building co-orbital systems capable of remaining with the target satellite for an extended period versus the cost in time, capacity, and surprise of launching and positioning a

---

[347] "Missile Defense Project, 'Standard Missile-3 (SM-3),' Missile Threat, Center for Strategic and International Studies" (CSIS, September 28, 2018), https://missilethreat.csis.org/defsys/sm-3/.

[348] Bryan Pietsch, "2 Russian Spacecraft Are Trailing a US Spy Satellite and Could Create a 'Dangerous Situation in Space,'" Business Insider, February 10, 2020, https://www.businessinsider.com/russian-spacecraft-trailing-us-spy-satellite-space-force-commander-report-2020-2.

large number of co-orbital systems just prior to conflict. Finally, a co-orbital threat such as the system the Russians seem to have developed is useful only against the single target it is following in any useful time-frame. In low Earth orbit, it is extremely fuel-intensive to change orbital parameters to rendezvous with another object quickly. These factors make co-orbital kinetic systems potentially useful but also extremely threatening pre-conflict and relatively costly.

This leaves the third option mentioned in the Aerospace report, using directed-energy weapons (DEW) or other forms of energy to damage a satellite or interfere with its ability to communicate. DEWs are potentially extremely attractive weapons for disabling low Earth orbit satellites. In theory, a DEW could fire multiple times, patiently engaging target satellites sequentially as they pass overhead in the course of their regular orbits at relatively low cost to the attacker, which might take several days to accomplish. These systems could also be positioned deep within an attacker's homeland protected by layers of air and missile defenses from direct retaliation. A further advantage of an anti-satellite DEW system is that it would not generate any significant debris in comparison to ASATs.[349] It is perhaps for these reasons that China and Russia are exploring the concept of using DEWs against satellites.[350] These advantages seem to point to ground-based DEW systems as the perfect anti-satellite weapon for low Earth orbit, but fielding an effective system faces many technical challenges. Directed energy as an anti-satellite weapon is potentially ideal, but it must overcome a myriad of difficulties. Even the lowest Earth-orbiting satellite is at least 250 kilometers away with geosynchronous satellites matching the Earth's rotation at

---

[349] Mike Gruss, "U.S. Official: China Turned to Debris-Free ASAT Tests Following 2007 Outcry," *Space News*, January 11, 2016, https://spacenews.com/u-s-official-china-turned-to-debris-free-asat-tests-following-2007-outcry/.
[350] "Challenges to Security in Space," 20, 29.

36,000 kilometers of altitude. In the case of constellations of remote sensing satellites, they are most commonly going to be found in orbits of between 250-500 kilometers to be operationally relevant and cost-effective. This scopes the problem faced by DEW, whose largest technical challenge lies in targeting and overcoming the absorption, scattering, and turbulence effects of the atmosphere between the ground and space.[351] At first blush, the atmospheric scattering problem would seem to be the more difficult for a ground to space DEW firing on a vertical path than for a DEW designed to defeat drones or missiles firing over a horizontal path, but this is not true. Interestingly, on a clear day, there are fewer atmospheric molecules per centimeter squared on a vertical path from sea-level to space than there are on a horizontal path between two points at sea-level 10 kilometers apart.[352] In the event of rain or other atmospheric conditions, this does not remain true. Potential weather interference is most likely why the Soviets attempted to place an anti-satellite DEW on an aircraft to further reduce atmospheric attenuation problems during the Cold War.[353] The second major challenge with DEWs as anti-satellite weapons, targeting, is eased by the relative predictability of satellite orbits. Despite traveling far faster than anything moving within the atmosphere, satellites are predictable in their orbits. Predictability allows an attacker to accurately determine with a very high degree of accuracy where a satellite will be in its orbit at any

---

[351] John Stupl and Gotz Neuneck, "Assessement of Long Range Laser Weapon Engagements: The Case of the Airborne Laser," *Science & Global Security* 18, no. 1-60 (2010): 4.

[352] Robert M. McClatchey and John E. A. Selby, *Atmospheric Attenuation of Laser Radiation From.76 to 31.25 Um* (L.G. Hanscom Field, Bedford, Massachusetts: Air Force Systems Command, USAF, Optical Physics Labratory Project 7670, 1974), 10.

[353] Noah Shachtman, "Look Out Above! Russia May Target U.S. Sats With Laser Jet," *Wired*, June 13, 2011, https://www.wired.com/2011/06/is-a-russian-laser-aiming-for-u-s-satellites/.

time, though precision aiming will require real-time tracking using a ground-based targeting radar.

A final advantage of using DEW against optical remote sensing platforms is that the optics on the target satellite are already staring at the Earth and magnifying many different wavelengths of light onto a focal plane. Energy from a DEW directed at a remote sensing satellite from the area being observed would be amplified by the target satellite's optics easing the power requirements for disabling or damaging these types of remote sensing platforms. Avoiding this difficulty would force remote sensing satellites to look away or shutter their optics when passing over areas with known anti-satellite DEWs essentially achieving the military objective of the attacker of imagery denial without needing to engage.

Each category of anti-satellite weapons systems has advantages and disadvantages as active denial measures against remote sensing platforms. ASATs are cost-effective against legacy systems and a proven capability though they quickly become cost-prohibitive against constellations of inexpensive satellites as well as being high-debris generators. Co-orbital systems can be pre-positioned to strike at a moment's notice though they are also costly as well as dangerously escalatory pre-conflict. Finally, DEWs show the most promise as an effective active measure against remote sensing systems with the proper research and testing.

The threat that remote sensing satellites pose to military forces cannot be ignored or dealt with through only passive means. Active measures are necessary to manage the operational threat that adversary remote sensing satellites pose to military forces. Even if effective active measures are developed and fielded, the threat from remote sensing satellites will not only be from adversary satellites but also from domestic commercial systems as well as third-party systems that do not belong to belligerent nations. While passive measures will remain a possibility against these systems, as demonstrated in this section, an active approach must be taken to limit observation. Kinetic options applied to non-belligerents and satellites owned by domestic corporations are likely to be poorly received, so other options must be explored, namely regulatory and diplomatic approaches to limiting the operational risk posed by these non-adversary systems.

REGULATORY APPROACHES AND DIPLOMATIC OPTIONS

Active measures are necessary against adversary remote sensing systems but should be a last resort against domestic commercial systems or those owned by third parties. These systems still represent an operational threat since the imagery they capture can become publicly available or accessible for purchase and provide an adversary with valuable intelligence. In situations where the adversary nation does not possess any significant domestic remote sensing capability, the active measures discussed above are largely unnecessary, and a combination of regulatory and diplomatic options becomes the primary method of limiting the distribution of valuable overhead intelligence.[354] Currently, the US has the largest commercial remote sensing market and is likely to continue to lead the market due to an increasingly friendly regulatory structure, a robust industrial base, and lucrative government contracts. The remaining global commercial market will probably remain concentrated in close US allies and partner countries. This presents the US with particular difficulties in managing these remote sensing threats since using active military measures against domestic or allied commercial systems is not a politically palatable option. This section will analyze the US regulatory structure and methods for controlling domestic commercial

---

[354] There is risk that nations opposed to US actions will provide a disadvantaged opponent with imagery from national level systems. This risk is mitigated by the fact that nations are hesitant to provide third-parties access to raw imagery and reveal national capabilities (and limitations) and by the time that making a decision to release even blurred imagery or intelligence to a third-party requires. These practical limitations prevent this source of imagery from being a real-time operational threat but does present challenges from an intelligence perspective.

remote sensing. It will also discuss how diplomatic measures accompanied by reciprocal agreements and international notifications could be an effective control measure for allied and third-party systems. The goal of this section is to demonstrate that regulatory and diplomatic controls can be effective complements to military means of controlling remote sensing intelligence, limiting the inadvertent operational and intelligence risk that these systems represent. An alternative means is to commercially purchase all available sensitive images of a battlefield with the provision that they cannot be used by other parties though such a strategy is increasingly untenable given the proliferation of imagery providers.

US regulation of commercial remote sensing systems began in 1984 with the passage of the Land Remote Sensing Commercialization Act.[355] This act was primarily intended to privatize the Landsat program, but it also included provisions to allow the Secretary of Commerce to issue licenses for commercial remote sensing satellites. The Department of Commerce quickly delegated this authority to the National Oceanic and Atmospheric Administration (NOAA), where it has remained.[356] The 1984 act was far from perfect though it did establish a framework for licensing commercial remote sensing systems and included many of the philosophical underpinnings of the current law that remain in effect today. The 1984 act was superseded in 1992 by the Land Remote Sensing Policy Act, which removed some of the more egregious licensing conditions, including the ability of the Secretary of Commerce to "terminate, modify, condition, transfer, or suspend licenses" without any legal

---

[355] "Land Remote-Sensing Commercialization Act of 1984," Pub. L. No. 98–365, 15 USC 4201 (1984).

[356] Dorinda Dalmeyer and Kosta Tsipis, "USAS: Civilian Uses of Near-Earth Space," *Heaven and Earth* 16 (1997): 47.

recourse for the licensee.[357] Included without substantive change in an updated 2010 National and Commercial Space Programs legislation, the 1992 act remains the foundational legal basis of US remote sensing licensing.

The basic tenants of the 1992 remote sensing act are relatively benign but do include several national security caveats. As part of the law, a US-licensed commercial operator must operate "the system in such a manner as to preserve the national security of the United States and to observe the international obligations of the United States."[358] Further, a licensee is required to inform the secretary whenever they enter into any agreement "with a foreign nation, entity, or consortium involving foreign nations or entities."[359] Other basic requirements include providing the orbital characteristics of the system, satisfactorily disposing of the satellite, and informing the secretary of any deviations to its orbit. At the surface level, these requirements seem fairly reasonable requests for a commercial provider to comply with the international obligations of the US with respect to orbital debris and account for national security. Where ambiguity quickly presents itself is with what is meant by the requirement to operate in a manner that preserves national security. Commercial providers and various government agencies are very likely to have different interpretations of what constitutes protecting national security.

An example of this conflict of interest and opinion is found in the release by Planet of imagery of the Iranian attack on Al-Assad Air Base hours after the attack. This imagery provided Iran with detailed post-strike battle damage assessment information that it would otherwise

---

[357] Land Remote-Sensing Commercialization Act of 1984, sec. 403a(1).

[358] "Land Remote-Sensing Act of 1992," Pub. L. No. 102–588, 15 USC 5623 (1992), sec. 5622(b)1.

[359] Ibid., sec. 5622(b)6.

have not had access to. Using this data, Iran could then judge the effectiveness of its targeting systems and the impact of its strikes on specific targets on Al-Assad, a clear national security risk. Alternatively, the rapid release of detailed imagery into the public sphere allowed the American people and the international community to independently determine that the number of missile strikes and that the amount of damage that they had inflicted was limited. This served to calm media speculation and support the narrative that the missile strike was merely a face-saving exercise for Iran, a clear national security gain.[360] Planet's release of imagery could then have different national security interpretations depending on perspective and subsequent actions. In this case, Iran did not conduct follow-up strikes, so in hindsight, Planet's release of imagery did not harm national security. This example demonstrates the ambiguity behind the seemingly straightforward requirement to preserve the national security of the US levied on commercial imagery providers.

If the US government had chosen to exercise regulatory control over Planet and control the release of its imagery, the regulatory options are limited. Presidential Decision Directive 23 (PDD-23), signed by President Bill Clinton in 1994, introduced the concept of modified operations colloquially known as "shutter control." PDD-23 stipulated that commercial imagery providers might be required "during periods when national security ... may be compromised, as defined by the Secretary of Defense or the Secretary of State, respectively, to limit data collection and/or distribution by the system to the extent necessitated by the given

---

[360] Shane Harris et al., "'Launch, Launch, Launch': Inside the Trump Administration as the Iranian Missiles Began to Fall," *Washington Post,* January 8, 2020, https://www.washingtonpost.com/national-security/us-officials-knew-iranian-missiles-were-coming-hours-in-advance/2020/01/08/b6297b4c-3235-11ea-a053-dc6d944ba776_story.html#click=https://t.co/SV4hrun4FG.

situation.".[361] Shutter control is a powerful regulatory tool that in practice could be used to prevent US-licensed commercial providers from
imaging everything from an individual Air Base to an entire theater of
military operations. However, despite its usefulness as a regulatory tool,
shutter control has never been invoked.

There are a variety of challenges to invoking shutter control that have
likely prevented it from being implemented. First, invoking shutter control would almost certainly trigger a legal challenge. This legal challenge
would probably not come from the licensed satellite owner. Instead, it
would likely come from news agencies or other entities seeking access
to the denied imagery unless there was broad consensus that the justification for invoking shutter control demonstrably supported national security. A situation which the example of Al-Assad above shows is difficult to prove under even the most seemingly clear-cut circumstances.
Second, the use of shutter control could have long-term repercussions
on the health of the US commercial remote sensing industry. It would
demonstrate the vulnerability of US-licensed providers to government
interference, potentially making the US a less attractive licensing environment.

Finally, there are logistical challenges to invoking and verifying the
effective execution of shutter control. With the growing number of remote sensing license holders in the US, active verification of compliance
is not reasonable so the government would be reliant on voluntary compliance from license holders. Given that the civil penalty cap that the
Secretary of Commerce can impose on an imagery provider for violating
the terms of their license is just $10,000, a licensee might simply decide

---

[361] "Presidential Decision Directive 23: US Policy on Foreign Access to Remote Sensing
Space Capabilities," March 9, 1994.

that the cost of compliance is more than the price of the punishment.[362] Maliciously, a provider could also conclude that the value of the shutter-controlled imagery is worth much more than the fine and sell it despite the government order. This scenario is possible, though unlikely. The US government is the largest single purchaser of commercial satellite imagery under the EnhancedView contract with the US National Reconnaissance Office (NRO) alone worth $300 million per year for Maxar technologies.[363] In an industry with an estimated global revenue of just $2.2 billion, US-based imagery providers are unlikely to risk the possibility of lucrative future contracts with the US government by intentionally ignoring shutter control requests.[364] Shutter control is a powerful regulatory tool for controlling domestically licensed remote sensing systems, but an alternative approach is necessary for foreign commercial systems.

Foreign commercial remote sensing systems can be broadly broken into three categories: allied, third-party, and partly adversary-owned with each requiring a slightly different approach. Allied commercial systems can be addressed through diplomatic channels, though the degree of control that allied countries have over their remote sensing industry varies, and any request would have to be matched by restrictions on US commercial companies. Canada is an example of a nation with remote sensing regulations that closely mirror those of the US, including the inclusion of a provision that the Minister of Defense can "interrupt

---

[362] "Licensing of Private Land Remote-Sensing Space Systems," 15 CFR 960, Vol. 71, No. 79 § (2006), pt. 960.15.

[363] Theresa Hitchens, "NGA Re-Ups Maxar Imagery Contract," News, Breaking Defense, August 28, 2019, https://breakingdefense.com/2019/08/nga-re-ups-maxar-imagery-contract/.

[364] "Commercial Satellite Imaging Market Statistics, Trends | Forecast - 2026," Allied Market Research, accessed May 5, 2020, https://www.alliedmarket-research.com/commercial-satellite-imaging-market.

or restrict" the operations of a licensee on national security grounds.[365] This is essentially the same language used in US law, which grants the Secretary of Defense the ability to direct modified operations (shutter control) of US licensees. With its regulatory structure, Canada, as a close ally of the US, would be both receptive and capable of limiting the operations of its satellites upon the request using its similar regulatory mechanisms. However, it would certainly expect reciprocal restrictions on US systems. While Canada uses the same basic approach to security as the US with modified operations directives used at the discretion of the Defense Department, not all Western nations take the same regulatory approach.

Germany takes a different approach to remote sensing regulation than either the US or Canada. German law for remote sensing platforms is very sensitive to the possible use of German commercial imagery for military purposes and its impact on domestic security as well as on foreign policy. Its regulations require licensed operators to conduct a sensitivity check of all data transactions against a government database, taking into account data quality, target area, and the individual making the request.[366] Transaction controls avoid the complexities of attempting to regulate the technical aspects of remote sensing systems as the US has done and instead focuses on controlling the product. This control by the German government would allow for a quick response if they judged a request by a foreign government to limit the release of imagery to be valid. Since German remote sensing law is intended to support the national commitment to peace and is sensitive to endangering foreign security interests, it is likely among the most receptive nations to

---

[365] "Remote Sensing Systems Act (Canada)," Pub. L. No. S.C.2005, c. 45 (2005), sec. 14(5).

[366] "National Data Security Policy for Space-Based Earth Remote Sensing Systems" (German Federal Ministry of Economics and Technology, December 1, 2007), 5.

diplomatic requests to limit imagery distribution. Alongside France, Germany is also unique among European Union (EU) members in that it possesses an overarching national policy governing remote sensing.

Managing the remote sensing security threat through diplomatic means with the broader European Union presents a more challenging problem than with Germany or France. Outside of the US, the member states of the European Union collectively have the largest commercial and privatized remote sensing market, with some smaller members such as Finland possessing highly capable commercial providers. Remote sensing companies based in these less-regulated EU member states present a much more difficult challenge since the EU does not have clear overarching policies governing remote sensing. The lack of an EU-wide regulatory mechanism for controlling the release of satellite imagery to protect domestic or foreign national security presents a challenge. Even if the nation in receipt of the diplomatic overture accepts a request as valid, they may find it legally impossible to impose any sort of limiting controls on the providers based within their borders. If allied nations do not possess the regulatory framework or legal authority to prevent their commercial providers from releasing imagery adequately, then these individual providers must be treated in the same manner as third- party commercial systems.

Third-party commercial systems present a significant challenge for any nation attempting to deny observation of military operations. Unlike products from third-party national systems—which are unlikely to be shared outside the owning government due to concerns over revealing capabilities and limitations—commercial providers operating from neutral nations will likely consider hostilities between other nations as an opportunity. Operationally this means that they are just as much a threat as adversary systems, but active measures cannot be used against them without a careful assessment of the risk of angering the host nation. Diplomatic overtures would seem to be the best approach and certainly a necessary step in limiting the release of data from third parties, but alone they are unlikely to be effective or timely. Neutral nations may be slow in responding to diplomatic overtures for innocent or malicious reasons. Once hostilities have begun, the normally slow pace of the diplomatic process will create unacceptable risk. An alternative to negotiations is to develop a mechanism that provides ample notice and quickly and effectively warns operators that imaging of specified areas is not authorized and is done at the risk of damage or interference to the imaging satellite. Aviation Notices to Airmen (NOTAM) provide a possible framework for how this mechanism could effectively function.

NOTAMs provide aircraft with information in an internationally recognized format warning of hazards or airspace restrictions. They are an outgrowth of the Convention on International Civil Aviation hosted by the US in 1944 which established international guidelines for civil aviation. The convention does not apply to military aircraft, but the regulatory mechanisms and processes that are the result of it are generally adhered to by military aviation during normal operations. Among the guidelines in the convention is an understanding that civil aircraft operating for non-civil purposes in the airspace of a nation may be dealt with by "any appropriate means."[367] It is a stretch to translate this understanding and its meaning into the space domain. Still, if a similar agreement applied to space systems it could provide the legal framework for nations to interfere with the operations of third-party commercial satellites which become threats to security when transiting over sovereign territory. For military operations outside of sovereign territory, which is more likely for the US, the NOTAMs mechanism could simply provide clear and unambiguous warning that third-party systems should not image an area. Those systems which violate this notice by pointing their optics at the Earth in these areas may be damaged by

---

[367] "Convention on International Civil Aviation" (International Civil Aviation Organization, 2006), 3, https://www.icao.int/publications/Documents/7300_cons.pdf.

active DEW systems or, in the case of SAR systems, may be actively interfered with if they are detected radiating energy.

The final category of commercial systems that might necessitate a diplomatic or regulatory approach are those with a significant ownership stake by an adversary. This is not as clear-cut of a category as it at first seems since many commercial systems are operated by international consortia and may be partially owned by companies based in the territory of both sides in a conflict. Multi-party ownership creates an added difficulty for determining the degree of aggressiveness in managing these satellites. Some commercial providers will be based in an adversary's territory and have contracts with their host government making them equivalent to adversary national assets. For other commercial systems, the threshold for treatment as an adversary system is difficult to discern. Determining a threshold for designation as an adversary controlled system will ultimately require a judgment call at the national level balancing the diplomatic risk against the operational risk of taking active measures.

Diplomatic and regulatory approaches to controlling the release of remote sensing data are a necessary complement to active and passive military measures (see Figure 2). This section demonstrated that there is no simple solution to mitigating the operational risk from non-adversary remote sensing satellites. Diplomatic means are the best approach with allied commercial systems, while third-party systems may require a more aggressive approach. Further, complexities in determining the risk posed by commercial systems, as well as assigning ownership, present a real challenge. Cutting through the complexity by developing and exercising a NOTAM type mechanism, in this case a Notice To Space Personnel (NOTSP), to protect sensitive military operations is the most straightforward approach, but it requires enforcement. This enforcement requires dedicated on-site assets capable of tracking and engaging any ISR asset transiting overhead with both destructive and non-destructive effects. A comprehensive and intensive multi-part strategy that includes both diplomatic and active measures is a challenging, but necessary, part of limiting the impact that non-adversary remote sensing can have on military operations.

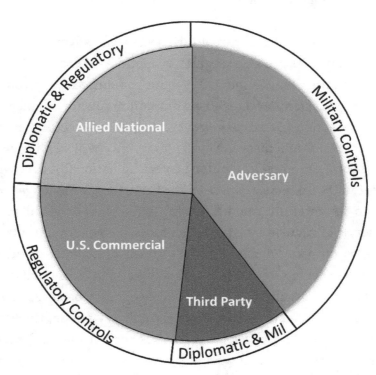

Figure 4. Approaches to Remote Sensing. Each remote sensing satellite will need to be managed broadly by category. Author.

CONCLUSION

A resolution convergence that will lead to the near-ubiquitous space-based observation of the Earth is coming, a situation that cannot be ignored by military planners. Already an intelligence threat, remote sensing satellites are rapidly developing into an operational threat to military forces. Passive-only measures of managing the risk from remote sensing satellites will become increasingly ineffective unless accompanied by active measures to limit the observation of friendly forces. A variety of systems that generate these active measures though directed-energy weapons may be the most cost-effective approach for this mission and China and Russia are already developing this capability.[368]

Not all remote sensing threats are necessarily adversary controlled, and so require diplomatic or regulatory methods of control. The US regulatory structure for commercial systems has shifted away from relying primarily on system-level technical limitations toward reliance on shutter control and broad language governing national security as its regulatory control mechanism. As a regulatory mechanism shutter control is, in theory, an efficient tool for protecting national security but one which the US has never exercised for fear of legal challenges or doing harm to its domestic remote sensing industry. For allied nations, a patchwork of regulatory controls exists, which those nations may be willing to enforce when asked to through diplomatic channels. For third-party systems or those that are unwilling to accommodate foreign security concerns, a NOTAM/NOTSP concept may be necessary to prevent observation. The NOTAM concept allows for appropriate forewarning that imagery of a specified area is not welcome and attempts to image the area will be met with an active response. Also, such declarations must necessarily be geographically broad so as not to reveal to adversaries specific military operational intent for certain smaller regions. Such a concept currently has no legal framework to rest on and would either need to be declared unilaterally or developed as a norm acceptable over sovereign territory or regions with active combat operations. Either way, active measures against non-adversary satellites would require a careful analysis of the associated risk. The figure below provides

---

[368] "Challenges to Security in Space," 20.

a summary outline of approaches for handling various satellite systems by conflict level and ownership.

		Level of War		
		Peacetime	Tension	Conflict
Satellite Owner	**Adversary National and Commercial**	Passive measures (denial and targeted deception)	Increased passive measures (denial and targeted deception) Dazzling + limited non-destructive interference	Non-destructive: cyber attacks, jamming of links Destructive effects (Lasers, ASATs & other space weapons)
	Third Party Systems	Passive measures (denial)	NOTAMs & diplomatic efforts	NOTAMs escalating to dazzling and non-destructive attacks
	Allied National & Commercial	Passive measures (denial) Shared regulatory controls	Diplomatic efforts	Continued diplomatic efforts, NOTAMs escalating to non-destructive in the event of serious security violation
	US Commercial	Regulatory limitations on highly capable systems + passive measures	Shutter Control	Shutter Control

Figure 5. Methods of Control. Example measures that can be applied across the spectrum of conflict to control remote sensing, note that measures build from right to left though that does not mean that peacetime control measures should cease in conflict. Author.

In an era of ubiquitous imagery remote sensing satellites will provide an overwhelming military advantage to the side that is best able to leverage them for its own gain while denying its opponent access to them. Despite this seemingly obvious conclusion, there seems to be very little acknowledgment of the threat that these satellites will pose to operational forces in the future. Historically intelligence tools that promoted strategic stability by allowing clear observation inside an adversary's borders, remote sensing satellites are quickly developing into a critical enabling tool for achieving strategic victory by destroying adversary forces wherever they may be on the globe. Full recognition of the scale of the threat and the opportunity that these systems present may not come until a nation is able to successfully exploit its advantage in utilizing and controlling space to inflict rapid defeat on a near-peer military power. When that day comes, military space will truly have come of age as a warfighting domain.

CHAPTER 7: WHEN DIPLOMACY FAILS: ANTI-SATELLITE WEAPONS

BY JOHNATHON MARTIN AND BRANDON BAILEY[369]

INTRODUCTION

Anti-satellite weapons and the satellite systems they target are at the very heart of space warfare. In the simplest of terms, anti-satellite weapons (ASATs) are the primary tools of conducting war in space, with their goal being to diminish, or threaten to diminish, an adversary's space power. ASAT weapons are not science fiction, nor are they new. They are serious business and their development and employment must be weighed carefully by decision makers prior to and during a war in or involving the space domain. In this chapter, we survey many types of ASATs, including direct-ascent missiles, directed-energy weapons, co-orbital weapons, nuclear weapons, electronic weapons, and cyber-weapons. We believe cyber-weapons and attacks are the most poorly understood category of ASATs and the least developed in terms of space warfare theory. Therefore, we devote much of the discussion to cyber-weapons.

THE VALUE OF THE TARGET

Even when the Space Age was in its infancy, it didn't take war planners and military strategists long to realize the value in denying an

---

adversary their satellite capabilities. Just over two years after the first satellite was placed into orbit, a Bold Orion missile intended to shoot down satellites was tested.[370] Although it missed by four miles, it was considered a success since four miles was close enough to do the job had the missile been equipped with a nuclear warhead.

Thor 278 (did not fly) Johnston Island (Program 437)   03644,03645

Figure 6. Program 437 Nuclear ASAT on Johnston Island.[371]

Just how much value there is in denying an adversary their satellites' capability depends on how much value the adversary is able to get from the satellites to begin with. Thus, before decision makers and war fighters can accurately evaluate the value of ASATs, they must first appreciate the value satellites themselves provide. This value can be difficult to explicitly quantify since satellites usually provide and transmit information of varying types and for different purposes. Nonetheless, the value can be said to be "great."

In today's world, satellites are tremendously valuable to warfighters engaged in all domains — not just space. Among other services, satellites provide warfighters positioning data, communications, missile warning, weather data, and intelligence information that effectively serve as force multipliers. Loss of these satellites could be devastating. This was well stated in a 2015 interview when General John Hyten, then Commander of Air Force Space Command, commented: "Without satellites, you go back to World War II. You go back to Industrial Era warfare."[372] Another commentator has even gone so far as to say that "satellites have become integrated into 21st-century society, much as electricity and mass communications became integral to 20th-century modernity."[373] Further, the value in space-based capabilities provided by satellites to warfighters will only continue to grow for the foreseeable future. It is difficult to overstate the importance of satellites to the

---

[372] 60 Minutes, "The Battle Above". April 16, 2015.

[373] "Space-based communications, navigation, weather, and remote sensing services make our daily lives better, and contribute to saving lives and property. Consumers enjoy the benefits of satellite services, usually without realizing their source; governments and businesses use space services for high-stakes purposes. For all of us, satellites have become integrated into 21st-century society, much as electricity and mass communications became integral to 20th-century modernity. Next time you think about space, think about that." from https://aerospace.org/paper/valueof-space

modern military and to national security writ large, especially for geopolitical superpowers.

Of course, satellites provide value beyond just to military users. Satellites provide information to the masses, weather data, support our modern banking system, and much, much more. Their key role in society, even outside of their direct support to warfighters, gives adversaries additional options to "make it hurt" or, in more traditional terms, to achieve greater or more diverse effects on the opposition.

As mentioned already, space provides many of the types of capabilities that an adversary would be greatly advantaged by subverting in a conflict. Two important maxims can be derived from this and are useful to keep in mind:

> *The more value a nation derives from satellites, the more value an adversary can derive from space weapons.*
>
> *The more value a nation derives from satellites, the more that nation is incentivized to develop capabilities, including space weapons, to protect their capabilities/advantage.*

Not all nations value or will seek to leverage satellite capabilities to the same extent or in the same ways as other nations. It is well known that the United States has both established a substantial lead in space capabilities and become reliant upon it. The CEO of Aerospace Corporation said it well in a 2018 interview: "That supremacy in space has enabled us to have the world's greatest warfighting capabilities... More and More every day, literally, we become more dependent on it.... And our adversaries know that.".[374]

By our maxims above then, adversaries, notably Russia and China, are greatly incentivized to develop, deploy, and use ASAT capabilities. The impetus for the United States then becomes protecting those

---

[374] https://www.politico.com/story/2018/04/06/outer-space-war-defense-russia-china-463067

capabilities, which may include ASAT capabilities of its own to target foreign ASATs or as an attempt to deter adversaries from employing ASATs.

Successfully targeting satellites and the capabilities they provide can significantly reduce or eliminate an enemy's ability to create and project power from space, which in turn can lead to significant strategic and tactical military advantages. Such advantages can prove to be key to achieving broader military and geopolitical objectives.

ANTI-SATELLITES & SPACE WEAPONS

What constitutes an ASAT? Is an ASAT the same thing as a space weapon? And for that matter, what even constitutes a space weapon? A survey of existing literature leads to the conclusion: there is simply no consensus.[375][376] That said, anything that targets the satellite can be thought of as an ASAT. This includes direct-ascent missiles, co-orbital kinetic-kill vehicles, lasers, nukes, and a variety of others. They can be launched from the sea, air, or land or they can be space-based. ASATs are a subset of a larger group known as space weapons. Space weapons are any system whose use destroys or damages objects in or from space.[377] The key difference is that ASATs target satellites specifically, while space weapons may have other targets besides satellites, both in space and elsewhere. As stated, space weapons may target satellites (and thus also qualify as an ASAT), but they may have other targets as well. For instance, space weapons can be designed to damage a target on the ground or attempt to intercept an intercontinental ballistic missile mid-

---

[375] Johnson-Freese, J. (2014). *Heavenly ambitions: America's quest to dominate space.* (p.81). Philadelphia, PA: University Of Pennsylvania.

[376] Johnson-Freese, J. (2017). *Space Warfare in the 21st Century: Arming the Heavens.* (p.67). New York, NY: Routledge.

[377] MOLTZ, J. C. (2019). *POLITICS OF SPACE SECURITY: Strategic Restraint and the Pursuit of National Interests (3rd ed.).* (p.43). Stanford, CA: Stanford University Press.

flight. Space weapons include weapons that are space-to-space, space-to-ground, space-to-air, or space-to-sea.

The following survey is not an exhaustive list or explanation of every type of space weapon or ASAT, but rather briefly examines the most commonly discussed types of space weapons. We devote significant attention to cyber-weapons as they are the least understood type of space weapon.[378]

DIRECT ASCENT

Direct-ascent ASATs (DA-ASATs) missiles are weapons launched from Earth on a suborbital trajectory to strike a satellite in orbit. They may be launched from land, air, or sea, equipped with an explosive payload or intended to physically collide with the satellite. Both DA-ASATs and the satellites they hunt travel at extreme speeds, and thus collisions or payload explosions deliver a tremendous amount of force to the target. Such forces lead to inevitable and irreversible destruction of the satellite.

This type of attack is likely to be attributable to the launching state and will certainly be detected by a number of observers. These weapons can produce significant orbital debris, which can indiscriminately affect other satellites in similar orbits. While for some orbits a strike can be conducted such that most of the generated debris will re-enter Earth's orbit relatively quickly, that is not a given. If conducted haphazardly, debris can remain in orbit for hundreds or even thousands of years.

---

[378] Cyber weapons can be classified as a space weapon that is not an ASAT if only the ground system is targeted, and can also be considered an ASAT if targeting the space segment.

Figure 7. ASM-135 ASAT.[379]

For these reasons, DA-ASATs are considered extremely aggressive and highly escalatory. Use of DA-ASATs is widely considered to be irresponsible - even when debris generation is minimized. To date, no country has conducted a kinetic physical attack against another country's satellite, but four countries—the United States, Russia, China,

---

[379] By Paul E. Reynolds (USAF) - Originally downloaded from http://www.losange-les.af.mil/SMC/HO/SNAPSHOTS%20IN%20SMC%20HISTORY.htmImage is a cropped version of this: Image page(image ID DF-SC-88-08413), Public Domain, https://commons.wikimedia.org/w/index.php?curid=227452

and India—have successfully tested direct-ascent ASAT weapons against their own targets.

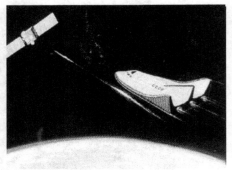

Figure 8. Russia ASAT concepts 1986. Paul Szymanski.

CO-ORBITAL ASAT

A co-orbital ASAT weapon differs from a direct-ascent weapon because it is first placed into orbit, typically in a close or intercepting orbit of the intended target. Since they are placed into orbit, co-orbital ASATs can remain dormant for days or even years before activating to attack the target.[380]

---

[380] https://csis-website-prod.s3.amazonaws.com/s3fs-public/publica-
tion/200330_SpaceThreatAssessment20_WEB_FI-
NAL1.pdf?6sNra8FsZ1LbdVj3xY867tUVu0RNHw9V; pg. 3.

Figure 9. Istrebitel Sputnikov Russian Co-Orbital ASAT[381]

Co-orbital ASAT weapons can take many forms, but are typically themselves satellites that host an offensive capability. One such capability is a kinetic-kill vehicle (KKV). A KKV can either be the satellite itself or hosted by the satellite. When deployed, it can physically intercept the target satellite. Like a DA-ASAT, this can cause a tremendous amount of debris. However, if the orbits are similar, the relative velocities between the KKV and the target satellite can be much smaller, resulting in less debris. Nonetheless, using a KKV to attack a satellite is still an aggressive and escalatory action, especially if discovered by the general public.

Another possible variant of a co-orbital ASAT would be a satellite that conducts a rendezvous and proximity operation (RPO) or a zero-

---

[381] By Ronald C. Wittmann - http://www.dia.mil/history/art/images/anti_sat.jpg, Public Domain, https://commons.wikimedia.org/w/index.php?curid=5975979

proximity operation (ZPO) to interact with a target satellite in some way. This could vary from breaking the solar panels off[382] to spray-painting an optical lens.[383,384]

Though they are considered separately in the following pages, it is worth noting that both nuclear warheads and directed-energy weapons can be hosted co-orbitally as well, technically making them co-orbital ASATs. Co-orbital ASAT weapons require sophisticated capabilities to detect, track, and guide the weapon into a target satellite. The likelihood of being able to attribute an attack from a co-orbital ASAT depends greatly on the specific mechanism the ASAT uses to attack (e.g., KKV, RPO, etc.), which orbit it is in, and the space situational awareness capabilities of other nations. Co-orbital ASATs can have irreversible or reversible impacts depending on specific capabilities of the weapon. The Soviet Union tested co-orbital kinetic ASAT weapons repeatedly during the Cold War, but no known instances of co-orbital attacks have taken place.[385]

NUCLEAR WEAPONS

Nuclear weapons can also be considered a form of ASAT weapon. Strictly speaking, a nuclear weapon can be deployed as either a DA-ASAT or as a co-orbital weapon, but nonetheless merits its own discussion. Let us also mention upfront that detonating or placing

---

[382] As made popular by the Netflix series Space Force.

[383] As described in 60 Minutes; *The Battle Above,*
https://www.youtube.com/watch?v=zcKT7ZHFauo

[384] NASIC Competing in Space

[385] Defense Against the Dark Arts in Space (2021) https://csis-website-prod.s3.amazo-naws.com/s3fs-public/publication/210225_Harrison_De-fense_Space.pdf?N2KWelzCz3hE3AaUUptSGMprDtBlBSQG, pg 3

nuclear weapons in orbit is banned by the Partial Test Ban Treaty of 1963 and by the Outer Space Treaty.[386]

Similar to a nuke used terrestrially, the use of a nuclear weapon in space would have large-scale, indiscriminate effects that would be attributable and publicly visible. A nuclear detonation in space would immediately affect satellites within range of its electromagnetic pulse (EMP), and it would also create a high radiation environment that would accelerate the degradation of satellite components in the affected orbital regime.

The United States and Soviet Union both tested nuclear weapons in space in the 1960s, albeit with an ASAT capability exclusively in mind. A number of other countries have the nuclear capabilities required to conduct a nuclear detonation in space.[387]

Use of a nuke in space is the most escalatory and aggressive action possible within the space domain. If a nation wished to eliminate an adversary's ability to use their space capabilities, a much more effective and less apocalyptic course of action, for instance, would be to physically destroy the associated ground stations.

DIRECTED-ENERGY WEAPONS

Directed-Energy Weapons (DEWs) are a class of ASATs that seek to damage targets with highly focused energy, traveling at or near the speed of light. Such weapons are capable of a wide range of effects such

---

[386] While China is not a party to the Partial Test Ban Treaty, nearly all spacefaring nations are parties to the OST. This makes it illegal, under international law, to "place in orbit around the earth any objects carrying nuclear weapons or any other kinds of weapons of mass destruction, install such weapons on celestial bodies, or station such weapons in outer space in any other manner."

[387] You don't have to be able to be terribly accurate per say, depending on the orbit and yield of the warhead.

as blinding optics, causing components to heat to the point of failure,[388] or simply preventing communications systems from operating properly. DEWs can take several forms including lasers, high-powered microwaves (HPM), particle beams, and jammers.[389]

They can be land, sea, air, or space-based. However, DEWs such as lasers and particle beams require extreme amounts of power to be able to deliver destructive amounts of energy.[390] It is therefore likely not possible with current technology for such types of DEWs to be space-based - and, if possible, certainly not practical. In addition to not requiring nearly as much power to cause interference, jammers have other unique considerations and are much more likely to be used in a space war for the foreseeable future compared to other DEWs, if for no other reason than they are readily available and inexpensive.[391] Therefore, we consider jammers separately in the following section.

Lasers can have both reversible and irreversible effects. Lasers can be used to temporarily dazzle or permanently blind sensors on satellites, cause components to overheat, or degrade other subsystems and components such as solar panels.[392] They can also cut through steel, aluminum, and other materials, which can potentially cause pressurized vessels, such as satellite propellant and oxidizer tanks, to explode.

A satellite lasing system requires high beam quality, adaptive optics (if being used through the atmosphere), and advanced pointing control

---

[388] United States, United States Air Force. (2004, August 2). *Counterspace Operations: Air Force Doctrine Document 2-2.1.* (p.34). Retrieved from https://fas.org/irp/doddir/usaf/afdd2_2-1.pdf

[389] Note that not everyone considers jammers to be directed energy weapons, however, they are DEWs by definition.

[390] This is because their effectiveness decreases with the square of the range to the target.

[391] https://www.securityprousa.com/products/satellite-jammer

[392] https://ndupress.ndu.edu/Portals/68/Documents/prism/prism_8-3/prism_8-3_Obering_36-46.pdf

to steer the laser beam precisely—technology that is costly and requires a high degree of sophistication. A laser can be effective against a sensor on a satellite if it is within the line of sight of the sensor and of the correct wavelength, likely making it possible to attribute the attack to its approximate geographical origin. Also of note is that terrestrial-based high-power lasers require atmospheric distortion compensation to be effective and provide satellite access only occasionally due to weather and repeating orbital tracks access constraints.

HPM weapons convert energy from a power source into radiated electromagnetic energy focused on the target. They create beams of electromagnetic energy over a broad spectrum of radio and microwave frequencies.[393] An HPM weapon can have a range of reversible or irreversible effects such as disrupting a satellite's electronics, corrupting data stored in memory, causing processors to restart, and, at higher power levels, causing permanent damage to electrical circuits and processors. HPM attacks can be more difficult to attribute because the attack can come from a variety of angles, including from other satellites passing by in orbit. The types of effects that lasers and HPMs tend to have do not produce visible indicators that are easily observed by an attacker to verify the attack.[394]

Particle beam weapons have long been discussed as potential ASATs. However, they are still years away from being realized. Unlike lasers, which burn the surface of a target, particle beams penetrate beyond the surface to affect interior hardware. Particle beam weapons work by

---

[393]https://www.onr.navy.mil/en/Science-Technology/Departments/Code-35/All-Pro-grams/aerospace-science-research-351/directed-energy-weapons-high-power-mi-crowaves#:~:text=Research%20Concentra-tion%20Area%3A%20High%20Power,on%20electronics%20within%20tar-geted%20systems.

[394] Space Threat Assessment (2021). https://csis-website-prod.s3.amazo-naws.com/s3fs-public/publication/210331_Harrison_SpaceThreatAssess-ment2021.pdf?gVYhCn79enGCOZtcQnA6MLkeKlcwqqks

accelerating particles without an electric charge—particularly neutrons—to speeds close to the speed of light and directing them against a target. A sufficiently powerful beam could generate enough heat to burn a target, igniting its fuel supply, melting it, and rendering it unstable, or frying the on-board electronics. The US Undersecretary of Defense for Research and Engineering Mike Griffin was quoted in 2019 saying, "We are deferring work on neutral particle beams indefinitely. It's just not near-term enough." Griffin emphasized the DOD will continue to forge ahead with development of lasers and microwave weapons.[395]

The United States continues to pursue directed-energy research in lasers and microwave energy, aiming eventually to deploy them on combat aircraft, with ground units, and aboard satellites.[396] Over the last twenty years, Chinese defense research has proposed the development of several reversible and non-reversible counter-space directed-energy weapons. Russia is reportedly developing an airborne laser weapon system intended for use against space-based missile defense sensors.[397]

JAMMERS & SPOOFERS

Jammers are weapons that interrupt or prevent communications between a transmitter and a receiver. This is done by generating a signal at the same frequency as the target signal at a higher power than the target signal, effectively raising the noise floor beyond what the receiver can continue "hearing" the target signal through.

---

[395] https://www.popularmechanics.com/military/research/a28942057/neutral-particle-beam/

[396] https://www.defenseone.com/technology/2019/09/pentagon-shelves-neutral-particle-beam-research/159643/

[397] Competing in Space, NASIC 2019, https://media.defense.gov/2019/Jan/16/2002080386/-1/-1/1/190115-F-NV711-0002.PDF

Jammers are among the easiest types of ASATs to field and can be based in any domain. They can target any receiver receiving signals into or out of the satellite, including the command and control uplink, telemetry downlink, and GPS signals. For communications satellites, jammers can also target the payload signals, such as voice or internet.

Command and control uplinks are easily targeted by uplink jammers which attempt to interfere with the signal going from the Earth to a satellite. Conversely, signals on the telemetry downlink can also be targeted using downlink jammers, which target the ground receiver listening for a signal from a satellite as it propagates down to Earth. Temporarily jamming the command uplink receiver (on the satellite) or a telemetry downlink receiver (on the ground) can be an effective way of temporarily denying an adversary access to their satellites.

When discussing jamming, spoofing is not far behind in the discussion. While they are different attacks, they often are intermingled when discussing electronic weapons. Sometimes discussed in the context of cyberattacks, spoofing is a form of electronic attack where the adversary tricks a receiver into believing a fake signal, generated by the attacker, is the authentic signal. A spoofer can inject false information into a data stream with the most extreme example resulting in a false command to a satellite being accepted as authentic and executed by the satellite.

Both jamming and spoofing are typically temporary and reversible because once they are turned off, communications can return to normal. Many types of satellite signals can be attacked with jamming and spoofing capabilities that can be repurposed from commercially available equipment or easily developed. Jamming can be difficult to detect or distinguish from accidental interference which makes attribution and awareness more difficult, whereas spoofing has a higher likelihood of detection and attribution. Multiple nations have demonstrated uplink jammers, including the United States, Russia, China, and Iran. While space-based downlink jammers are certainly feasible, there are no examples of such a system being tested yet.[398.399.400.401.402]

SPACE CYBER-WEAPONS

"...it is essential to protect space systems from cyber incidents in order to prevent disruptions to their ability to provide reliable and efficient contributions to the operations of the Nation's critical infrastructure." - Space Policy Directive 5, Cyber Security Principals for Space Systems[403]

The Trump administration enacted seven Presidential Directives related to space. The fifth of these, Space Policy Directive (SPD-5) was devoted entirely to space-cyber and established for the first time, national-level cybersecurity principles for space systems. SPD-5 was in many ways a wakeup call to the US space enterprise that cyber-weapons aimed at space systems were a serious threat and in need of attention beyond what had previously been given. And rightly so! Often considered as a monolithic threat, cyberattacks can take many forms, can have diverse entry and exploitation vectors, and can enable a host of crippling effects when triggered. Unfortunately, this complexity often leads to discussion of space cyber-weapons to be diminished to nothing

---

[398] https://www.wired.com/2011/06/iraqs-invisible-war/

[399] https://georgetownsecuritystudiesreview.org/2019/06/26/the-russian-edge-in-electronic-warfare/

[400] https://www.c4isrnet.com/battlefield-tech/space/2020/01/08/what-we-know-about-irans-counter-space-weapons/

[401]https://timesofindia.indiatimes.com/world/china/from-robots-to-satellite-jammers-china-looks-to-space-to-blind-deafen-enemy-us-report/articleshow/77916165.cms

[402] https://radionavlab.ae.utexas.edu/images/stories/files/papers/gnss_spoofing_detection.pdf

[403] Space Policy Directive 5: https://trumpwhitehouse.archives.gov/presidential-actions/memorandum-space-policy-directive-5-cybersecurity-principles-space-systems/

more than a hand-wave acknowledgment accompanying a black box description. Further, as space systems have continued to grow in complexity and interconnectedness, many more-than-qualified folks have simply resigned themselves to a "black box" view of space cyber-weapons. It is no surprise then that cyber-weapons aimed at space systems are the most poorly understood class of anti-satellite weapons.

We believe this is a dangerous situation. Space cyber-weapons are relatively cheap to develop, have a large attack surface to target, and offer unparalleled prospects for going undetected or unattributed. Thus, these types of weapons are particularly attractive for hostile actors to develop and employ and will almost certainly play a key role in future wars extending into space. Understanding them is a must.

While the effects of more traditional kinetic based attacks are usually rather obvious, the effects of cyberattacks can vary wildly. For instance, cyberattacks can draw into question the confidentiality or integrity of information gathered or produced by the system. Cyber-weapons can be used to affect the availability of the space systems, such as disrupting the ground site's ability to command the satellite. A hacked satellite could even be held for ransom.

Cyber-attacks can also have permanent impacts, such as causing depletion of the batteries or pointing an optical apparatus at the sun. The impacts could cause damage beyond just the attacked satellite. While causing the unnecessary firing of thrusters could be done to simply expend the propellant and leave the satellite uncontrollable, it could also be used to change the satellite's orbit and possibly cause a collision with another satellite. The orbit can also be changed to induce the satellite to re-enter the atmosphere and burn up, or worse still, cause damage on the ground.[404] In short, cyberattacks can enable the full spectrum of objectives: denial, degradation, disruption, deception, or destruction.

Table 3. Space Attack Definitions Derived from "AFDD 2-2"

Deception consists of those measures designed to mislead the adversary by manipulation, distortion, or falsification of evidence to induce the adversary to react in a manner prejudicial to their interests.

Disruption is the temporary impairment of the utility of space systems, usually without physical damage to the space segments. These operations include delaying critical mission data support to an adversary. Given the perishability of information required to effectively command and control military operations, this disruption impedes the effective application or exploitation of that data. Examples of this type of operation include jamming or refusing or withholding data support or spare parts.

Denial is the temporary elimination of the utility of the space systems, usually without physical damage. This objective is accomplished by such measures as denying electrical power to the space ground nodes or computer centers where data and information are processed and stored.

Degradation is the permanent impairment of the utility of space systems, usually with physical damage. This option may include attacks against the terrestrial or space element of the space system. For example, a ground-based laser could be used to damage the optics of an imaging sensor without impairing other functions of the satellite bus.

Destruction is the permanent elimination of the utility of space systems, usually with physical damage. This last option includes special operations forces (SOF) missions to interdict critical ground nodes, airpower missions to bomb uplink/downlink facilities, and attacks against space elements with either kinetic-kill or directed-energy weapons.

---

[404] See https://freebeacon.com/national-security/moscow-accuses-ukraine-of-electronic-attack-on-satellite/

In the context of a war, cyberattacks on space systems can have devastating impacts. As mentioned, compared to other classes of anti-satellite weapons, cyber-weapons are significantly cheaper and can be built much more quickly. They provide the user significant flexibility in their choice of effects to have on the space system - including actions that are reversible or irreversible. Cyber-weapons can destroy satellites without creating debris and can be conducted in silence, making it difficult to determine whether a critical satellite failure was the product of an adversary's aggression or simply from a naturally occurring system failure. While owning an offensive cyber capability will not necessarily win a war in space, failure to adequately protect against adversarial cyber-weapons can guarantee a loss in a space war.

THE BASICS

The range of possible attacks can make understanding cyber-weapons a daunting proposition. Further complicating the matter is that space systems themselves can vary greatly in both function and implementation and this impacts how, when, and for what purpose hostile actors might target them with a cyberattack. For instance, destroying a commercial satellite with a cyberattack may be done one way to achieve one effect, while temporarily denying a spy satellite may be done with an entirely different attack and purpose.

Though permutations abound, one can simplify and summarize these kinds of attacks. There is a way to depict cyber-weapons in a generalized and accurate manner. First, it's important to note that at the most basic level, a satellite and the associated ground station can be viewed as nothing more than two computers networked together over an RF-link. Both are required for the space system to operate correctly and therefore a successful cyberattack on either may cripple the system. Though the specific objectives of a cyberattack may require access to one computer or the other, access to one may be leveraged to gain access to the other computer. For example, if the goal is to destroy (or permanently disable) the satellite, an attacker may access the ground station and then leverage the RF-link to issue a command to the satellite that will result in its demise. In other words, attacking the ground can enable an attack on the satellite.

Just as an attacker may target the ground network or the satellite with a cyberattack, so also the attacker may target either the mission (i.e., the payload) or the satellite infrastructure (i.e., satellite bus). Akin to the space/ground relationship, an attack on the satellite bus can result in damaging the payload (such as controlling the satellite to point an optical payload at the sun to burn it out). When overlapped with the target location, a simple 2x2 matrix is created.

Table 4. Possible Cyberattacks Matrix

		Target Location	
		Space Segment (i.e., the satellite)	Ground Segment
Target Function	Mission (Payload)	1	2
	Infrastructure (Bus)	3	4

Let us explore a quick example of each. For square 1, a cyber-weapon may be designed to spoof the ground system and tell the satellite to simply turn the payload off. For square 2, a cyberattack may deny a mission by forcing the ground station to stop accepting mission data, such as communications or intelligence, from the satellite. For square 3, the attack may directly command the satellite to, for instance, turn off, spin uncontrollably, or fire the thrusters to make the satellite re-enter the Earth's atmosphere. For square 4, an attack on the ground system may prevent the satellite operator from commanding the satellite.

Of course, there is overlap among the squares and a single cyberattack may encompass multiple squares simultaneously. For instance, an attacker may take control of the ground system (square 4) to command the satellite (square 3) to point its payload at the sun (square 1) thereby preventing the mission of the satellite from continuing. This matrix can be decomposed to greater fidelity to identify and mitigate potential vectors cyber-weapons may use to attack a space system.[405]

In reality, we can be more specific as to what can be targeted from a cyber perspective, such as ground software, the command and control (C2) workstation, the front-end processors (FEPs), encryption devices, cross domain solutions/firewalls, the radiofrequency (RF) link, supporting ground infrastructure, satellite subsystems, etc. We will delve into some of these areas more deeply, but at their core, all cyber-weapons targeting space systems can be generalized and articulated by this matrix.

THE GROUND SEGMENT

In many ways, a cyberattack on the ground segment of a space system is just as attractive, if not more so, than attacking the satellite directly. Why is this the case? Let us first explain exactly what we mean by the "ground segment" and what it does.

As the name implies, the ground segment is the part of the space system that is located on the ground. Ground systems exist to serve two fundamental purposes: to tell the satellite what to do and to get data from the satellite. The ground system's most important element is a C2 workstation that is interacted with by some user to communicate to a

---

[405] A more thorough list can be found in Oakley, J. G. (2020). Cybersecurity for Space: Protecting the final frontier. APRESS.

spacecraft.[406] As commands are generated and issued by the user, the commands are processed by ground software and forwarded to the FEP which formats and frames the messages. From there the data is either sent to a crypto module to encrypt the data or, if encryption is not being used, sent directly to a modem for modulation, then to an antenna for a radiofrequency (RF) uplink transmission to the satellite.

For a transmission from the satellite - a downlink - the reverse occurs: the antenna receives data via RF, the modem demodulates, the FEP translates the data for delivery to the ground software where the user views the data. A downlink can include telemetry data, which gives the health and status of the satellite itself, or it can include payload data, such as imagery or communications from other users.

Attacking the ground segment, and specifically the C2 workstation, is the most direct way to execute a cyberattack on a space system. Attacking the C2 workstation and its associated ground network can disrupt or deny the ability of the system to effectively operate. Further, as described previously, it can also be leveraged to execute a cyberattack on the satellite itself. Such an attack eliminates the need for an attacker to replicate a command uplink transmission with a signal that is properly framed, modulated, and encrypted (e.g., spoofing). In effect, an attacker can simply leverage the existing pipe rather than try to create one themselves.

Much like the satellite, the C2 workstation is often physically unreachable by an attacker. However, the C2 workstation is typically connected to a network, usually with many nodes, connections, and interfaces. This is where traditional cyber vectors come into play as there are many places in a ground network that an attacker may gain access to and then pivot to gain downstream access to the C2 workstation.

---

[406] For our purposes here, we use satellite and spacecraft interchangeably.

The most pressing difficulty for a cyberattack to be successful against a space system is the access vector, which is the means by which an attacker accomplishes getting code into the target computer. For the ground segment, an access may be achieved into the space system by exploiting a connection on one of the ground computers with an external source of data (e.g., a connection with an external network such as the Internet, via insider threat, social engineering an employee to plug in media, software patches, etc.) These accesses provide the attacker the ability to deploy malicious code directly or enable a new access for the attacker to interact with the system in a more direct or more concealed manner. Even if an access into the ground segment is exploited, it is not necessarily trivial to use that access to penetrate to the satellite. However, as discussed above, an attacker need not necessarily access the satellite directly to achieve their objectives.

Since satellites are in space, the hardware is generally inaccessible. Therefore, cyber-weapons have to rely on pre-existing and generally well-protected data links into the satellite to get nefarious data onto the satellite's computers. There are two obvious ways an attacker can do this. The attacker can first gain control of the ground station and leverage the existing infrastructure to transmit commands or software to the satellite. Many satellite designs not only permit the processing of commands, but some of the commands may contain new software updates, configuration parameter changes, or even direct memory writes from the ground. Having the ability to make on-the-fly software updates to include direct memory writes provides an attack vector that requires mitigation protections. Traditionally, there is unfettered trust between ground systems and satellites. We expect that over time, the ground-to-space link as well as the on-board architectures will move away from trusted architectures to zero-trust architectures and operate under least privilege principles.

ACCESSES ARE PRECIOUS

The primary, and often only, protection satellites employ against cyberattacks are through encrypting the data links and requiring authentication of the data therein. While not sufficient to mitigate all cyberattacks, it does provide a good measure of defense. Improvements are needed with monitoring the command link for adversarial radio frequency attacks in addition to targeted monitoring of telemetry values that could indicate malicious commanding attempts.[407] Successfully penetrating the space system network can be exceedingly difficult when proper encryption and authentication are in use. While finding an exploitable vulnerability in the ground segment is the most viable path to conduct a cyberattack, if discovered, those vulnerabilities are easily patched and mitigated (if known). Therefore, it is important to note that access vectors are extremely precious, especially since one access may enable cyberattacks across multiple space systems that share a ground segment or common configuration. If an offensive cyber unit discovers a vulnerability, it keeps that vulnerability secret for use to deliver a cyber-weapon. If it is used stealthily, it might remain secret for a long time. Cyber weapons are a combination of a payload—the damage the exploit does—and a delivery mechanism: the vulnerability used to get the payload into the enemy network. Imagine that a nation state knows about a vulnerability and is using it in a still-unfired cyber-weapon, and that the United States learns about it through espionage. Should the United States disclose and patch the vulnerability, or should it use it itself for attack on other nation state's networks? If it is disclosed, then the nation state could find a replacement vulnerability that the United States doesn't yet know about. But if it doesn't, the United States is

---

[407] See *Satellite Telemetry Indicators for Identifying Potential Cyber Attacks.* Johnathon Martin. Aerospace TOR-2019-02178, The Aerospace Corporation, El Segundo, California (August 16, 2019). Approved for Public Release; Distribution Unlimited.

deliberately leaving itself vulnerable to a cyberattack. The world's militaries are investing more money in finding vulnerabilities than the commercial world is investing in fixing them.[408]

This generally creates a high threshold for willingness to use the attack vector before the attacker is ready to execute the cyberattack during a conflict. However, there are several activities that make using the access prior to war difficult to resist. Access to the network could allow for data to be exfiltrated which may include operational intelligence about the activities of the satellite; network-mapping allows the attacker to search for additional accesses or connections with additional space systems; implanting malware may allow for a resilient attack in a war time even if the access is severed; and testing the downstream attack builds confidence that the attack itself will achieve the desired effect when initiated during a conflict, which is analogous to increasing the probability of kill (P_k).[409] This is a delicate risk-reward ratio and should be contemplated carefully by senior decision makers.

The difficult nature of discovering, creating, developing, maintaining, and exploiting cyber-accesses against space systems without being discovered incentivizes creativity on the part of the attacker. One such way would be to inject or modify code prior to launch of the satellite. This could be done during design, testing and integration, or through the supply chain.[410] Protection from such an attack starts with recognizing that the whole-of-government challenge

---

[408] Schneier, Bruce (2014). https://www.theatlantic.com/technology/archive/2014/05/should-hackers-fix-cybersecurity-holes-or-exploit-them/371197/

[409] Of course, one also runs the risk that the targeted satellite system operators are already aware of the attack vector or access point, have a mitigation ready to activate, but have allowed the attackers access to remain in place until conflict arises in order to create false confidence in the capability an attacker believes they may have.

[410] Oakley, J. G. (2020). Cybersecurity for Space: Protecting the final frontier. (p.87-102) APRESS.

is far too wide-ranging and dynamic to be solved with money and by simply throwing more people at the problem.[411] Fundamental changes are needed where stronger governance and bill of materials are properly managed and tracked to the smallest detail throughout development and operations.

DETECTION

Detecting and mitigating cyber vectors and intrusions into the ground segment is quite similar to a traditional cybersecurity construct. Many of the same monitoring technologies can be leveraged on the ground; however, specialized technology is needed to extend the monitoring to include the telemetry, tracking, and control (TT&C) from the ground software to the antenna. Commercial and open-source software can be utilized for the monitoring, but customization is needed where specialized protocol decoders are required to process uplinked (i.e., commands) and downlinked (i.e., telemetry, mission data) packets to detect potential malicious values indicating your satellite is under attack. In addition to the ground segment monitoring, the space segment presents a unique set of challenges. While in orbit, satellites transmit two separate types of data to the ground. The downlinked data provides the mission data (communications, intelligence, imagery, timing information, etc.). This data type could provide indication that something isn't operating correctly but gives little additional information to diagnose why the anomaly may have occurred, especially since in most cases the only indication of a cyberattack would be an abrupt discontinuation of the data.

---

[411] Bisceglie, Jennifer (2020). Supply chain is under siege, agencies lack a coherent strategy
https://federalnewsnetwork.com/commentary/2020/12/supply-chain-is-under-siege-agencies-lack-a-coherent-strategy/

The other data type provides telemetry to the ground segment. This is designed to enable operators to monitor the health and status of the satellite, diagnose and troubleshoot anomalies, and ensure that the satellite is operating as desired. The downlinked telemetry provides important information needed for the satellite operators to properly manage the satellite safely. Given the complexity of spacecraft, it is unsurprising that the list of data types needed is extensive. These include data such as the operating mode of the satellite, the number of commands the satellite has executed, battery power levels, orientation of antennae, temperatures across the satellite, signal information, satellite location information, and so on.

The command uplink from the ground provides only a portion of the needed monitoring as it would detect attacks occurring from an authorized ground station. However, the data associated with the telemetry stream is the only truly viable source of information from the satellite to detect whether a cyberattack has occurred, is occurring, or whether an unauthorized user has interacted with the spacecraft when the attack is not initiated from the authorized ground station. To achieve a more complete cyber picture of the space system, monitoring is needed on the command uplink, the mission data downlink as well as the telemetry downlink. Unfortunately, the magnitude of data needed to be sent through the telemetry, combined with encryption overhead, limited bandwidth, and often limited visibility, leaves little room for robust cybersecurity information to be transmitted in the telemetry. In lieu of transmitting the information to the ground, cyber monitoring should also be occurring onboard the spacecraft to enable faster and more robust cyber intrusion detection capabilities. If on-board monitoring is not feasible, several parameters exist in most spacecraft implementations that provide a minimal capability indicating a cyberattack against a spacecraft and these parameters should be actively monitored on the ground.[412]

PROTECTION AND PREVENTION

So how does one go about protecting a space system from cyberattacks? Fortunately, some of the easiest defenses are also the most effective. Protection should start there. We have identified the three most effective defenses that every space system should contain. These defenses make a cyberattack on a space system significantly more difficult but still considerably more attractive than many other classes of ASATs.

First, every system should have an encrypted C2 link. Without it, it is all too easy for a sophisticated attacker to spoof your command signal and take control of your satellite. It is akin to leaving your front door unlocked and hoping you won't get robbed. Of course, the stronger the encryption, the better, but commercial-grade encryption makes developing and executing a cyberattack considerably more difficult.

Second, access to the C2 terminal in the ground system should be minimized as much as possible. This includes both physical and network access. Connections with a larger network may be unavoidable, but the allowance of traffic back to the C2 terminal should be restricted to the greatest extent possible to prevent an attacker from using your own C2 terminal against you.

Finally, authentication should be used on the C2 link to prevent replay attacks in which transmissions can be intercepted, recorded, and played back later. A successful replay attack can cause operations such

---

[412] See *Satellite Telemetry Indicators for Identifying Potential Cyber Attacks*. Johnathon Martin. Aerospace TOR-2019-02178, The Aerospace Corporation, El Segundo, California (August 16, 2019). Approved for Public Release; Distribution Unlimited.

as maneuver burns to occur multiple times.[413] It is important to note that authentication is useful only when paired with encryption. Authentication comes in the form of a changing value in the header of a command packet that the command processor on the satellite can recognize as being invalid. Examples of this are using a time stamp or a command counter that increments every time a command is received. Implementing authentication is both cheap and easy during the design phase of a space system and should always be used.

These three defenses are necessary, but not sufficient. As we go into more detail about protecting the system holistically (i.e., prevent breach), we should recognize two things at the outset. First, defending from cyberattacks is an ever-evolving process as bad actors are constantly adapting their tactics and attempting to find new accesses and vulnerabilities. Second, we should exhaustively work to ensure adversaries cannot gain access to the system, but we must also consider layered defenses that assume our initial "outer gate" has been breached (i.e., assume breach). The assumed breach mindset limits the trust placed within the system and assumes each component is not secure and probably already compromised. Strategies employed using this mindset tend to resemble more of a zero-trust model and leveraging a defense-in-depth protection strategy.

One of the fundamental problems with space system design is an assumption that protection at the system boundaries will be enough. For space, the boundary is often thought to be the communications link (i.e., radio frequency link) and the ground system in general. Little internal protection exists if the boundary is breached. Similar schools of thought existed in the beginning days of traditional cybersecurity, where border firewalls were providing the only protection from intrusion. This

---

[413] See *Security Threats Against Space Missions*. CCSDS Green Book. P. 3-8. https://public.ccsds.org/Pubs/350x1g2.pdf

approach proved to be faulty, and well-protected IT systems are now designed with risk-based defense-in-depth principles. Similarly, current and future space system designs must overcome the risk of an adversary breaching the boundary and operating unhindered inside the system.

Both large traditional developments and more modern rapidly developed space systems should ensure that they have a cyber-hardened design with defense-in-depth throughout. When cybersecurity protections have been deployed, the focus has commonly been on the ground segment with little research or guidance on securing the space segment (i.e., spacecraft). A space system should have cybersecurity protections applied to both the ground and space segments. Defense-in-depth has long been explained by using an onion as an example of the various layers of security. For example, on the space segment, the outer layer would contain protection such as governance, supply chain protection, and risk management. The middle layers would contain on-board logging, monitoring, and intrusion detection and the inner layers would be where the mission data and the flight software reside with protections such as encryption and software assurance to reduce risk.[414]

The following diagram, derived from one published by the National Air and Space Intelligence Center,[415] depicts a very high-level view of cyber threats for space systems. When applying a defense-in-depth strategy, security controls would need to be applied at all segments, especially the ground and space segment, to ensure the space system has a robust security architecture.

---

[414] Bailey, Brandon; Cybersecurity Protections for Spacecraft: A Threat Based Approach (2021). Aerospace TOR-2021-01333-REV A, The Aerospace Corporation, El Segundo, California. Approved for Public Release; Distribution Unlimited.

[415] United States, National Air and Space Intelligence Center. (2018, December). Competing in Space. (p.19). Retrieved June 30, 2020, from https://media.defense.gov/2019/Jan/16/2002080386/-1/-1/1/190115-F-NV711-0002.PDF

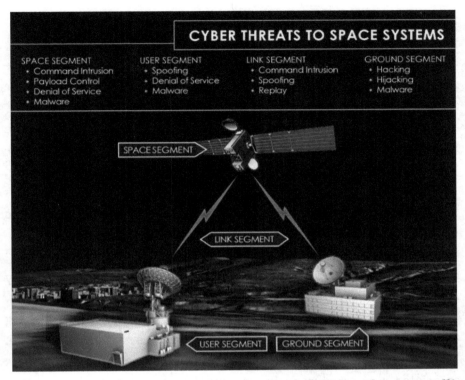

Figure 10. Cyber Threats to Space Systems. National Air and Space Intelligence Center (2018).

As previously mentioned, cyber-weapons are particularly attractive for adversaries to develop and employ during a conflict. To counter these weapons, careful planning years ahead of the conflict is necessary to ensure space systems will be resilient against cyberattacks in the future. Deciding what protections should be used on which segments in the architecture must be driven by a threat-informed risk management process. To manage risk, decision makers should assess the likelihood as well as potential impact of a successful cyberattack against the space system and then determine the best approach to deal with the risks: avoid, transfer, accept, or mitigate.

Not all risks can be eliminated, and no decisionmaker has unlimited budget or enough personnel to combat all risks. Selecting which protections will be used should be driven by the risk tolerance profile of each space system and its stakeholders. Many factors must be considered when generating a risk profile, such as the importance of the mission the space system is conducting or will conduct when fielded (are we talking about a small science experiment or a billion-dollar missile-warning capability?). Adversarial motivation to target a specific space system in a war must also be considered as the actual value and the value perceived by an adversary both affect the risk tolerance profile. Deciding what kind of protections to employ to protect space systems should also account for adversary capabilities as well as the difficulty to exploit the system.

For many military-focused systems, one must assume that during conflict the motivation is high and, depending on the specific adversary involved in the conflict, their capabilities are likely well developed. Therefore, the driving variable is the difficulty to exploit (i.e., gaining and maintaining access to) the system and similar systems in the future. This depends in large part on how a specific space mission and its associated space system is implemented and operated. The result is often a unique profile in which different threats have unique applicability that can change over time, depending on the degree to which conflict has been escalated.

Nonetheless, as discussed with encryption, authentication, and the C2 workstation, certain threat vectors and defenses against them are common across space systems. While aspects of threats will evolve over time, there are published space system threats, vulnerabilities, and mitigations mission designers should consider as starting points beyond those briefly discussed here.[416]

---

[416] Bailey, Brandon; Cybersecurity Protections for Spacecraft: A Threat Based Approach (2021). Aerospace TOR-2021-01333-REV A, The Aerospace Corporation, El Segundo, California. Approved for Public Release; Distribution Unlimited.

The most likely cyber threats to a space system during a conflict, or even during peacetime or a small military "crisis", would be exploiting the ground system to maliciously interact with the spacecraft via commanding or uploading custom malware, communications system spoofing resulting in denial of service and loss of availability and data integrity (i.e., command link intrusion), cyber-enabled communications system jamming resulting in denial of service and loss of availability and data integrity, and possibly a replay attack using recorded authentic communications traffic at a later time with the hope that the authorized communications will provide data or some other system reaction. More strategic adversaries would likely be establishing the accesses years in advance via hardware or software supply chain intrusions which would only be activated during the conflict period thereby making prevention difficult. Where prevention or detection methods may fail, recovery and response should step in. The spacecraft should provide the capability to enter the platform into a known good, operational cyber-safe mode from a tamper-resistant, configuration-controlled ("gold") image that is authenticated and has its integrity verified. Satellites generally contain various modes that can be an automatic response based on pre-set conditions. For instance, a safe mode can shut down certain non-essential activities if temperatures of certain components rise above safe levels. We are proponents of having a dedicated cyber-safe mode to allow recovery if certain anomalous conditions occur that correlate with indicators of cyberattacks.

In a cyber-safe mode, non-essential activities are shut down and the spacecraft is placed in a known good state using validated software and configuration settings. Within cyber-safe mode authentication and encryption should still be enabled and the spacecraft should be capable of reconstituting firmware and software functions to trusted and preattack states. That said, and more broadly speaking, any response and recovery protection features should not put the spacecraft in a more vulnerable state, allowing an attacker to use fault management systems to their advantage. In other words, protection mechanisms should make attacking the system more difficult, not easier.

Cyber ASAT Summary

Given the temperamental nature of cyber-accesses, it is not surprising that those who may have such capability have not exercised them and risked making the capability obsolete. During times of conflict, adversaries will be motivated to perform denial, degradation, disruption, deception, or destruction activities which will lower the threshold for use of cyber-weapons. So even in the absence of a highly publicized space mission failure attributed to cyberattack, these types of weapons will likely be a force to be reckoned with in a time of war. Multiple nations have published open-source doctrinal documents that show they consider both offensive cyber capabilities and electronic warfare as key assets for maintaining military advantage in a conflict extending into space.[417] We believe defense-in-depth is a substantial component of protecting from such attacks. This starts with designing cybersecurity into space systems before launch and continuing to improve system cyber security throughout the system life cycle.

One area to watch is on-board cybersecurity. Defense-in-depth principles have led to early consensus that security is needed to protect satellites even if the C2 terminal, the command link, or some other compromise occurs. System designers will have to balance the challenges of size, weight, and power with cybersecurity protection and ensure that the protections are not inadvertently making the system more vulnerable.

The protection of space systems is a must moving forward as space systems provide critical capabilities for the United States and its allies.

---

[417] National Air and Space Intelligence Center; *Competing in Space*, January 2016, https://media.defense.gov/2019/Jan/16/2002080386/-1/-1/1/190115-F-NV711-0002.PDF

The release of SPD-5 echoes this same sentiment and articulates the call to arms to address cybersecurity for space across government and commercial sectors. The barrier to entry into space has been drastically reduced and the "security by obscurity" model is no longer acceptable as the space industry continues to grow and space systems are increasingly interconnected. Implementing known best practices, as well as new technologies and processes along with proper risk management strategies can dramatically improve the cyber health of space systems and improve confidence that the system will be reliable in a time of war.

CHAPTER 8: ESTABLISHMENT OF THE UNITED STATES SPACE FORCE AS AN EFFICIENT SERVICE BRANCH

BY MICHAEL UNBEHAUEN

The creation of the United States Space Force, the newest branch of the US military, technically happened in December 2019, but its initial development is still unfolding in 2021. Strangely, the creation of this new branch was greeted initially by ridicule in US popular culture. (Netflix even created a mocking series around it.) However, anyone with even a slight awareness of military trends understands the importance of this development. This move shows the world that the United States is taking the next military domain seriously and likely marks the beginning of a global military priority shift[418].

However, as the US Space Force begins to organize as an independent military service, it needs to clearly define its mission[419]. The current Space Force that was established by the National Defense Authorization Act (NDAA) "does not exactly match the administration's earlier

---

[418] Acamar Institute, "Air & Missile Defense Year in Review: The Most Important Stories of 2020", *Acamar Institute*, JAN 17, 2021, https://www.acamarinstitute.org/post/air-missile-defense-year-in-review-the-most-important-stories-of-2020

[419] Michael Spirtas, Yool Kim, Frank Camm, Shirley M. Ross, Debra Knopman, Forrest E. Morgan, Sebastian Joon Bae, M. Scott Bond, John S. Crown, Elaine Simmons, "A Separate Space, Creating a Military Service for Space", RAND Corporation, 2020

guidance for the new service.".[420] The Trump administration's original proposal was to merge all Air Force, Army and Navy space activities under the Space Force. However, Congress only authorized transfers of Air Force personnel to the space service and the new Space Force is therefore essentially the old Air Force Space Command as its own new branch.

Pentagon officials are still hashing out which other space-focused units will move under the Space Force, which was almost exclusively created from the existing Air Force space enterprise[421]. Certain functions from other branches are now starting to be included. Nevertheless, these functions appear to be limited to satellite communications and theater warning. Incoming new units include those that operate Navy narrowband communications satellites and Army-run aspects of the Wideband Global Satellite Communications and Defense Satellite Communications System programs, among others[422].

Some experts have started to suggest that the current limitation of functions of the Space Force may impair its effectiveness. For example, besides the missile-warning mission which it inherited from the Air Force, the Space Force must also incorporate actual strategic missile defense[423]. Even the integration of the Air Force's land-based intercontinental ballistic missiles (ICBMs) into the Space Force has been

---

[420] Ibid.

[421] Rachel S. Cohen, "Nearly 4,000 soldiers, sailors and Marines applied to join the Space Force. Here are the 50 who made it", *Military Times*, June 30, 2021, https://www.militarytimes.com/news/your-air-force/2021/06/30/nearly-4000-soldiers-sailors-and-marines-applied-to-join-the-space-force-here-are-the-50-who-made-it/

[422] Ibid.

[423] Acamar Institute, "Air & Missile Defense Year in Review: The Most Important Stories of 2020", *Acamar Institute*, JAN 17, 2021, https://www.acamarinstitute.org/post/air-missile-defense-year-in-review-the-most-important-stories-of-2020

contemplated by some[424]. However, the Air Force personnel who control land-based ICBMs and the Army personnel who operate national missile defense systems will not be part of the US Space Force.

Nevertheless, there are certainly some strong arguments that justify a basic reexamination of military functions and personnel included in the new Space Force. Furthermore, it must also be considered that if the Space Force is limited to being just a force enabler rather than directly engaging in combat, then it will have difficulty demonstrating its effectiveness, justifying its existence as an independent service, and developing a distinctive identity[425].

HISTORICAL CONTEXT OF US MILITARY OPERATIONS IN SPACE

A closer examination of the role and history of US military operations in space could provide valuable context from which to analyze the development of the new US Space Force. The original incentive for the United States to put satellites in orbit was the need for a capability to monitor military developments in the Soviet Union, particularly those involving nuclear forces[426]. For the first two decades of the Space Age, most satellites were devoted to strategic missions supporting national decision-makers and US nuclear forces. Space capabilities became ever more tightly integrated with nuclear missions, both for strategic warning and for command and control[427].

---

[424] John "J.R." Riordan, Daniel "Sphinx" Dant, Timothy "Stepchild" Cox, "Time to Move ICBM and missile defense units to the Space Force", *Space News*, June 26, 2020, https://spacenews.com/op-ed-time-to-move-icbm-and-missile-defense-units-to-the-space-force/

[425] Michael Spirtas, Yool Kim, Frank Camm, Shirley M. Ross, Debra Knopman, Forrest E. Morgan, Sebastian Joon Bae, M. Scott Bond, John S. Crown, Elaine Simmons, "A Separate Space, Creating a Military Service for Space", RAND Corporation, 2020

[426] Ibid.

[427] Ibid.

Nonetheless, with the end of the Cold War, the trend toward greater military dependence on space-based services accelerated even more. Space became now also critical in US conventional military operations. In the 1991 Persian Gulf War, for the first time on a large scale, traditionally national strategic assets were tasked to support conventional combat operations [428]. Military communications satellites, originally designed to support command and control of strategic nuclear forces, were now being reconfigured to provide an unprecedented volume of bandwidth to conventional war fighters [429].

New generations of military communications satellites were developed to support conventional operations. Space capabilities are today of course crucial in US network-centric operations: Targets are identified by using space-based sensors; precision weapons are guided to their targets using GPS; and network components are linked via satellite communications. Blue-force tracking systems for better battlespace situational awareness are space-reliant. As a result of these developments, the US military's conventional warfighting capabilities have become increasingly fast, effective, and lethal [430]. However, these developments have also shifted the current military space focus to supporting conventional forces.

ARE ICBMS SPACE ASSETS?

ICBMs are large rockets, designed to reach targets many thousands of miles quickly and effectively away by transiting space on a ballistic trajectory [431]. They are using the same technologies which are used to

---

[428] Ibid.

[429] Ibid.

[430] Ibid.

[431] John "J.R." Riordan, Daniel "Sphinx" Dant, Timothy "Stepchild" Cox, "Time to Move ICBM and missile defense units to the Space Force", *Space News*, June 26, 2020,

launch satellites into orbit. Many of the launchers used by the US space program up unto the present were either retired ICBMs or technology which has directly evolved from them [432]. ICBMs are in all actuality, dual-use technologies, which operate in the space locality (near-Earth space) occupied by many of the systems conducting Space Force missions; they are, for all intents and purposes, space warfare systems. Since mass to orbit (space launch) or mass through ballistic delivery (IC-BMs) follows the same physics and space personnel are trained in this domain, it follows that space personnel are already optimized to integrate these missions [433].

It is planned that the Space Force will be the lead for the development of new rockets to lift satellites into space. As ICBMs as well as missile defense interceptor systems are being upgraded or replaced there will certainly be acquisition pressure from Congress to work together to find a common lift vehicle for satellites, nuclear warheads, and missile defense kill vehicles. Additionally, the Air Force's current ICBM force has a well-established cadre of maintenance specialists who are experts at maintaining rockets, a mission area which by necessity will be growing rapidly within the Space Force in the coming decades, as indicated by language in the National Defense Authorization Act calling for tactical space launch capabilities [434].

Both the space lift mission as well as the ICBM mission were somewhat neglected over the last few decades by the Air Force [435]. Placing the ICBM mission in the Space Force also disperses the nuclear triad from

---

https://spacenews.com/op-ed-time-to-move-icbm-and-missile-defense-units-to-the-space-force/

[432] Ibid.

[433] Ibid.

[434] Ibid.

[435] Ibid.

currently two services (Navy, Air Force) to three. The Air Force currently splits its support between nuclear bombers and ICBMs, tending to favor the aircraft and flight personnel over the missiles and the personnel who operate them, but never really having enough resources to handle both [436]. A division of the Air Force's nuclear missions with the Space Force would ensure a four-star on the Joint Chiefs of Staff to advocate for each leg of the nuclear triad. Although ICBMs may almost certainly open the US Space Force up to criticism that it should not be involved in terrestrial strike missions, such a direct combat mission may be beneficial for the definition of the new Space Force. In addition, it opens the possibility of at least conventional munitions being deorbited from space, or spaceplanes as conventional bombers.

Like the Army, Navy, and Air Force, the Space Force will operate in its own distinctive domain. But analysis indicates that its small size, even when compared with the Marine Corps and the Coast Guard, could pose a challenge. In addition, the current focus on space assets as enablers of combat operations instead of as employers of force could also impede the development of an independent identity [437]. From the history of the US armed forces, and of state-organized militaries in general, it appears that what is unique about them is that they engage in organized violence in the pursuit of national political objectives [438]. This role makes militaries distinct from other organizations. In the United States, military services gain their purpose, or mission, in that they train, organize, and equip forces to use violence (both passive via deterrent

---

[436] Ibid.

[437] Michael Spirtas, Yool Kim, Frank Camm, Shirley M. Ross, Debra Knopman, Forrest E. Morgan, Sebastian Joon Bae, M. Scott Bond, John S. Crown, Elaine Simmons, "A Separate Space, Creating a Military Service for Space", RAND Corporation, 2020

[438] Paula G. Thornhill, "The Crisis Within: America's Military and the Struggle Between the Overseas and Guardian Paradigms", RAND Corporation, 2016

threats or even cyberattacks, through escalations to physical violence) against other states and adversaries of the nation [439].

With the transfer of most Space Force personnel from the Air Force, many field-grade and senior space officers will have some ICBM operations experience owing to the fact that until very recently, the Air Force considered ICBMs as space mission and cross-trained personnel to do both [440]. But in the next five years or so, most of the space guardians will have had no interaction with any combat system capable of inflicting kinetic damage on an enemy. This is certainly not a desirable knowledge and experience gap for a military organization dedicated to the profession of arms. In addition, there is the danger that basic concepts, thought processes and functions such as shot doctrine, target selection, weapons mix or combined arms attacks applied by a potential enemy are not instantly understood by the US Space Force, though its current mission also encompasses missile warning (but not actual missile defense nor ICBM launches). ICBM and missile defense forces already understand and are engaged in offensive missile operations and can provide a foundation for the Space Force.

Then there is also the issue of ICBM operators and their role within the US Air Force. For a long time, these personnel have been treated as second and even third-class citizens by the Air Force. Over the past thirty years they have been shoved from Strategic Air Command to Air Combat Command to Air Force Space Command before ending up in Air

---

[439] Michael Spirtas, Yool Kim, Frank Camm, Shirley M. Ross, Debra Knopman, Forrest E. Morgan, Sebastian Joon Bae, M. Scott Bond, John S. Crown, Elaine Simmons, "A Separate Space, Creating a Military Service for Space", RAND Corporation, 2020

[440] John "J.R." Riordan, Daniel "Sphinx" Dant, Timothy "Stepchild" Cox, "Time to Move ICBM and missile defense units to the Space Force", *Space News*, June 26, 2020, https://spacenews.com/op-ed-time-to-move-icbm-and-missile-defense-units-to-the-space-force/

Force Global Strike command [441]. As space warfare operational art develops further, it will be critical that ICBM operations be coordinated by space warfighters. ICBM and space guardians currently lack a common frame of reference, even while operating in some of the same geological and astrometric spaces. The service which presents space warfighters is the Space Force, therefore it should be logical that all military space warfighting specialists need to be in the Space Force.

BALLISTIC AND HYPERSONIC MISSILE THREATS

The media has discovered the significance of missile warning provided by the Space Force through its legacy Space-Based Infrared System (SBIRS) in the Iranian ballistic missile attacks on US bases in Iraq. Another news focus has been the development of hypersonic weapons by Russia and China and the threat they supposedly represent for the United States. Today's US military lags Russian and Chinese developments in the field of hypersonic weapons and is pressed to find a quick solution for the defense against such weapons. Completely focused on nearly two decades of counter insurgency warfare, the US military neglected strategic planning, air and missile defense, and the military and technological modernization of Russia as well as the emergence of China [442].

Similarly, the development of the New Ground-based Interceptor (NGI) and homeland defense against intercontinental ballistic missiles has also been a reoccurring topic in the media. However, the intercept of such ballistic missile attacks would take place in space. Therefore, it could effectively be argued that strategic missile defense should be integrated into the new Space Force. With ongoing missile proliferation and

---

[441] Ibid.

[442] Michael Unbehauen, "Hypersonic Weapons Hype?", *Modern Diplomacy*, March 20, 2020, https://moderndiplomacy.eu/2020/03/20/hypersonic-weapons-hype/

constant improvements in missile technology, missile defense is a growing field of military interest and advancement.

Historically, the beginning of the development of rockets as long-range weapons in World War II is a brainchild of the identical thought and logic that prevails to this day in militaries that view themselves at a strategic disadvantage. The V-2 provided Germany with the advantage of attacking foes without developing a strategic bomber force. In addition, the V-2 could not be countered in the air by any known defensive systems of the time. Many non-Western military thinkers are still applying this rationale today. The difference, however, is that the V-2 was not a very precise weapon; today, there are precision guided missiles that have far overcome the shortfalls of the V-2, and thus make missiles even more attractive [443].

At the start of World War II, the German rocket program dropped to a relatively low priority. It was not until after the historic Battle of Britain, in which the German Luftwaffe had promised to dominate and crush Britain but then could not deliver, that rockets moved up on the German agenda. When it became apparent that the German plans of air dominance over England had to be abandoned as hopeless, and with Britain gaining air superiority, Hitler made the rocket program his top priority. Germany did not need air superiority to launch missiles at London from a safe distance. In addition, Hitler came to recognize the power of deterrence that originated from missile arsenals and regretted not having invested more into his missile program before the war. The same logic is prevalent today in North Korea or Iran, and understandably so, judging from their overall military disadvantage. Since WWII, air

---

[443] Acamar Institute, "Striving to Remain: Is Missile Proliferation a Requirement of Self-Determination?",*Acamar Institute*, Mar 15, 2021, https://www.acamarinstitute.org/post/striving-to-remain-is-missile-proliferation-a-requirement-of-self-determination

dominance has been the cornerstone of US military superiority and every country in the world understands that it cannot compete with the US Air Force. The key to balance this military disparity is missile technology. Just as Hitler focused on his missile program after he had to accept that Allied air forces dominated the skies, America's adversaries today focus on missile technology and capabilities. Missiles give them the capability to punch way above their weight class and prevents even highly sophisticated military powers from military action against these rocket systems.[444]

Therefore, missiles will not go away; they will not lose their appeal for militaries worldwide. They have and will even further change the geopolitical landscape. Proliferation of missile technology will likely continue to rise with the growth of private commercial space companies that are in possession of relevant technology for application in military missiles. This may happen through the mishandling of data by companies and cyber espionage, but history also shows other, more mundane, dangers. OTRAG, a German company, was the world's first commercial developer and producer of space launch vehicles. In the 1980s, the company got heavily involved in Libya's missile program when Muammar Gaddafi offered a testing facility and financial support for their commercial space project.[445]

With ongoing international missile proliferation and the obvious inability to stop or significantly limit this trend, the United States and its allies cannot avoid investing in efficient missile defense capabilities on the tactical and strategic levels. These investments must include not only upgrades and new missile defense systems, but also new sensor networks in space.

---

[444] Ibid.

[445] Ibid.

In addition to the ICBM threat, a new hypersonic threat has evolved. The speed of hypersonic weapons is typically the key focus in most discussions of them as a dangerous new weapon system. This is understandable, as their speed is certainly significant and poses a strong technical challenge in designing a system to counter their employment. However, it must be understood that speed is only one consideration for successful intercept. The ability for hypersonic missiles, or glide vehicles, to significantly maneuver and avoid a predictable trajectory is the critical feature that will be the biggest challenge to overcome.[446] Existing missile defenses are designed against ballistic missiles, which travel along a predictable trajectory with very limited ability to maneuver. Hypersonic weapons will negate current defense capabilities due to their greater speed and maneuverability relative to ICBMs.

In recognition of the growing missile threats, a multi-orbit network of space sensors that can detect and track both ballistic and hypersonic missiles is a goal now being pursued by the US Space Force, the Defense Department's Space Development Agency, and Missile Defense Agency.[447] The Space Based Infrared System (SBIRS) of geostationary missile-warning satellites has been in operation for decades. The Space Force is now investing billions of dollars in a new constellation of Next-Generation Overhead Infrared (OPIR) geostationary and polar-orbiting satellites to provide global early warning of missile launches.[448] In addition, sensor satellites closer to Earth in low orbits to detect and track

---

[446] Michael Unbehauen, "Hypersonic Weapons Hype?", *Modern Diplomacy*, March 20, 2020, https://moderndiplomacy.eu/2020/03/20/hypersonic-weapons-hype/

[447] Sandra Erwin, "Space Force, DoD agencies planning multi-orbit sensor network to track hypersonic missiles", *Space News*, June 21, 2021, https://spacenews.com/space-force-dod-agencies-planning-multi-orbit-sensor-network-to-track-hypersonic-missiles/

[448] Ibid.

maneuvering hypersonic glide vehicles and other advanced weapons that could evade current early warning satellites, ship and ground-based radar sensors are being developed.

To qualify as a hypersonic weapon, the weapon must be able to travel at least five times the speed of sound. The Russian Avangard hypersonic glide vehicle, the first operational hypersonic weapon, can achieve speeds between 20 to 27 times the speed of sound, according to the Russian government. In comparison, a traditional ICBM changes speeds throughout its parabolic flight (between boost, exo-atmospheric mid-course, and terminal phases) and achieves speeds averaging twenty times the speed of sound during re-entry into the atmosphere. By this definition, current ICBMs would also technically be hypersonic missiles.[449]

Russia's announcement of its first operational hypersonic weapon seems to have been a "Sputnik moment" for the US military. By 1957, the Soviet Union "had acquired the world's first ICBM, which also placed the first artificial satellite, Sputnik, in space. For the United States, this presented a substantial threat and challenge, amplifying fears about American weakness against a Soviet ICBM attack. This shaped the political support for the creation of an American anti-ballistic missile (ABM) system."[450] The first American ICBM was declared operational two years after the Soviet Union already had ICBMs. The reason for the American delay during the Cold War was due to a different strategic focus and to military leadership that was not adaptive in its approach. With over-whelming air superiority and capable intercontinental bombers, the US

---

[449] Michael Unbehauen, "Hypersonic Weapons Hype?", *Modern Diplomacy*, March 20, 2020, https://moderndiplomacy.eu/2020/03/20/hypersonic-weapons-hype/

[450] M. Unbehauen, G. Sloan, A. Squatrito," The U.S. Missile Defense Shield and Global Security Destabilization: An Inconclusive Link", *International Journal of Business, Human and Social Sciences*, May 1, 2019. https://zenodo.org/record/3299365#.Xm6JNI7Yqzz

Air Force did not take the development of ICBM technology seriously. Within the Air Force, many fighter and bomber pilots, the elite of the hierarchy in the Air Force and the main pool from which decision makers came, were opposed to the notion of American ICBMs, since they saw their traditional roles in danger and could not conceptualize a new form of warfare.[451]. The development of the Space Force must not be allowed to suffer from similar inability of military leaders to adapt to changing situations, unwillingness to encourage flexibility and innovation, or inner-service rivalries.

A viable defense against the hypersonic threat will rely largely on space-based sensors. The defense against the ever-growing threat to the United States through ballistic missiles also relies on space-based sensors to a large extent, as well as land-based sensors which fulfill a dual role for tracking satellites. And the engagement of enemy strategic ballistic missiles takes place in space. Nevertheless, missile defense functions are not included in the new Space Force. This stems largely from an antiquated division between the Army and Air Force regarding air and missile defense functions. Ground-based air and missile defense functions were given to the Army and the Air Force was made responsible for the missile-warning mission relying on satellites (the Space Force inherited the Air Force space functions). However, this strict division is today no longer applicable. For the sake of a more effective defense, the entire mission of missile defense related operations (missile warning and missile defense) should be unified under the command of the US Space Force.

---

[451] Michael Unbehauen, "Hypersonic Weapons Hype?", *Modern Diplomacy*, March 20, 2020, https://moderndiplomacy.eu/2020/03/20/hypersonic-weapons-hype/

GROUND-BASED MIDCOURSE DEFENSE (GMD)

Ground-Based Midcourse Defense (GMD) was designed as a defense against a limited ICBM threat that could potentially emanate from rogue states. When the GMD system was anticipated, it was done so mainly with the upcoming missile capabilities of North Korea in mind. Still, in 2004, when GMD became operational, many contested the decision to field the missile defense system, reasoning that North Korea did not have ICBMs at the time nor would it be able to have such a capability anytime soon. Today, the North Korean threat is real, and Pyongyang can potentially reach the American mainland with ICBMs and nuclear warheads[452].

Knowing today's reality, the establishment of GMD over 15 years ago proved to be farsighted. It must also be argued that, despite widespread criticism about the reliability and excessive cost of this missile defense system, GMD has already proven its tremendous security value. Without such a system in place, the US defense establishment would likely have viewed a preemptive military strike on North Korea as a necessity had Pyongyang obtained a nuclear ICBM capability. It is hardly conceivable that an undefended United States would have tolerated a nuclear armed, ICBM-capable North Korea. This preemptive strike may have resulted in a war on the Korean peninsula, with clear global implications[453].

GMD is the only US missile defense system that was specifically designed to counter long-range ballistic missiles threatening the US homeland. The current interceptors that the system uses are called Ground-Based Interceptors (GBIs). GBIs use a three-stage booster, giving GMD

---

[452] Michael Unbehauen, "The Case for Missile Defense and an Efficient Defense of the US Homeland", *Wild Blue Yonder*, 8 June 2020, https://media.defense.gov/2020/Jun/10/2002314039/-1/-1/1/UNBEHAUEN.PDF
[453] Ibid.

the necessary ability and power to perform intercepts over great distances. This range gives GMD by far the greatest coverage area of any US missile defense system. GBIs are basically ICBMs without a warhead and have similar ranges as ICBMs. GBIs travel with a speed of over 7 kilometers per second, exceeding 27,500 km/h, toward their target and release an Exo-atmospheric Kill Vehicle (EKV), which destroys the warhead of an enemy ICBM through kinetic energy in the midcourse phase of the threat missile's flight in space [454]. These kill vehicles are technological siblings of direct-ascent anti-satellite (ASAT) systems like those currently deployed by potential US adversaries Russia and China [455]. GBIs are launched out of refitted silos that were originally designed for US Minuteman ICBMs and use the same rocket stages that are used to launch satellites into space [456]. Just like ICBMs, ground-based interceptors are dual-use technologies, which will do their mission in the space locality (near-Earth space) occupied by a variety of systems conducting Space Force missions. Technically, GBIs and the EKV are space warfare systems.

The GMD missile defense system is operated by the US Army National Guard and there are currently no plans to integrate the GMD mission or strategic missile defense into the Space Force. Nevertheless, the present-day sequence of events in case of a potential ICBM launch toward the US homeland illustrates what in 2008 already, a

---

[454] Missile Defense Advocacy Alliance, "Evolution of GBI Boosters and Kill Vehicles", *Missile Defense Advocacy Alliance*, https://missiledefenseadvocacy.org/

[455] John "J.R." Riordan, Daniel "Sphinx" Dant, Timothy "Stepchild" Cox, "Time to Move ICBM and missile defense units to the Space Force", *Space News*, June 26, 2020, https://spacenews.com/op-ed-time-to-move-icbm-and-missile-defense-units-to-the-space-force/

[456] Michael Unbehauen, "The Case for Missile Defense and an Efficient Defense of the US Homeland", *Wild Blue Yonder*, 8 June 2020, https://media.defense.gov/2020/Jun/10/2002314039/-1/-1/1/UNBEHAUEN.PDF

congressionally mandated report on US defense space organization found: Leadership and organization for military space was "fragmented and unfocused"[.457].

If North Korea ever launched an ICBM, it would be the US Space Force that would likely be the first ones to detect such a launch through their SBIRS. This would alert all sensors within the defense architecture to search for and detect the threat missile. The US Army operates two forward based radars in Japan that would collect more precise data about the missile and pass it on. These US Army missile defense radars are vital for the missile-warning mission (a Space Force function) and fulfill a dual role for missile defense and space surveillance. Nevertheless, they are operated by active-duty US Army Soldiers and not the Space Force. Based upon the information of those Army radars, other radars operated by the Space Force would then track the incoming missile further and share vital data with the GMD system operators of the US Army National Guard for engagement. Also, in the mix would possibly be the Sea-based X-Band Radar (SBX) which provides discrimination capability for missile threats in midcourse over the Pacific Ocean for the GMD system. This discrimination of the actual warhead is of utmost importance to ensure a successful intercept. SBX is a highly capable discrimination radar that is mounted on a self-propelled former oil platform. Its ocean-spanning mobility allows it to be repositioned as needed to support homeland defense. The SBX vessel management, navigation, and physical security fall under the US Navy's Military Sealift Command, though the Missile Defense Agency (MDA) retains responsibility for communications, the X-band radar, and for mission integration. The radar operators are civilian contractors and employees of MDA.

---

[457] Michael Spirtas, Yool Kim, Frank Camm, Shirley M. Ross, Debra Knopman, Forrest E. Morgan, Sebastian Joon Bae, M. Scott Bond, John S. Crown, Elaine Simmons, "A Separate Space, Creating a Military Service for Space", RAND Corporation, 2020

Based upon the collected data from all these various sources provided through different military services and agencies, the US Army National Guard would then launch its GBIs and intercept the incoming warhead in space. Paradoxically, regardless of the engagement in space, the Army personnel who operate national missile defense systems are not and will not become part of the US Space Force.

Ground-based missile defense forces could be integrated with missile and space warning to form the core of a major command dedicated to terrestrial defense against space threats.[458]. Such an integration would arguably create more effectiveness, efficiency for homeland defense and increase independence, and sense of identity for the Space Force.

ADVERSARIES

The Russian Aerospace Forces, as the branch is known, combines elements of the space forces, air forces, as well as air and missile defense forces under a single command. In 2015, Russia integrated its air force branch with its space force and its separate air and missile defense branch. The reason for Russia's decision was that it defined the boundaries of their missions as entirely contrived and artificial, and concluded that the capabilities required for air defense, missile defense, and anti-satellite missions were closely related and multirole in nature.[459].

It has been falsely reported in the US media that the 2015 merger of the Russian Air Force and the Russian Space Force was doctrinally

---

[458] John "J.R." Riordan, Daniel "Sphinx" Dant, Timothy "Stepchild" Cox, "Time to Move ICBM and missile defense units to the Space Force", *Space News*, June 26, 2020, https://spacenews.com/op-ed-time-to-move-icbm-and-missile-defense-units-to-the-space-force/

[459] Matthew Bodner, "As Trump pushes for separate space force, Russia moves fast the other way", *Defense News*, June 21, 2018, https://www.defensenews.com/global/europe/2018/06/21/as-trump-pushes-for-separate-space-force-russia-moves-fast-the-other-way/

diametrically opposed to the Trump administration's creation of the US Space Force and the separation of space activities from the US Air Force. Such a statement or comparison is neither historically, nor operationally accurate: The role of the Russian Air Force is not comparable with that of the US Air Force. In the United States, the strategic defense concept after World War II was based upon a counter offensive air force which would attack any aggressor with utmost violence. This was in accordance with the popular view built on existing capabilities and the extensive US experience from WWII. In the Soviet Union, on the other hand, Stalin and the highest military leadership were reported to personally have encouraged the development of long-range intercontinental missiles soon after WWII. This stood in contrast to the US, where many prominent US scientists doubted that an ICBM was even feasible. Research in the US concentrated on jet engine propulsion instead.

The different strategic defense choices after WWII were decisive and are still impacting basic defense concepts today. The Soviets viewed rocket technology as promising. They needed a deterrent to neutralize US strategic air bases in Europe, and a means to hold Europe hostage against a US threat of action. A strong Soviet security position was needed; a deterrent force contributed directly to the defense of the Soviet Union. Technology offered the prospect of an impressive solution to the perceived threat. The Soviet leader Nikita Khrushchev would even boast that the strategic attack aircraft was obsolete and therefore had decided not to produce a large bomber force. Rockets and missiles instead were manifestations of a growing Soviet emphasis on new means for wielding power[460]. In 1959, the Soviet Union created a separate missile military branch, the Strategic Missile Forces. To this day the date of its formal foundation, December 17, is celebrated as Strategic Missile

---

[460] Center of Military History, "History of Strategic Air and Ballistic Missile Defense, Volume I: 1956-1972", *United States Army*, 2009

Forces Day in Russia. Soviet, and later Russian resources and doctrine were invested and geared toward its missile forces rather than its air force. Even today the Russian Air Force is in size or spending nowhere comparable with those of NATO or the United States. The dominant role that air power had achieved in Western military concepts was in Russia to a large extent filled by their Strategic Missile Forces. For some time, Russian Space Forces were part of the Russian Strategic Missile Forces, comparable with the situation in the United States where space functions were carried out by the US Air Force until the creation of the US Space Force.

With this historical background, it would be wrong to assume that Russia with its founding of the Aerospace Forces went the opposite direction than the United States and merged Space Forces with the Air Force. Russia incorporated its strategically less significant air force with its doctrinally important space and air and missile defense forces because Russia wants to raise the efficiency of their use through closer integration [461]. Here it is especially interesting that Russia appears to acknowledge the benefits of the integration of missile defense with space operations. The United States unfortunately does not seem to share this view for its armed forces. Russia chose not to integrate its Strategic Missile Forces with its Aerospace Forces (and thus its Space Forces) to prevent the dominance of Russian Strategic Missile Forces over the aerospace branch, which might negatively impact the effectiveness of space operations (as it was arguably the case in the US when the current functions of the Space Force were carried out by a fighter-pilot dominated Air Force).

---

[461] Matthew Bodner, "As Trump pushes for separate space force, Russia moves fast the other way", *Defense News*, June 21, 2018, https://www.defensenews.com/global/europe/2018/06/21/as-trump-pushes-for-separate-space-force-russia-moves-fast-the-other-way/

In China, the space force is part of the People's Liberation Army Strategic Support Force (SSF). This military branch is made up of space-, cyber-, and electronic warfare forces. It was created in 2015 and functionally and structurally, operates like the People's Liberation Army Rocket Force.

In the case of China, just as with Russia, there is less separation of strategic missile operations, missile defense, and space than there is in the US. The People's Liberation Army (PLA) has made it clear that it views midcourse Ballistic Missile Defense (BMD) and kinetic ASAT as similar capabilities under the singular umbrella of "space operations" rather than as two discrete mission types. The only distinction between the two is that midcourse BMD is a "space defense" mission while kinetic ASAT is a "space control" mission [462]. Furthermore, the PLA places its greatest emphasis on the ability to establish space superiority through non-kinetic and kinetic strikes against adversary satellites and space vehicles [463]. The ability to destroy ballistic missiles in space appears to be another (albeit less important) requirement [464]. There is also circumstantial evidence that suggests the SSF Space Systems Department is responsible for developing midcourse interceptors. The PLA SSF is tasked with overseeing the PLA's strategic space, cyber, electronic, and psychological warfare missions [465]. Given this mission set, the SSF's involvement in developing midcourse interceptors suggests that BMD and ASAT are both viewed as space-centric missions.

---

[462] Roderick Lee, "China's Recent Ballistic Missile Defense Test May Have Actually Been an Anti-Satellite Test", *China Aerospace Studies Institute*, February 09, 2021, https://www.airuniversity.af.edu/CASI/Display/Article/2497584/chinas-recent-ballistic-missile-defense-test-may-have-actually-been-an-anti-sat/

[463] Ibid.

[464] Ibid.

[465] Ibid.

PERSONNEL QUESTIONS

The overwhelming majority of US Air Force personnel working in space-related functions welcomed the creation of the Space Force. Traditionally, the Air Force has been culturally dominated by a leadership hierarchy that saw fighter-pilots at the top and viewed space operations as secondary at best. The culture within the other services was similar. The importance of space operations for the Army or Navy was not reflected in promotion chances nor adequately in the highest leadership functions. The creation of the Space Force was therefore viewed with great interest and hopes by space operators throughout the services. Therefore, when it became clear that the US Space Force was only a transformation of Air Force space functions into its own branch, many soldiers, sailors, and marines engaged with space operations were somewhat disappointed.

As the US Space Force announced that it would allow fifty volunteers from services other than the Air Force in its ranks, to its surprise nearly 4000 officers and enlisted members from the other services applied.[466]. This is to a large extent the result of years of neglect, marginalization, and misappropriation by all services of their space personnel, and the high number of applicants should have been by no means a surprise.

Only now, with the new Space Force, it seems that the services have discovered the true importance of their own space capabilities. There seems to be reluctance to giving up influence and ownership of space

---

[466] Rachel S. Cohen, "Nearly 4,000 soldiers, sailors and Marines applied to join the Space Force. Here are the 50 who made it", *Military Times*, June 30, 2021, https://www.militarytimes.com/news/your-air-force/2021/06/30/nearly-4000-soldiers-sailors-and-marines-applied-to-join-the-space-force-here-are-the-50-who-made-it/

missions[467]. A role in space means control over one's satellite overhead watch. But more so, it also ensures control of billions of dollars in acquisition, budgetary, personnel and contracting authority tied to space missions. With the potential of shrinking military budgets, the loss of a space missions means fewer options for a service to tap into when it needs to shift funds. This has especially led to a competition for control of space assets between the Space Force and the Army[468].

Another unresolved field of contention is the question of members of the National Guard and Reserve and their role in the Space Force. It is difficult to understand why the question of Reservists and the National Guard was not adequately addressed with the creation of the Space Force. Traditionally space functions within the Air Force as well with the Army have been to an exceptionally large extent supported by members of the National Guard or the Reserve.

The Space Force has currently about 6,500 active-duty members. But Air Force Reservists complete 26 percent of the Space Force's total mission[469]. However, the 2021 National Defense Authorization Act prohibited the Defense Department from establishing any reserve components of the Space Force until DOD submits a draft plan to the House and Senate Armed Services committees. In addition to many Reservists, there are approximately 2,000 space personnel in the Army and Air National Guards. National Guard units have taken on space missions for twenty-five years, and Army and Air National Guardsmen now make up 11

---

[467] Tara Copp, "Space Force's First Battle Is With the US Army", *Defense One*, May 20, 2021, https://www.defenseone.com/policy/2021/05/space-forces-first-battle-us-army/174174/

[468] Ibid.

[469] Brent D. Ziarnick, "Space Force Reserve too important to be dictated by active duty", *Air Force Times*, April 20, 2021, https://www.airforcetimes.com/opinion/commentary/2021/04/20/space-force-reserve-too-important-to-be-dictated-by-active-duty/

percent of personnel that works directly for the Space Force[470]. The Air National Guard has space units in seven states — Alaska, California, Colorado, Florida, Hawaii, New York, and Ohio — plus Guam[471]. Currently, the Air National Guard provides 60 percent of the Space Force's offensive space electronic warfare capability[472]. The Air National Guard also operates the nation's only survivable and endurable strategic missile warning / nuclear detection capability and provides the nation's strategic missile warning[473].

CONCLUSION

The US Space Force will not rise to its full potential if the original proposal to merge all Air Force, Army and Navy space activities under the Space Force is not realized. This should ainclude the ICBM mission as well as missile defense (especially as missile threats are growing). It is imperative for the Space Force to broaden its mission sets to include all space-related functions throughout the services. Further it must define its warfare functions to include its own combat operations, rather than focusing exclusively on support functions for other services. The Space Force also needs Congress to create a Space National Guard and a Space Reserve that incorporates Reservists and National Guard units who are part of the Space mission. The goal of an independent US Space Force will not be accomplished if major functions are carried out by members

---

[470] Rachel S. Cohen, "Plan for Space Force reserve component is 'fairly close,' National Guard boss says", *Defense News*, May 4, 2021, https://www.defense-news.com/news/your-air-force/2021/05/04/plan-for-space-force-reserve-compo-nent-is-fairly-close-national-guard-boss-says/

[471] Ibid.

[472] Ibid.

[473] National Guard, "Fact Sheet NG Space Operations", National Guard, https://www.nationalguard.mil/Portals/31/Re-sources/Fact%20Sheets/Fact%20Sheet_NG%20Space%20Operations_Mar2021.pdf

of the Army National Guard, Army Reserve, Air National Guard, and Air Force Reserve. If this situation persists, the Space Force is depending on personnel from other services and is therefore reliant on those services to carry out its core mission. The creation of the Space Force, despite how critically it is viewed by some, was a necessity that reflects current and future warfare realities. However, if the establishment of the Space Force will not be carried out efficiently and if it will not create an effective new military branch as its outcome, then the entire American defense capability could potentially suffer tremendously.

CHAPTER 9: SOLAR SCRAMBLE: ASTROSTRATEGIC
IMPLICATIONS OF PERMANENT SPACE SETTLEMENTS

BY DAINIUS T. BALČYTIS

INTRODUCTION

Nothing is as foundational to the human experience as the places we live in. And since the dawn of time, wherever we lived, whether in jungle villages or modern megacities, we also fought each other. Many theories even propose that civilization itself was as a result of settling down to develop agriculture by storing food surplus, and the resulting arms race between those who wanted to protect these valuable settlements and those who would try to sack them. As humanity ascends into the cosmos, this fundamental dynamic will follow us into space; however it will also inevitably change, as what it means to settle and build our new homes will change as well. Warfare in the cosmos might not happen at first with settlers' perceptions of infinite resources, but certainly will occur when these resources are threatened by other groups.

In this chapter we will discuss hypothetical implications of permanent human presence beyond Earth orbit in the context of grand strategy, space warfare and resulting political considerations. This topic has not been well explored, as there are still many questions looming about the practical aspects of settling space. Principles discussed in this chapter are not likely to materialize for some time to come. The ambition to establish extraterrestrial colonies exists since the 1950s (Ordway et al., 2003) and it appears that if the political, cultural and economic factors would align, there are no hard limitations stopping humanity from establishing permanent presence beyond Earth within the decade. Although this is not very likely now, it can be optimistically suggested that the innumerable advantages of space exploration (Crawford 2012) and the need to hedge against the existential risks on Earth (Bostrom 2013) will eventually direct humanity toward this route, whether it would take a decade or a century. Barring unforeseen hard barriers in material sciences or a civilization-scale catastrophe, we can extrapolate that humanity will sooner or later make use of and spread throughout the Solar system.

We will discuss the resulting dynamics of competition, which are likely to increase geopolitical tensions and cause a scramble for the key locations around the Solar system. We will review the possible impact of space settlements on astrostrategic thought. We will the discuss military, legal and political advantages and disadvantages of permanent human presence in space and the offensive and defensive considerations that will have to be considered. Finally we will present a case that long-term planning and managing of international tensions during the initial period of human expansion into space is of utmost importance.

DEFINITIONS AND ASSUMPTIONS

At the time of writing, barely six decades have passed since the launch of Vostok 1 with Yuri Gagarin on board and the beginning of human space exploration. Space sciences have advanced much since then, but they are still in their relative infancy. Meanwhile, discourse on space settlements and conflicts is at roughly the same stage as aeronautics were before the outbreak of World War - theoretical debate is lively, but there is no practical understanding of its full implications. While the technical side of space sciences has a robust and clearly defined terminology, discourse related to the theory of conflict in space and the future of human space exploration still has many nebulous terms which are used in different ways by different researchers.

Therefore, it is important to clarify assumptions under which the following discussion is based and explain relevant terminology.

Several different proposals for settling beyond Earth have been discussed, notably kick-started by Stanford/NASA Ames space settlement studies which began the debates in the 1970s (NASA Ames Research Center, 1975). While so far humanity has experimented only with orbital space stations (such as International Space Station or Russian "Mir" station), there is solid scientific and experimental backing (NASA Scientific and Technical Information Program Office 2004) that both space habitats and planetary settlements (while not without great challenges) are possible with the current level of technology. The question of human ability to settle in space appears to be a matter of resources and political will, rather than feasibility.

For the purposes of this chapter, we will consider three general types of space settlement infrastructure: orbital stations (enhanced versions of ISS), autonomous space habitats (such as O'Neill cylinders) (Globus 2006, Ashworth 2012) and settlements on astronomical bodies such as the Moon base plan outlined in the Project Horizon (Ordway et al., 2003), Artemis Program proposal (Smith et al. 2020) or an even more ambitious SpaceX vision for Mars (Cannon and Britt 2019). We will be referring to these categories together as space settlements.

While we have grown accustomed to seeing space settlements inhabited by people in science fiction media, in practice human-run space stations and habitats would make up only a small (but vital) proportion of humanity's space infrastructure. Most space settlements could be remotely controlled or even fully automated, with humans visiting them only for maintenance purposes. However, most of the future human population is likely to reside in planetary space settlements, which could be much fewer in number, but not constrained by the limitations of space stations. When discussing these space settlements which would have a permanent, endogenous human population, we will refer to them as space colonies. While orbital or space habitat space colonies are also possible, it is much more likely that they will develop on other planetary bodies as like Earth as possible.

Based on cost, safety and recent trend considerations, most of the space infrastructure is likely to be remote controlled or autonomous, without any humans present. While on Earth no one would call an automated outpost a "settlement", we argue that in astrostrategic context the prerequisite of human presence for the definition of "settlement" should be relaxed, as even unmanned or temporarily crewed space installations should be considered part of space settlement infrastructure. In the context of military analysis, their functional value and threat factors are not likely to be highly affected by the number of actual humans present[474]. In fact, human presence on a spacecraft is likely to reduce the chances of it having a military purpose because it would be much harder to sacrifice in the event of a space conflict. After all, with enough delta-v fuel and end-game tracking sensors, almost any unmanned mining drone, communications satellite or even a space station has the potential to be turned into a kinetic projectile.

Because of these reasons, in the context of this chapter, space settlement refers to any semi-stationary[475] installation that is built with the

---

[474] However it can be expected that rules of engagement and the repercussions of targeting a manned object are going to be very different. It is not difficult to imagine a future military argument being made in favor of manned space exploration with astronauts serving as the "tripwire force", or conflict escalation control "line-in-the-sand" akin to US deployment of troops on the German-USSR border in order to signal commitment and deter aggression.

[475] Orbital stations or space habitats are likely to retain maneuver engines for orbital station keeping and could regain limited mobility in cases of emergency, such as danger of collision or breakout of war, which is why we cannot consider them truly stationary, unlike planetary (and lunar or planetoid) settlements.

intention of utilizing it on a semi-permanent basis.[476] beyond the Earth's atmosphere.

Differentiation between orbital stations and autonomous space habitats can become blurry, as in principle both rely on similar technology, however in the context of space warfare it is valuable to differentiate them. Orbital space stations would be in principle dependent on the resources and support from the space body which they are orbiting. These stations can serve many purposes, such as scientific centers, industrial processing plants, transportation waystations, space tourist resorts, etc. However, even if they would happen to have a permanent population, they are never built to be completely self-sufficient, and their construction would be optimized for specialization and performing as part of a greater infrastructure grid. Meanwhile truly autonomous space habitats, as once advocated for by the L5 Society (Dorminey 2012), would likely be built at Lagrange points across the Solar system (Hibbs 1977) and contain their own systems to acquire or produce vital supplies and energy, allowing them to go without resupplies from Earth for years, if not indefinitely. While for economic reasons it is likely that very few of these space settlements would pursue a policy of complete autonomy, they would nonetheless have a much wider range of military and political options available to them, possibly even including the ability to relocate. When thinking about these three categories of space settlements,

---

[476] It must be noted that permanency might mean different things in space than it does on Earth. For example ISS would fall under our definition of a temporary space settlement, but it has already been in space since 1998 and theoretically, could continue to be renewed and recertified indefinitely, although it would become like the mythic Theseus' ship (https://en.wikipedia.org/wiki/Ship_of_Theseus). While this is unlikely, as eventually maintenance costs and mounting risks will inevitably make creation of a new station cheaper from cost-benefit analysis perspective, if said temporary space settlement would be of strategic importance, it is likely that it would continue to be utilized past its originally planned dates.

to help visualize, one can consider planetary settlements to be equivalent to cities, while the orbital stations are their dependent suburbs and the autonomous space habitats are the outlying provincial towns.

Table 5. Types of space settlement.

Space settlement type	Examples
Orbital space station	Mir; Almaz, ISS
Autonomous space habitat	O'Neill Cylinder
Planetary space settlement	Project Horizon; Artemis lunar outpost

For the foreseeable future all space settlements will need to be founded by an Earth polity. This founding polity, which we assume would hold a stake in control, utilization and protection of the said settlement, will be referred to as the metropolity.[477] While initially these metropolities are likely to be states or heavily state-funded private enterprises, opening of the space frontier is likely to entice corporations, religious foundations or other sub-state political entities to attempt in setting up their own space settlements.

Another important concept for this chapter is astropolitics, which we use to describe the political dynamics that extend the long tradition of geopolitical thinking into space (Dolman 2005, p.). While at the time of writing in 2021 astropolitics are merely a small side theater of geopolitics; as the importance of space for human society and economy grows, we can expect it to become ever more important, especially once the proliferation of space settlements initiates the scramble for real estate around the Solar system. However, it must be clear that within the foreseeable future, astropolitics will remain Earth-centered and will either deal with conflicts and interests of Earth metropolities in space or

---

[477] Based on the words metropolis (in Ancient Greek "mother-city") and polity.

alternatively use the space dimension and space assets to achieve their goals on Earth.

Downstream of astropolitics we find astrostrategy, which concerns the plans, policies and execution needed to achieve long-term goals as a result of national astropolitical considerations. Astrostrategy will be almost inevitably concerned with the practical side of space exploration —acquisition, protection and control of assets, expansion of the sphere of influence where hard or soft power can be projected, mitigating risks of perceived threats and balancing any competitors. In case of a complete laissez-faire approach from the Earth governments, where (either by design or incompetence) space exploration is left entirely to the private interests, astrostrategies would nonetheless materialize, only instead of being formed in the cabinet, they would instead be formed in corporate boardrooms (much like the British occupation of India in the 19th century by commercial interests). Based on performance over the 2010s, it appears that in 2021 only China has a consistent long-term astrostrategy, most recently evident in becoming the second nation to successfully land a Mars rover (Reuters 2021), with milestones stretching as far as 2050 (Goswami 2018). The USA has only a short-term astrostrategy (most milestones discussed in strategic documents appear to end by 2030) and planning is further complicated due to strong effects on the program by American domestic political trends and presidential elections. Meanwhile Russia, EU and India appear to be mostly pursuing a range of disparate smaller objectives, which cannot be called coherent astrostrategies at this point.

Analysis provided in this chapter operates on three axiomatic assumptions, which have been discussed in much finer detail elsewhere:

The first assumption is that pursuing space settlement and colonization is scientifically and economically worthwhile in the long term and that humanity will proceed at a faster or slower pace to continue this endeavor. While it is very likely that the ebb and flow of politics, inevitable testing disasters, corruption scandals and economic crises, deaths and births of great space pioneers and scientists will affect exact time-lines, the general trend will remain oriented toward ever more complicated and more varied human activity in space. A perfect example of this was the 1960s race to the Moon for purely political purposes that was halted soon after the first man landed, but now has restarted fifty years later. This is the weakest of the assumptions and there are many factors that could render it void, but for the time being it seems to hold true.

The second assumption is that the principles of astropolitics are related to those of geopolitics and that development of human presence in space will continue to be semi-anarchic in nature and constrained primarily by the balance of power, economic and social interests and other factors back on Earth. Idealistic Cold War treaties, such as the *Treaty on Principles Governing the Activities of States in the Exploration and Use of Outer Space, Including the Moon and Other Celestial Bodies* (henceforth Outer Space Treaty) (Johnson 2018) or *The Agreement Governing the Activities of States on the Moon and Other Celestial Bodies* (henceforth Moon Treaty)(United Nations Treaty Collection 1984) have served an important purpose in their time, but today they are mostly obsolete. In the current multi-polar confrontational political climate neither the UN nor the space powers will enforce these treaties in full unless it benefits their interests. They are still going to be used as ammunition for space law-fare, but with limited effect. As evidenced by the introduction of the Artemis Accords (NASA 2020), which both in spirit and letter contradict UN treaties, a new chapter of space law is about to be written and it is likely to be about as unanimous as the current debate related to the freedom of navigation in the South China Sea. It should also be noted that eighty-nine countries on Earth never ratified the Outer Space Treaty (Arms Control Association 2020).

The third assumption is that warfare waged in space will be waged within the realm of the known laws of physics, human biology and psychology. It is possible that the coming century could hold many marvelous and terrifying discoveries, such as development of a strong artificial intelligence or a breakthrough in genetic engineering, which could change aforementioned factors so drastically that this analysis would be rendered moot. Nonetheless, we will proceed under the assumption that the men and women who will contest these new frontiers are in principle brothers and sisters to those who read these pages. It is also assumed that modern day and future humans will have the same motivations and attitudes as humans have always had, even in ancient times, when it comes to warfare, whether terrestrial, or space-based when it comes to strategies and tactics. All warfare is always between human minds who transmit will and intent onto their adversaries through military equipment and personnel, even within the bounds of the unfamiliar physics of orbital dynamics.

TAXONOMY OF SPACE SETTLEMENTS

Based on the assessments of the challenges and opportunities of putting humans into space, it seems that the three most feasible types of space settlements are orbital stations, space habitats and planetary settlements. It is important to quickly overview and compare their key characteristics, which will also affect their military profiles.

Orbital space settlements have already seen successful prototypes, notably in the shape of Russian Mir (1986 – 2001) and the International Space Stations (1998 – present). While neither one was intended for permanent habitation, both contributed immensely to our understanding of construction and human habitation in space conditions. Based on this experience currently there are a number of initiatives for further research into orbital settlements, both manned and unmanned. There have been discussions for a long time about developing a private orbital space station industry, notably Bigelow Aerospace invested around 500 million US dollars in pursuit of this goal (Little 2008). While the company unfortunately was forced to stop operations in March 2020 due to COVID-19 pandemic (Foust 2020), Bigelow Airspace has managed to develop a few working prototypes of inflatable space habitats, one of which still serves attached to ISS (NASA 2016; Thomson 2015). While some of these initiatives might fail due to political or business reasons, the expertise and knowledge that is being developed is setting the stage for ever cheaper LEO (Low Earth Orbit) stations, which could lead to their proliferation. While American private companies are experimenting, Chinese state-led space enterprises are also following suit and while their exact plans are seldom specific enough to judge how credible they are, they have plans to construct a space station based on the successes of the Tiangong "Heavenly Palace" program (Wall 2016). Furthermore, Russia is planning to remove their modules from ISS by 2024 and form their own space station (Selding 2015). If these events take place as planned, there would be at least three manned space stations in LEO within a decade and this could even spark further competition between US, China and Russia.

While LEO stations themselves are not going to affect astropolitics considerably, they will serve as an important testing ground, which (if successful) will provide the required expertise to expand the range of space operations and consider establishing orbital settlements around other objects in the Solar system, such as the Moon first with other planets to follow. From a military standpoint, stations in LEO are a relatively easy target for even the current level of anti-satellite (ASAT) technology, if we take examples such as Chinese test in 2007 (Kan 2007), Indian test in 2019 (Tellis 2019) and the Russian test in 2020 (Weitering 2020) as possible indicators of capability. The high vulnerability and cost of orbital stations make them poor military assets. However, we would argue that orbital space settlements will grow in importance when established in non-Earth orbits. Despite the costs, they are still the cheapest of the three settlement types to establish, their technology is well tested and putting them far enough away from Earth will increase their survivability in the event of space confrontation near Earth. Orbital settlements would be semi-mobile—just like current orbital stations, they would be equipped with engines and have a limited capacity to relocate (or even evade attacks when given enough warning), although that wouldn't be their main mode of operation. This means that they could be constructed in Earth orbit and then stationed in lunar or Martian orbits, where they would be outside of immediate Earth-based ASAT weaponry range but not localized weapon systems and space-to-space ASAT's, while providing an invaluable beachhead for further expansion and supporting other operations.

Another method of settling space is establishing extraterrestrial planetary settlements[478]. First known studies have been conducted by Americans in 1959 under Project Horizon (United States Army 1961) and by Russians under Korolev in 1960s under Zvezda plan (Lindroos n.d.; Wade 2019). In both cases plans were for military bases to be used in the context of the ongoing Cold War, but neither came true. Since then, and a wider and much better panoply of designs have been presented, but due to the relative stagnation of space ambitions with the end of the Space Race, none has come to fruition. However, since the rise of SpaceX and Elon Musk's vision for human settlements on Mars (Brown 2019), the idea of extraterrestrial planetary settlements has reignited public discussion. Advances in material science and robotics have made building planetary settlements in situ a plausible proposition (Arnhof 2016) and SpaceX has achieved unprecedented success in the field of cheaper, reusable rockets, which would be the backbone of any plans to colonize Mars or other places around the Solar system. Its example has ignited an ongoing race with Blue Origin, Virgin Galactic, ULA (United Launch

---

[478] Lunar and planetoid settlements also fall under this category. Hypothetical planetoid settlements are much harder to categorize, as they could theoretically be given engines to move them around, like orbital stations or space habitats, however we argue that due to high energy expenditures required to change their orbits and low likelihood of this being the case, they should be classified as planetary for the purposes of this chapter.

Alliance) and others (Reddy 2018), but so far only SpaceX remains unabashedly committed to the clear vision of extraterrestrial planetary settlements. However, it must be noted, that despite this, there is still a lot of skepticism about the proposal to settle Mars, both on the feasibility and desirability aspects (Drexler 1984, Coates 2018, Bharmal 2018, Levchenko et al. 2019).

Nonetheless, even if Musk's vision of a settlement with a population of one million on Mars by 2050 (McFall-Johnsen and Mosher 2020) does not materialize, it seems the current trend ensures that SpaceX-led technological breakthroughs at least will allow development of a Moon base and possibly a prototype base on Mars itself, which might or might not, be manned by humans. However even if extraterrestrial planetary settlements are not adopted by humanity widely for the purposes of colonization, they could still serve an important purpose which other types of settlements cannot—extension of political claims to other planetary bodies[479]. Settling of humans to establish control of resources and claims of sovereignty dates to ancient times and presence of citizens or other protected groups is being instrumentalized by polities to this day in various contexts. In most recent times, the Russian Federation as a matter of state policy regularly issues its passports to people in disputed regions, which are later used to legitimize interventions on their behalf, as in Georgia in 2008 or Crimea in 2014 (Lachert 2020). NATO countries also have a history of interventions based on the R2P (Responsibility to Protect) concept (Carati 2017). One way or another, wherever there will

---

[479] Currently no space power will admit to planning to extend their political claims to space. However, in numerous previous cases when technological means allowed countries to reach previously inaccessible territories, whether overt or covert carving out of the zones of influence followed. For examples, see scramble for Africa which followed medical inventions of the mid-19th century, Western Hemisphere colonization after proliferation of ocean-going caravels, Arctic tensions intensifying as it is becoming more accessible due to global warming.

be colonies, some authority will move into the power vacuum to either claim authority over them or to protect them from the claims of authority by others. Naturally, such carving of spheres of influence is two steps away from declaring sovereignty over territories in space and this would run directly against the provisions of Outer Space and the Moon Treaties, however gradual astropolitical legitimization is likely to sideline these treaties in the long term.

The final type of space settlements is what we would classify as space habitat settlements. These would be massive settlement-stations, potentially built in stable orbits or Lagrange points, utilizing zero-gravity advantage for advanced engineering solutions, which could be subsequently located almost anywhere in the Solar system. The most famous example of this would be O'Neill cylinder designs, which span up to twenty miles in size (National Space Society 2021). These habitats could potentially house thousands of inhabitants or act as space hubs for massive asteroid mining operations, which could also have factory modules and processing plants to provide in-space manufacturing capacity. We have neither existing examples of them, nor are there any notable initiatives striving to promote them at this time, as they would present unprecedented mega-structure engineering challenges. Furthermore, this idea has not yet penetrated public imagination in the same way as extraterrestrial planetary or orbital settlements have, so the chances to see any space habitats to be developed within this century are quite low. However, it must be noted that Jeff Bezos in the famous Blue Origin Moon lander concept unveiling speech indicated his hope that future of human space expansion will be driven by O'Neill colonies, although he stressed the potential for humanity to outsource industrial production (along with pollution) to space, rather than to colonize it (Brown 2019). It is very possible that once space infrastructure is developed enough to allow relatively cheap transit to orbit, possibly following the asteroid mining boom, it would open the possibility for space engineering innovation and space habitats could become a viable option. Notably, if metropolities were inclined to follow UN legal foundation, these space habitats could provide a legal loophole to allow bypassing Outer Space and Moon Treaties and enabling an effective mass settlement of the Solar system, while utilizing its resources, without laying any sovereignty claims on extraterrestrial territories.

FUTURE OF SPACE SETTLEMENTS AND THE POSSIBILITY OF A SOLAR SCRAMBLE

In the absence of an effective international space law framework, currently the Solar system presents itself as the ultimate frontier, non-governed, unclaimed and very hard to access and yet full of possibilities. As the launch costs per kilogram are gradually falling (Fox 2018), the entry barriers to the space market are decreasing. Sooner or later the floodgates will gradually open and then the space economy is very likely to experience a boom (Greason and Bennett 2019). This is very likely to lead to a situation like the navigation and shipbuilding advances which began the Age of Sail and suddenly opened up the whole world to the European nations. Similarly, the exploration and settlement process is likely to begin with a few government-supported high-profile missions, but soon taken up by private interests willing to take great risks, while expecting (literally) astronomical profits.

At the current moment it seems that the Solar scramble will be initiated by American entrepreneurs and relatively quickly followed by Chinese and possibly Indian, Russian or European companies (although secondary space powers are quite far behind and are likely to join either the US or China as junior partners, rather than pursuing their own course). As of 2021, political interest in the space issues is still relatively limited - this can be judged by how seldom space questions are raised during presidential debates or seriously considered on the national stage, in comparison with other more mainstream issues, such as healthcare, education or immigration. However, there are signs that this might soon change. Establishment of the US Space Force in 2019 (Mack 2020), the

Chinese-Russian space cooperation agreement (Goswami 2021), the announcement of the Artemis program and the growing public interest in the SpaceX Mars vision are all signs of the growing importance of space.

For now, the attention is still far from that experienced during the heyday of the Space Race in the 1960s, however this is likely to rapidly change with the first space settlements and arguably space will come to either dominate or at least get a significant prominence on the national agendas. It can be argued that this would happen due to two primary factors.

First, humans tend to perceive reality through stories, which require human protagonists and clear challenges to be overcome. Apollo missions had these elements—astronauts were heroes, the Moon itself was the challenge and competition with the Soviet Union created a powerful narrative. In Kennedy's words it had to be done "before this decade is out" (NASA 1962) and the US achieved that goal with flying colors. However, as space programs became more conservative and smaller in scale, the sense of drama and excitement diminished, reducing public interest and funding for them, which led to a feedback loop that caused a gradual retreat of space from the public imagination. However, as soon as the first space settlement is established, new protagonists will appear and the sense of wonder will return, causing public interest in it to explode. It has already been widely speculated that reality TV might be the first export from the first off-Earth colony in the context of the unsuccessful Mars One initiative (Williams 2019).

The second possible reason is that the beginning of the permanent human presence outside of the LEO would likely coincide with the beginning of a new space economic revolution, both in support industries on Earth and in extractive industries in space. Having a space program would no longer be just a matter of prestige, but it would also determine having access to all the future space economic activity. Political and economic elites would be drawn to these opportunities, making them even more important. Not being in favor of "astronomization" of economy would be akin to not being in favor of industrialization in the 19th century or not being in favor of digitalization in the late 20th century. Once the integration of space and Earth economies begins through off-Earth settlement and resource extraction, it could become possibly one of the most dependable sources of economic growth due to the effectively limitless frontier. Even in the short term, the space economy is expected to triple, reaching 1 trillion USD by 2040s (Morgan Stanley 2020).

With these incentives and under these conditions, it is possible that a Solar scramble to claim as much of the newly opened opportunities by the nation-states would begin. As they currently stand, the United Nations Outer Space Treaty and Moon Treaty are unenforceable and will be of limited utility for resolving practical questions and conflicts that will appear because of the competitive dynamics already causing the Solar scramble. In the absence of an established and effective legal framework, realpolitik will dominate the scene. When settling disputes, the rule of presence will come to play the greatest role—whoever happens to arrive somewhere first will be the one to exploit the resources and build infrastructure. If other states would complain, they are likely to be invited to resolve differences in bilateral deals. There will be a lot of strongly worded letters and media drama, but effectively there will be about as much action to change anything as there is currently to restore sovereignty for Tibet. Absent a radical toward a united American-Chinese-Russian consensus on global affairs, existing UN mechanisms are too outdated and weak to either update or enforce the framework, so they are just going to be conveniently circumvented and laid to rest alongside the Treaty of Versailles (routinely violated during World War II) and other, once very important, but now irrelevant, documents. Conceivably, China could abrogate the Outer Space Treaty ten minutes before they land a man on the Moon, and then claim the whole celestial body for themselves. Would this be any different from China's claims to the South China Sea? Also, with eighty-nine countries that have never ratified the Outer Space Treaty, could commercial operators launch from their territory, claim all the Moon for a given country, and then have the country lease back all Moon resources for ninety-nine years for commercial exploitation?

However, it is also unlikely that any power would be eager to escalate tensions without a strong reason. Long-term, it is likely that major space powers will work out between themselves an understanding or possibly even a written agreement of sorts, like mare clausum claims of 15th century (Davenport and Robertson 2008), although this time instead of Spanish and Portuguese sea powers, we could see American and Chinese space powers making the claims. Russia, India and Europe might join this framework later, but having in mind the timelines and economies of scale required to develop the required infrastructure to meaningfully participate in this race, they are likely to play secondary roles and lay claims to locations of secondary importance. Remember, Spain claimed ownership of the entire Western Hemisphere with Columbus's voyage. It took military might to hold on to a minimal number of these claims, with many other powers laying subsequent claims that only endured due to their strenuous military actions.

Currently in the public perception there is little differentiation between different space locations, all of it commonly being portrayed as a uniform nothingness; however, nothing could be further from the truth. As Dolman (2005, p.52) accurately points out:

> "What appears at first a featureless void is in fact a rich vista of gravitational mountains and valleys, oceans and rivers of resources and energy alternately dispersed and concentrated, broadly strewn danger zones of deadly radiation, and precisely placed peculiarities of astrodynamics. Without a full understanding of the motion of bodies in space, in essence a background in the mechanics of orbits, it is difficult to make sense of this panorama."

Not all space real estate is of equal value and while it is not commonly understood at the political level, it is a well-known fact for subject matter experts. When this knowledge trickles down to the policy maker level, there will be much more drive to secure these "mountains and valleys, oceans and rivers."

Lagrange points might become attractive locations for future deep space colonies. Lagrange points are exceptional since structures built there can remain locked by the gravitational pulls of the two bodies (either Earth-Moon or those of another celestial body pair such as Sun-Earth) without any additional expenditure of fuel. There are many uses for them, for example these points could make great space shipyards, where new vessels could be built in zero gravity with the resources from the mined asteroids or brought up from the Moon. However, they are limited—every pair of celestial bodies has only five of them and different Lagrange points have different utility, so having presence there before it gets crowded would be desirable and may possibly have to be defended in the future.

While explaining the value of the orbital high ground to the public might still be complicated, the concept of taking control of celestial bodies will be more mentally accessible. The need to maintain the astropolitical balance of power will limit this somewhat and claims are more likely to be unpronounced and only de facto enforced with "safety zones", "warnings to avoid collisions", "permission request protocols" or otherwise presented in ways to minimize diplomatic consequences, while exerting maximum control in pursuit of national interests. A precursor to this can already be seen in the American Artemis Accords, which establishes "safety zones" under section 11 (NASA 2020), although it can be expected that means to enforce these will become much more sophisticated in the future.

However, Americans are very unlikely to be the only ones in space. If one accepts the premise that the current Chinese plan to have a permanent lunar base by 2030 would succeed (Wall 2019), an event of this magnitude would likely create a paradigm shift toward more intense astropolitical competition. In practice it does not matter whether China would explicitly outline any legal claims on the surrounding area. A Chinese base on the Moon (scientific or otherwise), that started expanding and might serve as a staging ground for building of further settlements would create political tension. Part of it would be motivated by the fear of missing out on the economic opportunities, another part of it would be lobbying by reinvigorated private space interests and as always, national prestige and eventual defense considerations would come in to play important roles in the national debates. Together, these factors are likely to cause a new Space Race which will shape the astropolitical dynamics of the Solar system and humanity for the next century, or at least until the first space war.

EFFECT OF SPACE SETTLEMENTS ON ASTROSTRATEGIC DYNAMICS

Space is a domain in which laws of combat operate under a qualitatively different rule set. The nature of the cosmos itself preconditions any human endeavor in space to deal with immense forces, zero friction, zero gravity and vast distances. Furthermore, there is no such thing as absolute stealth in space. While it might be possible to evade detection due to different factors (most of which would include one or another form of human error), if both sides are assumed to have adequate technological base and sufficient monitoring infrastructure, space war is very likely to be an almost perfect information game.

It is important to realize that in outer space the line between tools and weapons is very thin. For example, almost any remotely controlled space vessel or satellite can be weaponized if sufficient propellant is available. Even the smallest satellites, if well aimed and possessing on-board tracking sensors, at orbital speeds could destroy anything else currently in space, (for example ISS—which is giant in comparison with most other satellites). Lack of friction and potentially limitless acceleration potential means that in the outer space the very concept of armor (as utilized by militaries from ancient infantry to modern tanks) at our currently technological level is simply rendered obsolete[480]. The only type of space settlement that would be an exception to this rule would be planetary settlements on planets with atmosphere (for example Mars). The atmospheric friction would act as a natural shield and potential to build deep bunkers would allow increased to protect against most low-power space-to-space weaponry. There should be no doubts however, that specialized anti-planetary munitions would be able to safely penetrate the atmosphere and destroy the bases, for example "rods from God" or similar kinetic or nuclear bombardment, not too conceptually different from those considered for use here on Earth (Sproull 2017).

In relation to space settlements, from these assumptions follow three astrostrategic conclusions:

1. *Any permanent installation with 3-D printing or other type of configurable in situ manufacturing capacity becomes a potential weapons platform.*

The basis for such capabilities is already under research at DARPA (DARPA 2021). As resupply or rescue missions in crisis situations are very problematic, it is very likely that as soon as it becomes feasible, every space settlement will be equipped with its own manufacturing capacity, at first for minor repairs and replacement parts, but eventually for expansion of operations as well. ISS is already utilizing a 3-D printer for exactly these reasons (Goldsberry 2019). Hypothetically, a scientific base with a single multi-purpose 3-D printer, appropriate materials and

---

[480] Currently the only armor considerations that comes into play during space vehicle construction are heat-shields and protection against micro-meteorites, such as the Whipple shield. As launch energy costs are among primary design drivers, every pound of armor would mean a pound less of cargo and economic incentives dominate the engineering. There is a possibility that eventually a new generation of space vehicles would be built from extraterrestrial materials directly in Lunar or Earth orbit, but most likely no armor thickness will ever match the lightspeed potential for acceleration of hypervelocity projectiles in frictionless space.

qualified assembly crew could print another dozen 3-D printers within a short time span and then use all of those 3-D printers to rapidly manufacture the rest of upgrades and modules required to transform the formerly scientific base into a military outpost. While this is most realistic in planetary settlements with readily available materials nearby, this could theoretically be done with orbital or space habitat settlements as well, although it might be easier to detect their changing nature. Some materials and parts, such as advanced electronics or synthetic materials not available in space, might need to be pre-positioned or smuggled into the base prior to the conflict. However once manufacturing capability, essential materials, design software and qualified personnel are available, any space settlement would have the potential to become a military asset. In addition, any civilian human settlement is a potential base for basic resupplies (food, oxygen, fuel, raw materials, volunteers) for any military force. Having this in mind, military planners should assume that all space settlements will play a part in the Solar system security equation and will have to be monitored —the distinction between "military bases" and "civilian settlements" will become blurred.

2. *Space settlements are likely to be treated as potential military assets and consequently to become targets in the event of a space war.*

Attacks may take the form of monitoring, quarantine, capturing, or neutralizing. For space settlements, resisting strikes or hiding are not feasible options, so two strategies left are defensive interception or preemptive attack. It is too early to judge which one of these two would be more practical, but we should presume the tendency to prefer first strike, ingrained in military thinking, is going to favor preemptive strike strategies. Unfortunately for space admirals, there are likely to be a lot of incentives creating a prisoner's dilemma not too dissimilar from that faced by the nuclear deterrence planners on Earth. Balance of power will be carried over into the space dimension and play a big role in astrostrategic planning. Escalation management will be important to avoid unwanted conflict. While the art of conducting a space war is still in the blueprint stage, we can already predict that battlespace awareness and having accurate, up to date information is going to be of extreme importance. We will see attempts to keep close track of all space vehicles, mass estimates, licensing of vehicles with distinct identification codes, positioning of space assets, changes in orbits and communication patterns. In the longer term, access to off-Earth sources of propellants (such as water) and other key resources will also be monitored, as well as some orbit clusters or choke points which could be used as potential attack vectors or blind spots. All of this when taken together will create a high-stakes environment, where first strike will have a great advantage.

3. *Space settlements will have either explicit or implicit "buffer zones."*

This will be valuable for self-protection, especially the further away from Earth and the rest of space vehicles they find themselves, where the zones will be easier to establish and harder to contest, while enforcing such zone in LEO or elsewhere close to Earth will be very difficult. For example if Europeans would have a scientific space settlement in the orbit of Venus, they would most likely be very concerned if Russians, without formal invitation, would launch a small, relatively cheap satellite on a trajectory that could potentially be diverted to hit the space settlement. Depending on the situation and political developments back on Earth, this might be resolved in a few different ways, but the most likely scenario is development of etiquette of respecting these concerns and warning or even requesting permission from the owner of the space settlement when approaching its vicinity. This vicinity, which we could call "buffer zones", most likely will be of the size and shape as determined by the likelihood of the entering space vehicle to pose threat to the settlement and settlement's own ability to respond to it with interception strikes or evasive maneuvers. There might be several levels of threat zones where escalatory self-defense responses are allowed as the threat comes closer (e.g., green, yellow, and red warning zones where shoot down is permitted if unauthorized access to red zones). When eventually a new international law framework is negotiated, these buffer zones are likely to solidify and become part of established space law, possibly like the concept of territorial waters in the international maritime law. While it is possible and even likely that there could be astropolitical actors who might try to claim either exclusive or universal right to the complete freedom of navigation in space, this is likely to produce similar frictions to those faced by modern Earth nations in sensitive areas such as the South China Sea, the Greenland-Iceland-United Kingdom (GIUK) gap or the Eastern Mediterranean. Just as Americans of today would react very badly to the presence of Russian nuclear submarines off the coast of Florida, so Americans of tomorrow are not likely to tolerate dangerously close (by astronomical standards) fly-bys of future Russian space vehicles. It might take a few close calls or even an open space confrontation for the politicians to recognize that these buffer zones are real and need to be either respected or ignored at the peril of diplomatic incident or even more general escalation.

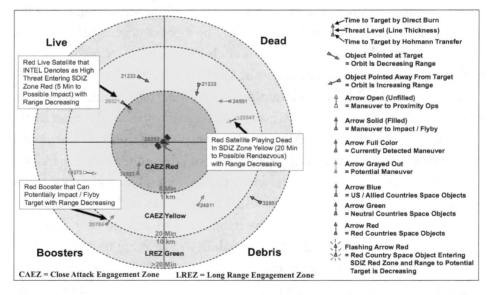

Figure 11. Possible Defense Warning Zones for Orbital Space Settlements—View 1. Paul Szymanski.

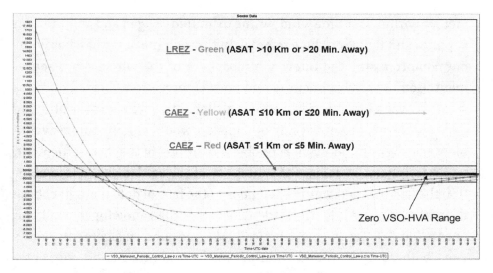

Figure 12. Possible Defense Warning Zones for Orbital Space Settlements – View 2. Paul Szymanski.

OFFENSIVE MEASURES AGAINST SPACE SETTLEMENTS

In hypothetical space war there will be at least four methods to neutralize a space settlement. First and the most obvious method is a direct kinetic attack, delivered either via interplanetary or spaceship weaponry. Discussion of potential delivery mechanisms and space weapon systems is outside of our topic, so we will not discuss it in detail, but there are numerous ways how even with current technology Earth could launch rockets to bombard hypothetical Martian settlements. It is enough to remember that the space program was born from ICBM research and all the advances made in civilian rocket science since then can just as easily be converted back into weaponry.

A second method to neutralize a space settlement would be an unlikely plan to capture it. This has never been attempted before and would likely be extremely dangerous. In some ways attacking a space settlement would be comparable with trying to board a hostile submarine underwater, but without any of the benefits which attackers enjoy in Earth combat conditions. Attacking force would have to achieve victory within a set time window due to limited oxygen and ammunition supplies and figure out how to break in through the outer hatches without compromising the internal atmosphere of the whole space settlement. Combat environment would be even more complicated once inside, because a lot of tactical options available on Earth (such as utilizing explosives or outmaneuvering opponents) would simply not be available when fighting in claustrophobic conditions of a space settlement, while trying not to damage the integrity of the settlement (not to mention the fact that determined defender in the face of defeat might choose the option of "scuttling" the settlement rather than allowing it to fall into enemy hands). Troops hypothetically waging such engagements would need both equipment and training on the scale that is not currently available to achieve a victory under such extreme conditions. Because of this reason, if the current trend in robotics and automation developments continues, it is quite possible that such missions would be carried out by expendable boarding robots, which could be sacrificed in case of failure. Due to these reasons, it is very unlikely that we will see this kind of space combat developing soon, or ever. But it is not completely out of the question once there are more space assets worth fighting over. Victory in such a space boarding action would allow a capture of the space settlement which could be of immense value both monetarily and strategically.

A third option to neutralize a space settlement is to blockade it. As much as we can foresee development of the technology and space exploration, it is a safe bet to say that at least for the next century any space settlements, whether planetary, orbital or habitats, will require support and supplies from Earth. This strategy will be very hard to utilize against automated settlements, as they potentially could be able to remain under blockade for decades if not centuries on a stand-by mode. However any settlements with human colonists will be vulnerable to this tactic and are likely to eventually surrender, especially if the besieging force would selectively destroy outer modules required for continued survival, such as solar panels, greenhouses, waste processing plants and other vital systems. It might even be possible for the attacking force to use electronic warfare to jam all incoming and outgoing communications, to completely isolate the settlement and break the will to resist quicker. Nonetheless, just like with ancient fortresses, a properly fortified planetary settlement with underground facilities would be able to hold out for years and if equipped with manufacturing capabilities, to even strike back. Furthermore, blockade would require dedicating both time and resources for such operation and having in mind that modern warfare paradigm tends to call for lighting action, blockades are more likely to be either a political tool in the phase leading to a space war or a fallback option in case the initial gambits would not succeed, and space war would take a slower pace.

The final method to neutralize a space settlement would be through the employment of clandestine means or special operations. As is clear from Cold War history, intelligence services are known for their ingenuity and there are likely hundreds of ways to use covert means to take control, destroy or otherwise incapacitate a space settlement.

For example, even with current technology, the attacker could send a scientific mission going past the planet or the moon where the settlement is located. In passing, this alleged (or even real) scientific satellite could drop a landing device disguised as a booster or some other unremarkable piece of junk and let the long trajectory and gravity do the rest. Infiltrator capsule wouldn't register as much more than a speck unless somebody was closely inspecting the skies for it. Capsule could contain a drone swarm or a rover that would land on the planet and proceed toward the target, potentially covering thousands of miles to eventually reach it. This might take weeks if not months, but eventually it would arrive and pre-position itself. Then, either at a set hour, or more likely, after receiving an encrypted signal, its AI would proceed to follow the most appropriate scenario, finding vulnerabilities and sabotaging the settlement. On a space settlement, every single system is important, almost any damage could be critical. If this rover were to carry explosives, it could not only destroy or seriously damage the settlement, but also remove any evidence of its presence there, allowing plausible deniability and leaving the blame to a tragic space accident. Alternatively, said infiltrator could destroy communication arrays or other critical infrastructure and pave the way for other types of attacks to come.

Other covert methods could include a cyber warfare approach to take control of the settlement. Fully automated settlements would be especially vulnerable to this attack vector because there would be no human on station to realize what is happening and take corrective action. Some space powers might precisely for this reason retain human presence on board space settlements. Despite all the technological advances, humans remain the most versatile answer to any unforeseen problem their space assets might face. However these same humans are prone to errors, their presence increases the number of vital systems, and they are susceptible to psychological warfare or infiltration at the recruitment stage. Striking the right balance between humans and machines will be an important decision to protect space settlements.

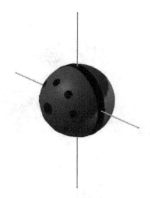

Figure 13. Potential Space Mines Employed Against Orbital Space Settlement (Size: 1 Meter in Diameter). Paul Szymanski

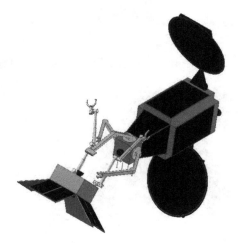

Figure 14. Potential Space Maintenance Robots Fighting Each Other in Space. Paul Szymanski.

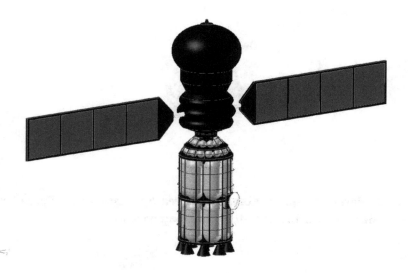

Figure 15. Potential Planetary Bombardment System. Paul Szymanski.

Defensive Measures to Protect Space Settlements

As we have just discussed, space settlements have many vulnerabilities and attackers will have many different attack vectors. That does not mean that space settlements are sitting ducks. In the perennial race behind offense and defense, the defending side has its own advantages, such as the ability to preposition resources and weapons and to set up kill zones, barriers, obstacles or fortifications. And, most importantly in space warfare, the defending side requires much less fuel, which would take up a significant payload of whatever craft the attacking side would be utilizing and leaves the defense with relatively more capability and optionality. Below we will briefly explore some aspects of the defense of space settlements.

In a space war, just as on Earth, camouflage, evasion and deception techniques will play a large role. In war time or during periods of high alert, space habitats and orbital settlements are likely to change their orbits, inclinations and speed at irregular intervals, to make opponent identification and tracking efforts more difficult. This would also provide limited passive evasion capability in the case of surprise attack.

Meanwhile planetary settlements will be stationary and such measures will not be available to them. However, there are likely to be dummy space settlements, both to confuse the opponents regarding the size of the operation and to serve as decoys in the case of attack. While initial construction and preparation of a space settlement is a very expensive affair, once the beachhead is complete, it becomes much cheaper to build additional add-ons and expansions. Large sections and vital parts of the settlements are likely to be located underground. So, the burgeoning small town of white domes around the location of the star port might be nothing more than secondary greenhouse or recreational facilities, while the real settlement is in the process of being excavated under the red Martian desert a few kilometers away. At the outset of the space war, a first phase kinetic strike might destroy the visible surface facilities, but the core of the settlement would remain safe. Even if the enemy were to figure out the true location of the settlement, not only would the underground location provide additional protection against possible bombardment, but it would also conceal the true extent of the base. Building secondary outposts could also provide potential fallback options. In case of a conflict breaking out on Earth, settlement might get months or years long preparation periods before opponent's weapons could reach them (unless they would have pre-positioned space assets). In addition, it would probably be difficult to attack all parts of a large settlement, and an adversary might simply attack key elements such as power and oxygen generation, command centers, or transportation hubs to isolate the settlement, etc. Since it's so vastly expensive to build and maintain a space settlement, a smart adversary might just cripple it enough so that they surrender, and the adversary now owns something very valuable instead of completely destroying it.

In addition to this, space settlements at risk of becoming targets in the event of space war are very likely to contain ASAT (anti-satellite) weapon systems for self-defense. They would need to be adapted from current Earth-based versions to suit the conditions of wherever the space settlement would be located, but eventually a separate branch of anti-orbital defensive weaponry is likely to emerge that would be specialized to answer different kinds of threats. Space settlements are likely to maintain constellations of early warning satellites in their vicinity, which would also serve as forward observation posts to provide strategic warning and mark targets for long-range defenses. A lot of these future weapon systems in principle would likely follow the design principles like either active rocket interception systems, such as the Israeli "Iron Dome" or the multitude of close-in weapon systems (CIWS) employed in the navies, such as the American "Phalanx" or Russian "Kashtan" systems. Such point-defense systems would have to either try to destroy incoming missiles through superior speed and accuracy of intercepting fire, or through overwhelming numbers. However, the space domain is also going to open possibilities to use some weapon systems that are not feasible for employment on Earth. For example, laser weaponry in the vacuum of space would be much more efficient and could be used to heat up incoming missiles to either divert them off-course or pre-maturely activate their explosive payloads. Positive results from research conducted by the Congressional Research Service (2021) indicate that railguns are also likely to eventually move from the pages of science fiction books to see adoption for both offensive and defensive purposes.

However the least obvious part of defending space settlements is going to be the non-kinetic systems of the defense. Space settlements will have to maintain very high levels of cyber security and electronic warfare readiness, as their isolated nature and the low cost-high return proposition of these attack vectors is going to tempt any potential attacker. Furthermore, space settlements will ensure that any colonists or visitors are thoroughly screened to ensure that threat of infiltration, sabotage or sedition is minimized. But the highest return on investment for space settlements in their defense is likely to be lobbying in favor of strict space laws of war. While as previously established, currently active UN space law is neither up to date, nor universally accepted, eventually certain new baseline principles are nonetheless likely to develop and upon them, hopefully, a functional body of space law that will be reflective of the new reality. As law conference catering budgets are orders of magnitude cheaper than developing new ASAT weapon systems, it could be a worthy attempt to prevent unrestricted warfare against space settlements and build in as much protections as possible, though verification and enforcement would be problematic, especially if destruction of a space colony cannot be attributed to any entity for certain due to the vastness of space.

FUTURE PROLIFERATION OF OPERATIONAL DOMAINS

It must also be noted that extraterrestrial presence will have a major impact on the understanding of operational domains in military organization. Currently human involvement in space is so limited that most of current space national interests fall under the Space domain in the US (or some countries still treat them as part of Air or a joint Aerospace domain, for example the Russian Federation) (TASS 2015). After the establishment of the first space settlements, it would soon become clear that operating on extraterrestrial bodies, either to ensure internal security within settlements and or in the case of hypothetical combat with an external adversary, has much more in common with fighting on Earth than with satellite and ASAT warfare that dominates concerns of today's warfighters in Space operational domain. While in the initial stages (which could take decades) space defense will be solely conducted under the aegis of a Space Command, sooner or later the diverging needs will become more prominent as human presence in space proliferates from dozens of individuals to tens of thousands or more. In addition, the vast distances involved do not allow for good command and control of remote space colonies that cannot be directly monitored from the Earth in a timely manner. It is likely that the US Space Force will expand its expertise and technology further toward building and countering space weapon platforms, monitoring and interference systems, astronomical range weaponry and other orbital domination technologies. Concerns of space superiority are discussed in more detail elsewhere (Szymanski 2019, Dolman 2012).

However, there will be other, smaller in scale, but very important defense considerations which will need to be addressed by the "boots on the other ground." Among these will be ensuring security of the space settlements, conducting rescue and rapid response operations, enforcing international law and national control over space assets, detecting and repelling potential sabotage attempts both within settlements and in the external areas of operation (such as mining outposts, monitoring stations, etc.). So far in academic literature not much consideration has been given to ground combat on extraterrestrial bodies, however it will become extremely important. In the 20th century we have witnessed a repeated pattern of failure to accurately judge limitations of the firepower and air superiority-based power projection. In the US case, remote bombing campaigns and air superiority did not deliver desired results in Germany, Vietnam and Serbia, until they were combined with other types of pressure. It is likely that in the early stages of space settlement similar mistakes will be made and all resources will be concentrated on maintaining space superiority, which (similarly to the Navy and Air Force of today) is critical for power projection and control of transport lanes. However, no matter how much firepower one might possess, in the age of space settlements, extraterrestrial ground forces, whether human or robotic, will be a necessary component to take control of objectives and establish the new status quo, especially when taking control of resources or settlements. There may also be competing colonies on the same planet that conceivably would come into conflict with each other.

Warfighting on the Moon and other planetary bodies will have a completely different set of circumstances, goals and challenges. In terms of both tactics and strategy, most likely the Moon domain will require adoption of heavily modified principles from all current domains. Another challenge will face space admirals when it becomes clear that lessons learned on the surface of the Moon will be different from those required to fight on Mars, Titan, Europa or other celestial bodies. As it always happens, first Moon warfighting tactics and technologies will be based on the Earth school of military doctrine. Then there will be an attempt to export them and build on them for other planetary bodies. However radically different atmospheres, temperatures, acidity levels, surface terrains, gravities and day-night cycles will mean that space rovers, combat tactics or drone swarms developed for the Moon are likely to have trouble on other bodies and would require adaptations to work properly. The Moon is likely to be the first of several new combat domains as militaries realize that the only way to achieve necessary levels of adaptability to warfighting terrain is to specialize for each planetary body. Possibly, with time, we will even see a separate Mars Army and Mars Air Force (unfortunately a Mars Navy is unlikely for the next few thousand years even with the best terraforming predictions). Even development of Heinleinian "space marines" is possible as the hypothetical need to capture orbital habitats is going to be a separate, very nasty and complicated business, comparable to modern close urban combat, only without air support and with a high probability of accidentally destroying the very objective you are fighting for.

While thoughts above are just speculations at this point, military thinkers considering space settlements should be aware that every new planet will present a completely new set of challenges. Earth-centric grand strategy, especially of the American kind, assumes a mostly interchangeable nature of assets, for example a US marine company or an F-16 stationed in Iraq can be (with minimal adjustments) easily redeployed to the Baltics, Taiwan or Alaska. This is likely to be much less the case in a space grand strategy and proliferation of operational domains should be considered when considering the long-term view of space colonization, as military planning will have to be capable of reinventing itself for every new environment.

It must be noted, that hopefully, space conflicts, in whatever form or shape they would eventually materialize, would not necessarily occur (either simultaneously or sequentially) in all these domains, yet it is likely that the leadership would nonetheless plan for and prepare for all of them.

UTILITY OF SPACE SETTLEMENTS IN MILITARY PLANNING – DISADVANTAGES

From these astrostrategic dynamics, there is a high likelihood of polities eventually going to war with each other in space, via space or over space. By this we mean that space is a combat domain, where battles could be waged, it also provides an attack vector to various force multiplier technologies for Earth-based combat and, finally, and most importantly—space contains both resources and chokepoints which will entice the polities to compete. All these three modes of conflict, either together or individually are what we refer to as space war.

In this hypothetical future conflict, space settlements will play a large role, so in this section we will review the advantages and disadvantages of the space settlements from the perspective of their metropolities. We will first consider the associated disadvantages that would have to be considered when planning the founding, control and defense of space settlements and then review why, despite these drawbacks, they are conferring significant advantages which will dominate the debate around this issue.

EXPENSIVE & CIVILIAN

First and arguably the most crucial disadvantage of the space settlements is that they are expensive. Especially during the early development phase of human expansion across the Solar system, every settlement will be a unique undertaking and will require a lot of resources and political capital. Furthermore, there will be a high chance of early failures and deaths. No matter what stringent precautions will be taken, the path of human progress to the stars will be paved with bodies of dead astronauts. Nonetheless, putting humans on Mars or other planets (or at least their orbits) will be a matter of prestige and we can expect at least a few human-manned (likely not continuously) space settlements to appear within the next few decades. Due to high costs and political considerations, these programs are likely to be presented as primarily science and economy oriented (whether it is true or not).

Private companies, under the aegis of the Space Commerce Act (or a similar legislative framework) (Posey 2020) are also likely to establish space settlements, with profit being the main motivator, but it is almost certain that their settlements will be primarily automated or remotely controlled to cut down the costs and risks of human loss of life. Elon Musk and his vision for human-driven expansion into space is an inspiring idea, however it must be noted that it is an exception to the rule and most other financial ventures are not likely to have such a strong preference for human participation over their profit factor.

While militaries are likely to play a part in the establishment of these settlements, it is very unlikely that any purely military space bases would be established by the US in the foreseeable future. This means that it will be very complicated to test space-based weapons and it will be done primarily in secret, in computer simulations or under the facade of scientific experimentation. Unless the geopolitical climate drastically deteriorates and space militarization becomes both acceptable and desirable from a security planning point of view, space settlements initially are likely to be within the civilian domain until the first space conflict breaks out. Keeping space at least officially demilitarized might serve to prevent an arms race in space, but this fragile equilibrium is not likely to last indefinitely; however when the peace breaks down, the most dangerous mistakes might occur during a rapid armament of previously civilian space objects, especially by the powers that will be trying to "catch up" with the rest.

LOGISTICS & MAINTENANCE

The next disadvantage stems from the first one—due to lack of military involvement in the initial settlement planning, in the event of any space conflict, all space settlements are likely to be very soft targets. While theoretically fully self-sustainable space settlements are possible, practical implementation of this idea is still far in the future. Most likely the first space wars will happen during the first century of humans venturing out into the Solar system and before truly self-sustaining space settlements are widespread. Until that is the case, all space settlements will require regular resupply missions. Depending on the type and nature of the settlement, the need for supplies and maintenance will be different. At the very top of the list will be human-inhabited space settlements, which will require regular supply runs both to deliver materials and items vital for the functioning of the settlement and to bring back and forth humans themselves. Even if the settlement is permanently inhabited, it is still likely that humans will be regularly visiting Earth (for example for medical procedures, most of which are complicated under low gravity conditions (Drudi et al. 2012)).

Meanwhile fully automated, remotely controlled, or occasionally visited space settlements might require only once-a-decade visits, to deliver spare parts that would be inefficient to produce in-situ, to perform external checks on the functioning of the machinery, and to provide shipments back to Earth of whatever industrial processes and materials that are being produced. Nonetheless, either option implies predictable and most likely regular supply lines, which will make for great targets. Unlike attacking settlements directly, for opponents disrupting supply lines will be both technically easier and much less costly in terms of public relations, as they are going to involve fewer (or possibly even zero) casualties and can remain hidden from the general population. These supply lines will present multiple surprise attack vectors over long distances from hidden ASAT's which will be orders of magnitude cheaper to utilize when compared to the costs of setting up and supplying settlements. This will create an undesirable investment asymmetry from defenders' point of view. As a result, any spacefaring nation wishing to establish space settlements will have to be both willing to risk exposure of their space assets and to plan for contingencies where their supply lines might be compromised.

DELAYED COMMUNICATIONS

Space will also bring back distance-induced communication delays which humanity has not experienced since the invention of the telegraph. Any communications will be delayed, especially on the outer reaches of the Solar system. For example, electromagnetic radiation messages from Earth to the Moon would be facing a delay of merely 1.3 seconds, while those to Mars would take between 3 and 21 minutes. Sending the message to Jupiter's moons could take between 33 and 53 minutes (Kennewell 2019). Realistically, this time is doubled because it will take the same time to send the answer back (if Earth can make instant decisions and there is no delay in replying, which for complicated situations is rarely the case). While it is relatively easy to overcome this communication time gap in civilian situations, in cases of space conflict such a delay could mean devastating defeats or dangerous events unfolding before details (which might require political decisions) could be communicated back to Earth.

The communication gaps open a strategic window of opportunity within which opponents can try to exploit their first mover advantage to take out defenses, sow confusion and interrupt or cut off communications, with space settlement defenders completely on their own. Longer communication lines also open new possibilities for electronic warfare (EW) applications. One can easily imagine an equivalent of space Pearl Harbor unfolding without Earth even being aware of it, to only wake up to a fait accompli, where the attackers have already achieved their objectives and defenders will have no options but to radically escalate or to settle for a losing peace—a fear shared by many analysts. These communication delays were prevalent throughout most of human history, especially for remote colonies separated from their mother country by vast oceans and requiring months delay in message transmission. This is the reason that, for the United States at least, embassies include US military forces. This is a minor, almost imperceptible disadvantage while humanity operates only within cislunar space, but as our reach extends further into the cosmos, the communication delay factor will become an ever more crucial part of space settlement control & defense planning. Because of this, distant settlements would require greater degrees of autonomy to make their own quick self-defense decisions, which might lead to complete political autonomy from Earth.

Table 6. Possible space weapons release authorities for remote settlements or systems based on traditional air defense doctrine. Paul Szymanski.

Space Autonomous Operation	In space defense, the mode of operation assumed by a space system/settlement after it has lost all communications with human controllers or Earth-based authorities. The space system/settlement assumes full responsibility for control of weapons and engagement of hostile targets, based in accordance with on-board surveillance and weapon system control logic. This automatic state may occur on a regular basis due to orbital movements outside regions of ground coverage and control.
Space Positive Control	A method of space control which relies on positive identification, tracking, and situation assessment of spacecraft within a Space Defense Area, conducted with electronic means by an agency having the authority and responsibility therein.
Space Weapons Hold	In space defense, a weapon control order imposing a status whereby weapons systems may only be fired in self-defense or in response to a formal order.
Space Weapons Tight	In space defense, a weapon control order imposing a status whereby weapons systems may be fired only at targets recognized as hostile.
Space Weapons Free	In space defense, a weapon control order imposing a status whereby weapons systems may be fired at any target in orbital space of defined altitude and inclination, not positively recognized as friendly.

ADDITIONAL CONSIDERATIONS

Active Space Defense	Direct defensive action taken to destroy, nullify, or reduce the effectiveness of hostile space actions. It includes the use of anti-satellite weapon

systems, defensive counter-space weapons, electronic warfare, and other available weapons not primarily used in a space defense role. See also Space Defense.

Passive Space Defense
All measures, other than Active Space Defense, taken to reduce the probability of and to minimize the effects of damage to space systems caused by hostile action without the intention of taking the initiative. These measures include camouflage, deception, dispersion, and the use of protective construction and design. See also Space Defense.

Space Centralized Control
In space defense, the control mode whereby a higher echelon makes direct target assignments to fire units.

Space Decentralized Control
In space defense, the normal mode whereby a higher echelon monitors unit actions, making direct target assignments to units only when necessary to ensure proper fire distribution or to prevent engagement of friendly spacecraft. See also Centralized Control.

Broadcast-Controlled Space Interception
An interception in which the interceptor is given a continuous broadcast of information concerning the space defense situation and effects interception without further control.

Close-Controlled Space Interception
An interception in which the interceptor is continuously controlled to a position from which the target is within local sensor range.

TYRANNY OF DISTANCE & DECENTRALIZATION OF CONTROL

Furthermore, because of the same reason, normal command & control (C2) mechanisms would not function well, necessitating a normally unseen delegation of authority to the settlement governance bodies and field commanders. While this approach would solve one set of problems, it raises another one.

In the early stages of colonization, the settlements would be too dependent on Earth to consider any independent courses of actions. However, if one would imagine a hypothetical permanent settlement of 10,000 people[481], this population would relatively quickly develop their own culture and sense of identity, as well as their own objectives, all of which might be quite different from those of their founding metropolity. While this goes slightly beyond the time scope of our analysis, the future generations of the settlers are very likely to have not much in common not only with the nation or company which originally established the settlement, but with the Earth population in general, both due to genetic and cultural drift. However, if we would limit our consideration of the developments until the end of the century, limited control is still going to raise certain concerns of military nature. Competing space powers will have a lot of incentive to infiltrate and compromise space settlements. This could be done in numerous ways. Infiltration of astronaut preparation programs is likely (which is very hard nowadays but would become much easier once the programs are expanded from dozens of graduates to thousands). Other methods could be bribery, blackmail or threats, as per any intelligence agency handbook, either targeting space settlers themselves or their relatives and interests on Earth.

It is even possible that other states might simply approach space settlement with a better support deal in exchange for a change of allegiance. Let us just imagine a scenario, where Country A establishes a space habitat, but after two decades, due to a large recession on Earth and a radical change of political discourse, it starts heavily cutting their space settlement funding. Then Country B steps in and offers the space settlement's governor to take up the burden of the resupply missions

---

[481] Although according to Salotti (2020) the number could be as low as 110.

and even promises additional funding, political attention and other resources. If this was a permanent settlement, with settlers intending a permanent habitation and colonization, they would be very much interested to ensure the continuation of their way of life. Taking historical examples as a reference, it is likely that initial colonists would be driven by some strong incentive to leave Earth and colonize space, such as idealism, religion, or ideology. Unlike current professional astronauts, who have their homes on Earth and practice space as their profession, future colonists are likely to be much more inclined to see their new home as part of their identity and try to continue their space habitation even if the support from their founding metropolity declines. This would create political friction as the interests of the space colonists and their Earth compatriots would sooner or later diverge and space colonies would become quasi-independent political actors.

The record of colonization in antiquity exhibits similar dynamics. For example ancient Greeks colonized the shores of the Mediterranean from Gibraltar to the Levant and even established colonies as far as the Crimean Peninsula in the Black Sea. Almost all those distant colonies kept amicable relationships with their mother cities (giving us the word metropolis), but within a generation or two these colonies drifted into the spheres of influence of powers that had a closer and more present impact on their material and political situation. Even in modern times there are cases of such dynamics. For example, while the United Kingdom and Australia have a shared historical and cultural heritage, today's Australian economy is de facto reliant on Chinese trade, while Britain makes up only a fraction of total import and export volume (Office of the Chief Economist 2020). At the time of writing it appears that this trend will continue and Australia will continue to drift further away from its British roots. After all, it is from the Australian history discourse that we inherit the idea of the "tyranny of distance" and how it was shaped by it, as coined by Blainey (1966).

Alternatively, a metropolity might lose interest or ability to maintain the colony and then decide to relinquish their control of it. There are plenty of examples of such behavior, for example the Louisiana Purchase, acquisition of Alaska from the Russians or handover of Hong Kong back to China by the United Kingdom. Furthermore, space settlement populations might have much more to gain as brokers and legitimizers of space power in their vicinity. It becomes hard for a state to justify the presence of their operations on Mars if the Martians themselves oppose it[482]. This means that from the perspective of modern nation-states, space settlements will have to be not only protected from outside, but also monitored for cultural and political drift if they wish to preserve their sovereignty over them and access to their resources. One possible way to do that would be the maintenance of a significant presence of Earth-born professionals, which would be regularly rotated to ensure that they do not integrate into the local community. Such practice has been widely used throughout history from the Ottomans to modern diplomatic services; however, it has its disadvantages as well, which would need to be considered. Another alternative method is for the metropolity to lavish considerable supplies and benefits, including political, on their space settlements that they consider critical for Solar System defense – essentially bribing them to stay within their sphere of influence.

LONG-TERM COMMITMENT & PLANNING

An often-overlooked consideration in any space settlement initiative is the need for sustained, possibly multi-decade planning and commitment from the part of the state founding the colony. This is less of a given than one would assume. It is sometimes argued that democracies are

---

[482] Interestingly, SpaceX is already trying to sneak in a (possibly as a joke?) a clause in their Starlink internet user terms of service (ToS) agreement about recognition of Martian independence. While it's just a gag now, at some point in the future it could be used to establish a legal precedent (Delbert 2020).

quite short-sighted in their long-term planning due to the dependence on the election cycles and the approval of public opinion (Spurling 2020, Garrì 2010). If proven true, this would pose a great issue for the space colonization ambitions; operation of a space settlement cannot be simply suspended when the budget needs to be rebalanced or when the trends in the opinion polls change. Nonetheless, we have some good practice examples of both megaprojects and complicated long-term endeavors, such as the Large Hadron Collider (12 years to build, 1995 - 2007), La Sagrada Familia (139 years, started in 1882 and still ongoing as of 2021) or the Panama Canal (33 years, 1881 - 1914) (Premierline 2019). However it is far from guaranteed that we can maintain this same focus and dedication for a century or more straight, which would be a more relevant timescale when planning space colonization.

Two of the biggest space programs in the history of humankind suffered extreme setbacks within a few decades of their launch. NASA's ambitions were curtailed in the 1970s due to the change in political priorities and have not recovered the same level of prestige or financing since, while the Soviet program got even worse treatment due to the collapse of the USSR, with a much-reduced presence under the Russian Federation. Having in mind long-term volatility of geopolitics (very few polities seem to maintain both high economic output and high internal solidarity for more than a couple of centuries), one cannot guarantee that either a space program in question or even the state running it would survive long enough to see it through and reap the benefits. The same goes for private investments; we must remember that out of today's Fortune top 500 companies, only roughly 3 in 10 are older than 120 years (Rapp and O'Keefe 2018). And this does not consider all the mergers, downturn periods, changes in leadership and other challenges these companies had to deal with in the meantime. Building sustainable colonies is going to take decades or possibly even centuries. If these plans would involve terraforming, the process might take even thousands of years, at least based on our current level of technology.

Corporate and state interests are likely to cooperate in settling of space, however neither seems to be immune to the danger of collapsing before their task would be complete.

Any foresight exercise for space warfare should first accept the premise that normal military planning horizons are not applicable. Possibly the only currently existing warfighting domain where planning comes even close to the required long-sightedness is naval procurement. Both development and building of the vessels to maintain the necessary naval state of readiness versus adversaries can require detailed planning many decades into the future. While the appropriateness o comparisons between space and the sea is often debated, we would argue that at least in terms of planning, there are some similar dynamics. Just as the US Navy is already making predictions about the future balance of power in the oceans and plans its capabilities as far as the 2050s (Panter et al., 2020; Office of the Chief of Naval Operations, 2019), it is wise to expand the planning horizon when thinking about space settlements.

RISK OF CATASTROPHIC FAILURES & SABOTAGE

Another factor to be considered would be future catastrophes and their management. While the space industry is widely known as a world leader in terms of safety best practices, accidents will nonetheless happen. Especially with an exponential increase in rocket launches and humans in space starts, there inevitably will be tragedies. And while loss of professional astronauts is greatly mourned when it happens, if tragedy hit a whole space settlement with dozens or hundreds of civilians, it is likely to cause great loss of trust in a space program and have wider political repercussions. A major space settlement disaster could cause space industry stock collapse overnight and stain the reputation of space settling proponents for decades. A good reference point for this could be the 1986 Chernobyl nuclear power plant disaster, which ingrained itself in the public mind. Even today, over three decades since the accident and after major overhauls in security procedures and advances in nuclear reactor technology, the name of that Ukrainian town still haunts any conversation about wider adoption of nuclear energy, despite its numerous benefits. While localized, unmanned, small-scale disasters can be brushed away with a press statement and a few months of waiting, large-scale disasters involving human casualties are not likely to be acceptable to the public. The space industry, especially in its early stages, will not be able to afford a Chernobyl-type disaster without severely compromising the long-term prospects of space settlements.

This fear will create dark incentives for hostile actors to sabotage or nudge events toward situations where rival states might suffer loss of life or even wholesale destruction of their space settlements. While plausible deniability will be maintained, covertly such plans will be discussed, or maybe even implemented. Currently this would be complicated to achieve, but once the number of targets and space access opportunities would increase, the probability of terrorists, political radicals or intelligence agencies considering such options will grow. Such a disaster could set back their rivals and at the same time win a public relations victory, especially if the bad actor country goes in to rescue survivors. In case of two or more competing space powers, the losing participant will always have an incentive to seek to even the playing field by these darker means. It would be extremely difficult to determine who attacked a transiting carrier space vehicle in the deepest of space, much like even today it is next to impossible to truly determine the causes of an orbiting satellite failure near the Earth. Even the great risk of exposure could make it valuable. Imagine how different our history books would look, if the King of France would have paid off a few reliable men to sign up onto Christopher Columbus's expedition and detonate gunpowder on his ships, before departing under the cover of the night back to shore. While the route from Europe to Americas would no doubt be discovered sooner or later, such an event could delay it by decades and potentially in that time swing the advantage away from Spain. Who knows, maybe Latin America would be called Francophone America instead. Small amounts of force applied at crucial points can turn the tables in radical ways and because of this, security against sabotage should be taken seriously.

As a matter of fact, in 2018 a hole drilled from the inside of the spacecraft was discovered on the ISS. While this event is still under investigation at the time of writing and exact reasons for this are not known, it has been widely speculated that the hole might have occurred because of attempted sabotage (Associated Press 2018). Russians have claimed that their investigation found the origin and reason of the hole, (Howell 2019). In 2021 Roscosmos accused a NASA astronaut of drilling the hole, which NASA denied.[483] While this incident is for now shrouded in mystery and possibly might have been a result of some accidental circumstances, it serves as a useful proof of concept for sabotage in space. For the time being space has an advantage of isolation—unlike the alternative history thought experiment of French sabotaging Columbus, the hypothetical astronaut-saboteur cannot just "sail back" to Earth after completing his mission. However, sabotage could be caused via variety of different vectors. Cyberspace is one, allowing the attackers to hack life support systems, communications or navigation interfaces, and these are just the juiciest of targets. Hacked satellites could be redirected to either hit other support satellites or to hit settlements directly (Kallberg 2012). Another vector could be sabotage at blueprint level—inserting flaws or back-doors into technologies which could be used later. And without a doubt, automated, disposable space-drone sabotage will be considered. In the worst-case scenario such drones could destroy a few satellites to start a collisional cascade (also known as Kessler syndrome)

---

[483] Amy Thompson. "Russian Space Officials Try to Blame NASA Astronaut for Soyuz Air Leak in 2018: Report." Space.com, August 14, 2021. https://www.space.com/russia-blames-nasa-astronaut-soyuz-leak.

to turn whole orbits into killing fields for any kind of assets present there (Drmola and Hubik 2018). Future space settlement builders will have to consider and protect against all of these, and not just for the safety of the particular settlement, but for the continuation of the space program as a whole.

UTILITY OF SPACE SETTLEMENTS IN MILITARY PLANNING – ADVANTAGES

As we have just discussed above, space settlements have many vulnerabilities and from an astrostrategic perspective could often be considered liabilities. However while space settlements create many concerns for the metropolity, they also confer several advantages, which we discuss below.

LEGAL DIVIDEND OF PHYSICAL PRESENCE

Even in the legal vacuum regarding the possibility of extending territorial sovereignty to extraterrestrial space, establishing a physical presence there will provide three main benefits to the metropolity. First, if there is ever a legal framework created to allow for claiming of sovereignty over spatial bodies, whoever would already have people and assets present, would also have an extremely strong argument to establish their sovereignty in that space. As childish as it may sound, "I was here first" holds as strong in international politics as it did back in the sandbox. There is no indication that this would change once the scramble for the Solar system will start and most likely whoever will establish the first settlements, will also have the strongest claims.

The second advantage is that even if no formal sovereignty is ever established, the presence of a space settlement gives the metropolity the ability to establish de facto control and "host-guest relationship" quasi-sovereignty over whoever would attempt to enter the area. This can be done either through control of space traffic in the area, through demands for other states to consult metropolity on their plans for expansion in the vicinity and to otherwise exert at least soft (or possibly even hard) influence over the actions of other space powers in the area, while citing the requirements for safety and coordination of common usage of the space. Control might be as simple as charging space traffic "tolls" for transiting settled space to pay for safety beacons, space rescue services and security management. Extraction of resources and other economic activity will also be much easier to conduct in such conditions.

The third advantage, though most likely seldom used, would be to utilize the space settlement as a lawfare asset, seizing de facto sovereignty, even if there would be no formal declaration of such. For example State A might be planning to establish presence in a very promising location for resource mining and State B could strategically rush to deploy a small space settlement there to deny the opportunity of expansion to State A (possibly a reason for China sending an astronaut to the Moon is to claim sovereignty after renouncing the Outer Space Treaty, much like their extra-territorial claims in the South China Sea.) Ideally, this space settlement would be privately owned, possibly a family sized small religious community or a corporate research module. As there is no sovereignty in space, State A never had clear rights to these resources in the first place and now they cannot access them as that would endanger the newly built mini-space settlement. Their options remain either to seek legal recourse on Earth (which might take years and even then might be impossible to enforce) or to proceed with the original plan and force the new settlers off their settlement (most likely resulting in a public relations disaster). Either way, State B can disrupt a decade-long expansion plans for State A for a fraction of the cost and with plausible deniability of their direct involvement. Station-based space habitats would be even more versatile in this, as they could mess/threaten with the orbits of other states' assets. However it must be noted that such tactics would most likely be repaid in kind and could be one of the ways to lead to escalation which could result in a at least a localized space war, much like the many military incidents between early competing settlements in the New World Western Hemisphere that did not cause major warfare between adversary countries.

ECONOMIC BENEFITS & THE BEACHHEAD TO THE SOLAR SYSTEM

Another important advantage is that once a viable space settlement possessing in situ capability to produce fuel and building materials is established, any further expansion would increase exponentially, as further construction becomes by orders of magnitude cheaper and faster once the necessary materials no longer need to be shipped all the way from the Earth's gravity well. This means that there is a significant first mover advantage when establishing space settlements. If one would take American colonies in the Age of Sail as an example, what in 1600s were a few small villages of a few hundred people, in the 1700s became a bustling network of towns and cities and by the 1900s became a nation economically rivaling any of the states from the Old World. While immigration and imports always play an important role in the early stages of the settlement, endogenous growth eventually catches up and surpasses exogenous support. In many cases modern population numbers in the original colonies far surpass the populations of the founding countries, illustrating how humans increase breeding when they have excess space to expand into.

When the Thirteen colonies rebelled, it might have seemed at the time as if Britain lost their investment, as not only the direct profits were lost, but also the young US waged war against the United Kingdom within the next few decades. However in the long term it became clear that Britain benefited greatly, as the cultural affinity brought them closer despite political rivalry and they could later rely on the US as allies in the Great War, World War II and during the Cold War. Even today, despite centuries that passed since those original British settlers founded the colonies, the so-called "special relationship" remains in play (Reynolds 1985). As a result of it, English language became the lingua franca of the modern world and even downstream purely American achievements, such as the internet, continue to benefit Britain. For a relatively small initial investment and by agreeing to send off their religious radicals and political free thinkers across the sea, Britain made one of the best long-term investment decisions in the history of their nation.

Considering this, settling space should also be viewed as shaping the future of political landscapes for centuries in advance. While these considerations are beyond the usual strategic planning horizons in Western democracies, this perspective appears in other discourses, for example the Chinese point of view appears to be more driven by long-term considerations (Hofstede and Minkov 2010), which if applied to space, will yield exponential results. As the saying goes, a wise leader will never enjoy the shade of the trees he plants. In the same vein, the nation that would establish the first autonomous colonies in space will effectively define the character of post-Earth humanity and will eventually grow itself an ally with the resources of a whole other planet or more. While it would take centuries to mature, this is the best long-term investment any space power can make.

A common question raised in these discussions is consideration of why anyone would want to live in the cold, dark and deadly vastness of space. However, it must be noted that the adaptability of humans and the variance of our preferences for habitats is often underestimated. After all the Bedouin of the burning Sahara Desert, the Inuit of ice wastes of Greenland and Unangans of the remote Aleut islands are a living proof that human beings can love and consider home even in the most extreme and inhospitable of environments. There is no reason to presume that there will not be any humans who would find dwelling in space or other planets preferable to the Earth-based way of life and that their children won't cherish their homes as dearly as we do ours.

HEDGING AGAINST EXISTENTIAL RISKS

On a more pragmatic note, space settlements would also serve as humanity's proverbial eggs in a different basket. In a progressively accelerating technological landscape the number of existential threats has grown significantly over the past century and will continue to do so as we unlock, develop and proliferate new technologies. As Nick Bostrom argues in his "Vulnerable World Hypothesis" (Bostrom 2019), it is quite possible that just around the corner we might have some technologies which would make Cold War nuclear deterrence dynamics look like a child's play in comparison to the complexity of threats that are about to follow. However even the older nuclear, biological, chemical (NBC) threats are still there and, even if their threat is perceived to be lesser, their capability to inflict harm has not been diminished in the slightest. In any sufficiently long-term planning exercise one must consider the possibility of an event which will wipe out a significant proportion of humanity, potentially collapsing our civilization as we know it, or causing a great economic boom like happened in Europe at the end of the Great Plague.

If we assume that one of the ultimate goals of any military planning is ensuring the continuation of the state functioning against any odds, there are few more surefire ways to hedge your bets than to establish an "escape pod" space colony that could serve as emergency outpost in case of any global calamities on Earth (Gottlieb 2019). Unfortunately, it is unlikely that in the near future we could terraform or establish robust enough space settlements to support a whole civilization. However, it is not beyond our capability to establish an outpost with enough manpower, materials and knowledge to help us kickstart the rebuilding process of our civilization back on Earth. There are very few global catastrophes that could wipe out 100 percent of humanity. However, major threats could be more than enough to disrupt our civilization to the extent that it would effectively return us to Iron Age technology within a generation and it would be a very hard, long slog to get back to where we were before the calamity with the loss of so much human experience and technical know-how. While there is a common tendency to view human history as a progression toward ever greater complexity, there are many examples (fall of the Roman Empire being the most notable) that show that even without catastrophic conditions whole societies can crumble and return to more primitive states for centuries. In the age of interconnected global commons, even something as unglamorous as a natural pandemic like COVID-19 or a complete stock market collapse could, through second order effects, bring about a new Dark Age However, if humanity would be wise enough to establish a space settlement beforehand, our astronauts could in that case coordinate from space the rebuilding efforts and shape the new world in a way that would hopefully avoid the self-destructing dynamics that led to the collapse in the first place.

DIRECT SUPPORT TO EARTH MILITARY BRANCHES

Space settlements would also provide an opportunity to diversify military presence and provide support to all other branches on Earth. Their unapproachability would improve chances of deterrence, emergency communications, intelligence and, if required, even second-strike capability. A Moon settlement could serve as both an "unsinkable aircraft carrier" and an "indestructible communications satellite." In addition, military operations in space, and development of new concepts of operation, can only best be understood by cultures that live in space.

Space settlements would have an important role to play in nuclear deterrence considerations. All nuclear first strike plans depend on rapid and complete destruction of the enemy command and control system, disrupting its chain of command and ensuring that there is no or very limited nuclear retaliation. Existence of space settlements would complicate any such plan beyond feasibility, since an approach of a nuclear missile attacking the Moon would take days to complete and could easily be detected and dealt with in the vastness of space without affecting Moon populations. For a first strike, as well as near-simultaneously eliminating all land, sea and air targets (which is currently almost impossible), an opponent would now be required to take out space settlements. A surviving space settlement could serve as the command-and-control nexus for the guaranteed second-strike capability. For the time being, there is a strong norm and legal constraints that prevent placement of weapons of mass destruction in space. However, this norm might gradually erode or be outright ignored or just covertly hidden if the situation becomes dire enough. In any event, an unarmed C2 nexus could direct second-strike resources without violating international law.

If extraterrestrial settlements joined the fight[484], they could wield a devastating power of the gravitational well against any targets on Earth. For example, a mass driver built on the Moon (normally used to deliver materials from the Moon to Earth orbit and other parts of Solar system as required), could be used to accelerate pieces of lunar rock and launch them down the gravity well with a high degree of accuracy. Upon impact, due to the acceleration, these improvised munitions could have explosive yields like those of WMDs.

Almost anything in space can be weaponized. It would be very important to ensure that this fact is used to deter any aggression without antagonizing other states and shifting the balance of power too rapidly. Aggressive posturing by the owners of the first space settlements could either spark a race that will take humanity to the stars or light the nuclear powder keg on which humanity has been sitting on since 1945. However, if done gradually and transparently, it is possible that space settlements could be used to solve deterrence problems on Earth once and for all – first strike without retaliation will become an impossibility.

Finally, a space settlement could provide a platform to build vital infrastructure for supporting Earth-based forces. Most LEO satellites are greatly constrained by the volume of the payload, but constructing infrastructure on the Moon would allow building of advanced

---

[484]Presupposing that current demilitarized space law framework would be ignored - *inter arma enim silent leges.*

communication arrays, massive telescopes and powerful space object tracking infrastructure, which would give greater cislunar and Earth situational awareness than ever before. Also, space warfare may come to the point where if an adversary wants to start a war on Earth, he had better take out his opponents' space assets first before even attempting to attack on the ground. In addition, with excellent space domain awareness, a threatened country might be able to detect the build-up of adversary space assets in critical orbital choke points and frustrate his attack plans either on orbit or diplomatically at the United Nations. Either way, keeping conflicts off the Earth results in fewer human casualties, and space war might ultimately simply be fought between remotely controlled orbital machines.

SCIENTIFIC DIVIDEND

Space exploration greatly benefits numerous other fields of scientific inquiry. The space industry can be a proving ground for all the STEM and adjacent fields. Exceptionally stringent mission parameters and high funding allocation allow for state-of-the-art technologies to be tested in the harshest conditions and improved upon by the brightest minds. Numerous technologies that we are utilizing today were either born out of space research or heavily influenced by advances that were made in adjacent industries. Challenges and extreme conditions of space exploration force researchers to find new ways to apply technologies, and those applications then return to the military or civilian spheres. This virtuous cycle drove a significant part of innovations since the 1950s (European Commission Space Policy and Coordination Unit 2010).

As mentioned previously, building a space settlement would be very expensive because of the necessary research and development costs. However, the initial effort of building the first space settlement will result in permanent advances in both material sciences and engineering techniques, which will give the nation who builds it a head start in all future space construction efforts. Downstream synergistic effects of these advances are likely to be felt for decades in fields such as civil engineering, industrial safety, life support systems, applied chemistry, mining techniques, ecosystems science, communications and many others. Even in the medium term, the initial investment might be at least partially recovered through offering consulting advice and expertise to other nations and the private sector companies who would be interested in establishing their own space infrastructure.

Furthermore, once the space settlement is built, it will serve as an on-demand base for further scientific inquiry (Purves 2008). As any construction is likely to be done in stages, once the settlement will be expanded, different materials, alloys and techniques will be tested in the low gravity, low temperature and vacuum conditions. After the settlement is completed, this process will continue—national laboratories from across the world would see this as a prime ground to partner to conduct various experiments. Current experimentation on ISS is important, but relatively rudimentary due to space, logistical, safety and human resource constraints. Space settlements will have fewer restrictions regarding these concerns. For example, currently new spaceship engines are tested on Earth, and it is a difficult, expensive and dangerous process. Even after computer simulations are completed and ground tests are done, there always remains a question of how the machine will perform under actual space conditions. And while the diligence of engineers and extreme safety regulations keep mistakes and accidents to a minimum, having an opportunity to test some of the designs in space conditions could be a vital addition to the future space industry.

The importance of this value cannot be understated—it is much harder to develop processes, conduct experiments and achieve breakthroughs when simulating environments rather than working in the actual environments themselves. It will also open possibilities of relatively cheap low gravity research—for example 3-D printing of human organs (such as heart replacements) are likely to be much more efficient in orbit or on the Moon, because under Earth gravity fragile structures tend to collapse in the printing process (Glasure 2019). Low or zero-gravity laboratories would not have this issue. This is just one of many areas where space settlements will open new opportunities. It is not beyond the realm of possibility that within a century multi-billion-dollar biomedical organ replacement industries might be based completely off-Earth.

ASTROSTRATEGIC DYNAMICS FOLLOWING THE SETTLEMENT OF MOON, MARS AND BEYOND

In the short term space settlements are likely to remain white elephant projects that will pose immense costs to those space powers that are willing to engage in their construction while also exposing those powers to numerous liabilities and vulnerabilities that would come with such commitment. These issues may have contributed to the lag in development of human presence in space for the past few decades. However, when all is considered, once established, space settlements would start bringing ever increasing benefits both to the founding metropolity and humanity in general. While currently this process is very slow and space plays a relatively minor role in politics, society and military considerations, this will rapidly change once the current pioneering phase proves that space bound resource exploitation passes the test of cost-benefit analysis and initial investment thresholds are reduced. Then we are likely to see acceleration of attempts to utilize space and having a physical presence will quickly become a matter of necessity to maintain the astrostrategic balance of power.

Speculating beyond this is complicated; however, having in mind the importance of the matter and the scarce discussion on the issue, an attempt must be made. The following conjectures is very likely to be out of date within a few years, affected by political, technological and other developments which cannot be reasonably foreseen; however it presents one potential path forward from the perspective of how things stand in 2021. Below is the analysis of three projected phases of settling of the Solar system: Moon, Mars and beyond.

The Moon is going to become extremely important over the next few decades.

Its proximity to Earth, access to propellant (in the form of frozen water) (Basilevsky, Abdrakhimov, and Dorofeeva 2012) and low gravity make it an almost perfect beachhead for further exploration beyond cislunar space. The same attributes are likely to make the Moon into an economic bottleneck and strategic chokepoint of human expansion into the rest of the Solar system. The first serious tensions in space will be the result of states carving out areas of influence on the Moon, much like the Western Hemisphere was divided after the Age of Discovery. Even if unenforced, the taboo of space militarization is still likely to hold power over political decision-making and overt militarization is not likely to be attempted, unless one of the revisionist space powers decides to make a run for the first mover advantage. At this stage we would likely see only very limited militarization of space beyond the Earth's orbit, mostly defensive, focused on anti-access and area denial (A2/AD) technologies and protection of assets. Some space assets suitable for A2/AD might be dual use, but not overtly weaponized, making deployment more palatable to domestic and international audiences. The balance of power would still be dominated by confrontations on Earth itself, but LEO, cislunar space and the Moon would be seen as a promising side theater, where advantage could be gained (or lost) easier than on Earth. "Satellite gap", "lunar outpost gap", "ASAT gap" or similar comparative metrics might gain traction, similarly to the infamous "missile gap" of the Cold War (Preble 2003). Eventually, equilibrium of one sort or another would be reached on the Moon and the price of further confrontation there would increase as the status quo would become entrenched; confrontational focus would be likely to shift toward interplanetary expansion, with Mars being the most likely candidate.

Humanity begins limited attempts to colonize Mars.

At some point, depending on the technological base and the presence of ambitious spacefaring vision among the intellectual, business and political elites, Mars may become a place where space power is exercised. In the beginning, human presence on Mars would likely be much less confrontational than on the Moon. Distance from the Earth and dangers of early colonization are likely to force early Martian space settlements to cooperate with little regard to political situations back on Earth. Low population, massive territories and practically unlimited access to resources are likely to decrease the tensions between the colonists from different settlements, even if their founding metropolities continue confrontation on Earth.

While independent colonies on the Moon are not likely, Mars presents a much wider range of opportunities and some private interests, such as religious or ideological organizations, might decide to take the risk. Authoritarian states, such as China, might offer one-way settler tickets to Mars to death row prisoners or other disposable groups. Either way, initial space settlements will have to be heavily subsidized by their metropolities; it will be important to establish Martian presence as early as possible and having a Martian settlement is likely to become a matter of international prestige.

If at this time Earth polities are locked in a new Cold War, this process would be accelerated as this would likely be perceived as part of the ideological conflict illustrating superior political and technological capabilities.

The scramble for advantage will extend to the rest of the Solar system.

Space settlement would most likely begin with the Moon and Mars, but it would not be likely to stop there. As space settlements start proliferating and initial investment costs drop, planetary settlements would most likely dominate the field. (It is hard to estimate at this point whether orbital settlements and space habitats will be adopted en masse.) This is the point where the next steps for space powers will diverge. While establishing forward bases on the Moon and Mars seem to be the logical steps that would be followed by most space powers within a short duration, afterward they are likely to turn their attention to colonizing different parts of the Solar system, which is likely to also start the next round of military tensions. By the time Mars bases are properly established, this technological base for interplanetary travel and settlement building should be relatively mature with a proven track record. The first major disasters will likely have already happened, and the population will have had time to process the trauma.

While this speculation rests on a lot of assumptions, if they turn out correct, at this stage exploring and establishing bases on or near the other planets would become realistic. Furthermore, these less explored areas would offer an effective monopoly of action and freedom to impose their own rules, at least until other space powers catch up with them. In a hypothetical distant future where the Chinese establish a base on Titan, the American government would likely feel immense pressure to establish their own presence there or an equivalent one somewhere else. The Sputnik crisis effect would come back with a vengeance (Kennedy 2005). In addition, it is conceivable that some countries may establish secret bases on celestial bodies without the public becoming aware of them.

Comparing this stage with the earlier ones, there are likely to be cultural changes in the approach of the space powers to the issues. We must remember that the Moon is a special case, as it has a very strong presence in all human cultures. There is a common perception that the Moon belongs to all humankind and is to be shared by everyone, especially as it is the best steppingstone to the stars. However it is possible that this ecumenical attitude will not extend to other space objects. For example if a state settled one of the eighty-two currently known moons of Saturn, it might declare the whole moon to be within its "buffer zone." Most lay people are not even aware that Saturn has so many moons, so there might not be enough public support to take serious action in response to such unilateral proclamations. Some orbits, communication frequencies or time windows for launches might also become contested, especially when space traffic starts growing exponentially; however, they are unlikely to become points of great tension as the public is likely to have trouble visualizing such domains of conflict. However it must also be noted that interest in space colonization is likely to ebb and flow. We may speculate that after the establishment of the permanent settlement on Mars, further space exploration will excite the general population less and less. Any further advances could be seen as "more of the same" rather than breaking new ground and the novelty may wear off. Such an achievement hangover effect was seen after the Moon landings in the 1960s and can be observed in earlier exploration drives, such as Arctic exploration and the race to climb Mount Everest in the first half of the 20th century. By this time human space presence will have to be robust enough to sustain and justify itself economically without the added benefit of novelty and prestige. The only motivation that is likely to remain constant throughout all the different stages of space settlement will be idealistic motivation, as some humans just happen to be fascinated by the idea of space exploration.

Table 7. Phases of Space Settlement

	Lunar Colonization Phase	Interplanetary Colonization Phase	Divergent Colonization Phase
Speculative dates	Present to 2050s	2060s to 2090s	2100s and beyond
Key milestones	Permanent presence on the Moon, experimentation with orbital habitats	Presence on another planet (most likely Mars), permanent orbital habitats, expansion of Moon settlements & facilities	Streamlining of settling process, settlement on other planets, experimentation with space habitats

Key driving space settlement motivations	Ideological and Prestige	Economic, Prestige and Ideological	Economic, Ideological and Security
Number of metropolities sponsoring space settlements	1-3 (Most likely US, possibly China and less likely Russia or European Union)	2-10 (Likely that secondary powers would join, also possibly major private companies such as SpaceX or Blue Origin)	10+ (Other smaller states and private corporations could join the Solar scramble if technology becomes affordable)
Associated risks and costs	High	Medium	Low
Risk of space-borne military conflict	Low - Not enough interests and assets to have conflicts over.	High – Moon will become a chokepoint to the rest of the Solar system and scramble will escalate the tensions. Additional actors might destabilize the balance of power.	Medium – As self-sustaining space settlements proliferate and balance of power in space is established, risks should decrease, but not disappear.

CONCLUSION

Space settlements will be extremely important for any military and astrostrategic planning within the context of planning for expansion into space and preventing conflict. Both a liability and an asset, space settlements will play a crucial role in human expansion across the Solar system and beyond. The path toward human presence in space is likely to cause greater tensions and require increased capacity for long-term planning. Building, using and protecting space settlements will be a key part of astropolitical considerations. By their nature, space settlements will be the focus of human attention on space; this means that they are very likely to become the first places where spacefaring states will start brushing shoulders. Because of this reason it is impossible to study space settlements without considering legal, political, economic and military aspects of their presence, all of which are intertwined. Space appears to be limitless and there are unending horizons for humanity to explore. It is our duty to avoid getting into vicious escalation cycles of destructive competition between the space powers, while stuck on a threshold to infinity, beyond which all current human conflict will become obsolete. For this purpose it is important to research all aspects of future Space Age warfare to understand how to deter aggressors, assure allies, build effective legal and economic frameworks, and most importantly, on how to avoid ending life on our world, while trying to reach other distant worlds.

BIBLIOGRAPHY

Arnhof, Marlies. 2016. "Design of a Human Settlement on Mars Using In-Situ Resources." In 46th International Conference on Environmental Systems. Texas Tech University Libraries. https://ttu-ir.tdl.org/handle/2346/67561.

Arms Control Association. 2021. The Outer Space Treaty at a Glance | Arms Control Association. Available at: https://www.armscontrol.org/factsheets/outerspace..

Ashworth, S. 2012. "The Long-Term Growth Prospects for Planetary and Space Colonies." Journal of the British Interplanetary Society 65: 200–217. https://ui.adsabs.harvard.edu/abs/2012JBIS...65..200A/abstract.

Associated Press. 2018. 'Russia: Hole Drilled from inside Int'l Space Station Capsule'. Associated Press. 24 December 2018. https://apnews.com/article/87cb3a5a3f1740eda47a0a1811f96033

Basilevsky, A. T., Abdrakhimov, A. M., and Dorofeeva, V. A. 2012. 'Water and Other Volatiles on the Moon: A Review'. Solar System Research 46, no. 2: 89–107.

Bharmal, Zahaan. 2018. "The Case against Mars Colonisation." The Guardian, August 28, 2018. http://www.theguardian.com/science/blog/2018/aug/28/the-case-against-mars-colonisation

Blainey, Geoffrey. 1966. The Tyranny of Distance: How Distance Shaped Australia's History. Sun Books.

Bostrom, Nick. 2013. 'Existential Risk Prevention as Global Priority: Existential Risk Prevention as Global Priority'. Global Policy 4, no. 1: 15–31.

Bostrom, Nick. 2019. "The Vulnerable World Hypothesis." Global Policy 10, no. 4: 455–76.

Brown, Mike. 2019. "Blue Origin's Jeff Bezos Details His Radical Vision for Colonies in Space." Inverse.Com. Inverse. May 10, 2019. https://www.inverse.com/article/55709-blue-origin-s-jeff-bezos-details-his-radical-vision-for-colonies-in-space.

Brown, Mike. 2020. "Terraform Mars: Elon Musk Says a Mars City of 'Glass Domes' Comes First." Inverse.Com. Inverse. November 19, 2020. https://www.inverse.com/innovation/spacex-mars-city-terraforming.

Cannon, Kevin M., and Daniel T. Britt. 2019. 'Feeding One Million People on Mars'. New Space 7, no. 4: 245–54.

Carati, Andrea. 2017. 'Responsibility to Protect, NATO and the Problem of Who Should Intervene: Reassessing the Intervention in Libya'. Global Change Peace & Security 29, no. 3: 293–309.

Coates, Andrew. 2018. "Sorry, Elon Musk, but It's Now Clear That Colonising Mars Is Unlikely – and a Bad Idea." Phys.Org. August 2, 2018. https://phys.org/news/2018-08-elon-musk-colonising-mars-bad.html.

Congressional Research Service. 2021. "Navy Lasers, Railgun, and Gun-Launched Guided Projectile: Background and Issues for Congress." https://fas.org/sgp/crs/weapons/R44175.pdf.

Crawford, Ian A. 2012. 'Stapledon's Interplanetary Man: A Commonwealth of Worlds and the Ultimate Purpose of Space Colonisation'. ArXiv [Physics.Hist-Ph]. http://arxiv.org/abs/1207.1498.

DARPA. 2021. 'Orbital Construction: DARPA Pursues Plan for Robust Manufacturing in Space'. Darpa.Mil. 5 February 2021. https://www.darpa.mil/news-events/2021-02-05.

DARPA. 2021. 'Orbital Construction: DARPA Pursues Plan for Robust Manufacturing in Space'. Darpa.Mil. 5 February 2021. https://www.darpa.mil/news-events/2021-02-05.

Davenport, Frances Gardiner, and Dr J. A. Robertson. 2008. "Treaty between Spain and Portugal, Concluded at Alcacovas, September 4, 1479." https://avalon.law.yale.edu/15th_century/spp001.asp.

Dolman, Everett C. 2005. 'Foundations: From Geopolitics to Astropolitics'. In Astropolitik: Classical Geopolitics in the Space Age. London: Routledge.

Dolman, Everett Carl. 2012. 'New Frontiers, Old Realities'. Strategic Studies Quarterly 6, no. 1: 78–96.

Dorminey, Bruce. 2012. 'Death of A Sci-Fi Dream: Free-Floating Space Colonies Hit Economic Reality'. Forbes Magazine, 31 July 2012. https://www.forbes.com/sites/brucedorminey/2012/07/31/death-of-a-sci-fi-dream-free-floating-space-colonies-hit-economic-reality/.

Drexler, Eric K. 1984. "Space Development: The Case against Mars." Foresight Institute. October 1984. https://foresight.org/nano/Mars.php.

Drmola, Jakub, and Tomas Hubik. 2018. 'Kessler Syndrome: System Dynamics Model'. Space Policy 44–45: 29–39.

Drudi, Laura, Chad G. Ball, Andrew W. Kirkpatrick, Joan Saary, and S. Marlene Grenon. 2012. 'Surgery in Space: Where Are We at Now?' Acta Astronautica 79: 61–66.

European Commission Space Policy and Coordination Unit. 2010. "Summary Report: Space Exploration and Innovation." https://ec.europa.eu/docsroom/documents/1042/attachments/1/translations/en/renditions/pdf.

Foust, Jeff. 2020. "Bigelow Aerospace Lays off Entire Workforce." Spacenews.Com. March 23, 2020. https://spacenews.com/bigelow-aerospace-lays-off-entire-workforce/.

Fox, William James. 2018. 'Launch Costs to Low Earth Orbit, 1980-2100'. Futuretimeline.Net. 1 September 2018. https://www.futuretimeline.net/data-trends/6.htm.

Garrì, Iconio. 2010. 'Political Short-Termism: A Possible Explanation'. Public Choice 145, no. 1–2: 197–211.

Glasure, Elizabeth. 2019. "Zero Gravity May Allow Viable Human Organs to Be 3D Printed." Biospace.Com. BioSpace. July 23, 2019.

https://www.biospace.com/article/zero-gravity-may-allow-viable-human-organs-to-be-3d-printed/.

Globus, Al. 2006. "A US Space Program for Space Settlement." Alglobus.Net. 2006. http://alglobus.net/NASAwork/papers/NSS2006SpaceProgram.pdf
.

Goldsberry, Clare. 2019. "3D Printer on International Space Station Allows Astronauts to Recycle, Reuse, Repeat." Plasticstoday.Com. February 15, 2019. https://www.plasticstoday.com/3d-printing/3d-printer-international-space-station-allows-astronauts-recycle-reuse-repeat.

Goswami, Namrata. 2018. 'China in Space: Ambitions and Possible Conflict'. Strategic Studies Quarterly 12, no. 1: 74–97.

Goswami, Namrata. 2021. 'The Strategic Implications of the China-Russia Lunar Base Cooperation Agreement'. Thediplomat.Com. 19 March 2021. https://thediplomat.com/2021/03/the-strategic-implications-of-the-china-russia-lunar-base-cooperation-agreement/.

Gottlieb, Joseph. 2019. 'Space Colonization and Existential Risk'. Journal of the American Philosophical Association 5, no. 3: 306–20.

Greason, Jeff, and James C. Bennett. 2019. "The Economics of Space: An Industry Ready to Launch." Reason Foundation. June 5, 2019. https://reason.org/policy-study/the-economics-of-space/.

Hibbs, A. R.; 1977; Princeton Conference on Space manufacturing facilities: Space colonies, May 7-9, 1975, Princeton, NJ.

Hofstede, Geert, and Michael Minkov. 2010. 'Long- versus Short-Term Orientation: New Perspectives'. Asia Pacific Business Review 16, no. 4: 493–504.

Howell, Elizabeth. 2019. "Russia Says It Will Keep Source of Hole (and Air Leak) on Soyuz Secret— but NASA Wants to Know: Report." Space. September 21, 2019. https://www.space.com/russian-soyuz-hole-air-leak-source-secret-nasa-chief.html.

Johnson, Christopher Daniel. 2018. The Outer Space Treaty. Oxford University Press.

Kallberg, Jan. 2012. 'Designer Satellite Collisions from Covert Cyber War'. Strategic Studies Quarterly 6, no. 1: 124–36.

Kan, Shirley. 2007. "CRS Report for Congress: China's Anti-Satellite Weapon Test." Fas.Org. April 23, 2007. https://fas.org/sgp/crs/row/RS22652.pdf.

Kennedy, Ian. 2005. 'The Sputnik Crisis and America's Response'. University of Central Florida.

Kennewell, John A. 2019. "Communication Delay." Australian Space Academy. August 1, 2019. https://www.spaceacademy.net.au/spacelink/commdly.htm.

Lachert, Jakub. 2020. "Russia Hands out Passports to Its Diaspora." Warsawinstitute.Org. February 18, 2020. https://warsawinstitute.org/russia-hands-passports-diaspora/.

Levchenko, Igor, Shuyan Xu, Stéphane Mazouffre, Michael Keidar, and Kateryna Bazaka. 2019. 'Mars Colonization: Beyond Getting There'. Global Challenges (Hoboken, NJ) 3, no. 1: 1800062.

Levchenko, Igor, Shuyan Xu, Stéphane Mazouffre, Michael Keidar, and Kateryna Bazaka. 2019. 'Mars Colonization: Beyond Getting There.' Global Challenges (Hoboken, NJ) 3, no. 1: 1800062.

Lindroos, Marcus. n.d. 'The Soviet Manned Lunar Program.' Fas.Org. Accessed 2 May 2021. https://fas.org/spp/eprint/lindroos_moon1.htm.

Little, Geoffrey. 2008. "Mr. B's Big Plan." Airspacemag.Com. January 2008. https://www.airspacemag.com/space/mr-bs-big-plan-23798796/.

Mack, Eric. 2020. 'US Space Force: Everything You Need to Know on Its First Anniversary'. CNET. 20 December 2020. https://www.cnet.com/news/us-space-force-guardians-everything-you-need-to-know-first-anniversary/.

McFall-Johnsen, Morgan, and Dave Mosher. 2020. "Elon Musk Says He Plans to Send 1 Million People to Mars by 2050 by Launching 3 Starship Rockets Every Day and Creating 'a Lot of Jobs' on the Red Planet." Business Insider, January 17, 2020. https://www.businessinsider.com/elon-musk-plans-1-million-people-to-mars-by-2050-2020-1.

Morgan Stanley. 2020. "Space: Investing in the Final Frontier." Morganstanley.Com. July 24, 2020. https://www.morganstanley.com/ideas/investing-in-space.

NASA Ames Research Center. 1975. "Space Settlements." Nss.Org. Accessed April 22, 2021. https://space.nss.org/settlement/nasa/75SummerStudy/Design.html

NASA Scientific and Technical Information Program Office. 2004. 'Lunar and Planetary Bases, Habitats, and Colonies'. https://ntrs.nasa.gov/citations/20040045214.

NASA. 1962. "John F. Kennedy Moon Speech - Rice Stadium (September 12, 1962)." Nasa.Gov. September 12, 1962. https://er.jsc.nasa.gov/seh/ricetalk.htm.

NASA. 2016. "Demonstrating Technologies for Deep Space Habitation: Bigelow Expandable Activity Module." Nasa.Gov. 2016. https://www.nasa.gov/sites/default/files/atoms/files/2016-march-beam-factsheet-508.pdf.

NASA. 2020. 'The Artemis Accords: Principles for Cooperation in the Civil Exploration and Use of the Moon, Mars, Comets, and Asteroids for Peaceful Purposes'. https://www.nasa.gov/specials/artemis-accords/img/Artemis-Accords-signed-13Oct2020.pdf.

National Space Society. 2021. "O'Neill Cylinder Space Settlement." Nss.Org. 2021. https://space.nss.org/o-neill-cylinder-space-settlement/.

Office of the Chief Economist, Department of Foreign Affairs and Trade. 2020. "Composition of Trade Australia 2018-19." https://www.dfat.gov.au/sites/default/files/cot-2018-19.pdf.

Office of the Chief of Naval Operations. 2019 "Report to Congress on the Annual Long-Range Plan for Construction of Naval Vessels for Fiscal Year 2019." US Navy, February 2018. Last modified February 2018. Accessed April 22, 2021. https://www.secnav.navy.mil/fmc/fmb/Documents/19pres/LONGR ANGE_SHIP_PLAN.pdf.

Ordway, Frederick I., Mitchell R. Sharpe, and Ronald C. Wakeford. 2003 "Project Horizon: An Early Study of a Lunar Outpost." Acta Astronautica. Pergamon, February 11, 2003. Last modified February 11, 2003. Accessed April 22, 2021. https://www.sciencedirect.com/science/article/abs/pii/009457658 8901944.

Panter, Jonathan, Anand j Jantzen, and Jonathan Falcone. 2020 "The 100-Ship Navy." War on the Rocks, June 26, 2020. Last modified June 26, 2020. Accessed April 22, 2021. https://warontherocks.com/2020/06/the-100-ship-navy/.

Posey, Bill. 2020. American Space Commerce Act of 2020. https://www.congress.gov/bill/116th-congress/house-bill/6783/text.

Preble, Christopher A. 2003. "'Who Ever Believed in the 'Missile Gap'?': John F. Kennedy and the Politics of National Security'. Presidential Studies Quarterly 33, no. 4: 801–26.

Premierline. 2019. "The Longest Projects in Modern Construction." Premierline.Co.Uk. August 12, 2019. https://www.premierline.co.uk/knowledge-centre/the-longest-projects-in-modern-construction.html.

Purves, Lloyd. 2008. "Use of Lunar Outpost for Developing Space Settlement Technologies." In AIAA SPACE 2008 Conference & Exposition. Reston, Virginia: American Institute of Aeronautics and Astronautics.

Purves, Lloyd. 2008. "Use of Lunar Outpost for Developing Space Settlement Technologies." In AIAA SPACE 2008 Conference &

Exposition. Reston, Virginia: American Institute of Aeronautics and Astronautics.

Rapp, Nicolas, and Brian O'Keefe. 2018. "See the Age of Every Company in the Fortune 500." Fortune. May 21, 2018. https://fortune.com/longform/fortune-500-through-the-ages/.

Reddy, Vidya Sagar. 2018. 'The SpaceX Effect'. New Space 6, no. 2: 125–34.

Reuters. 2021. 'China Completes Historic Mars Spacecraft Landing', 15 May 2021. https://www.reuters.com/lifestyle/science/chinese-spacecraft-successfully-lands-surface-mars-xinhua-2021-05-15/.

Reynolds, David. 1985. 'A "Special Relationship"? America, Britain and the International Order since the Second World War'. International Affairs 62, no. 1: 1–20.

Salotti, Jean-Marc. 2020. "Minimum Number of Settlers for Survival on Another Planet." Scientific Reports 10, no. 1: 9700.

Selding, Peter B. 2015. "Russia -- and Its Modules -- to Part Ways with ISS in 2024." Spacenews.Com. February 25, 2015. https://spacenews.com/russia-and-its-modules-to-part-ways-with-iss-in-2024/.

Smith, Marshall, Douglas Craig, Nicole Herrmann, Erin Mahoney, Jonathan Krezel, Nate McIntyre, and Kandyce Goodliff. 2020. 'The Artemis Program: An Overview of NASA's Activities to Return Humans to the Moon'. In 2020 IEEE Aerospace Conference, 1–10. IEEE.

Sproull, Daniel C. 2017. "Kinetic Energy Weapons: The Beginning of an Interagency Challenge." InterAgency Journal. 2017. https://thesimonscenter.org/wp-content/uploads/2017/05/IAJ-8-2-2017-pg62-68.pdf.

Spurling, Bryden. 2020. "The Peril of Modern Democracy: Short-Term Thinking in a Long-Term World." United States Studies Centre. February 3, 2020. https://www.ussc.edu.au/analysis/the-peril-of-modern-democracy-short-term-thinking-in-a-long-term-world.

Szymanski, Paul. 2019. 'Techniques for Great Power Space War'. Strategic Studies Quarterly, Air University, Maxwell AFB, AL Volume 13 Issue 4 - Winter 2019. 21 November 2019. https://www.airuniversity.af.edu/Portals/10/SSQ/documents/Volume-13_Issue-4/Szymanski.pdf.

TASS. 2015. "Russia Establishes Aerospace Forces as New Armed Service — Defense Minister." TASS. August 3, 2015. https://tass.com/russia/812184.

Tellis, Ashley J. 2019. "India's ASAT Test: An Incomplete Success." Carnegie Endowment for International Peace. April 15, 2019. https://carnegieendowment.org/2019/04/15/india-s-asat-test-incomplete-success-pub-78884.

Thomson, Iain. 2015. "SpaceX to Deliver Bigelow Blow-up Job to ISS Astronauts." The Register. March 14, 2015. https://www.theregister.com/2015/03/14/spacex_inflatable_bigelow_iss/.

United Nations Treaty Collection. 1984. "Agreement Governing the Activities of States on the Moon and Other Celestial Bodies." https://treaties.un.org/pages/ViewDetails.aspx?src=TREATY&mtdsg_no=XXIV-2&chapter=24&clang=_en.

United States Army. 1961. "Project Horizon: Summary and Supporting Considerations." Gwu.Edu. September 21, 1961. https://nsarchive2.gwu.edu/NSAEBB/NSAEBB479/docs/EBB-Moon01_sm.pdf.

Wade, Mark. 2019. 'DLB Module'. Encyclopaedia Astronautica. 2019. http://www.astronautix.com/d/dlbmodule.html.

Wall, Mike. 2016. "China Launches Tiangong-2 Space Lab to Prep for 2020s Space Station." Space. September 15, 2016. https://www.space.com/34077-china-launches-tiangong-2-space-lab.html.

Wall, Mike. 2019. 'China Eyes Robotic Outpost at the Moon's South Pole in Late 2020s'. Space. 18 July 2019. https://www.space.com/china-moon-south-pole-research-station-2020s.html.

Weitering, Hanneke. 2020. "Russia Has Launched an Anti-Satellite Missile Test, US Space Command Says." Space. December 16, 2020. https://www.space.com/russia-launches-anti-satellite-missile-test-2020.

Williams, Matt. 2019. 'Mars One, the Plan to Make a Reality Show on Mars, Is Bankrupt'. Universetoday.Com. 14 February 2019. https://www.universetoday.com/141499/mars-one-the-plan-to-make-a-reality-show-on-mars-is-bankrupt/.

Chapter 10: Conclusions

By Paul Szymanski

There are many examples in military history where a supposedly inferior force bested a technically superior force on the battlefield. One needs only view recent history where 75,000 Taliban forces with 1940s weapons (AK's) readily beat 300,000 Afghan government forces with much superior military technologies from the United States ($85 billion of military equipment). *Wars are still fought between human minds*—not necessarily between technologies. This has been true since ancient Greek times to the present day.

Figure 16. As early as 175 AD, Lucian of Samosata envisaged Roman legions invading the Moon in his *True History*. London: A.H. Bullen, 1902. Illustration by William Strang.

This adage must be infinitely more applicable for this new area of conflict where one cannot even directly image the satellites "fighting" each other. Knowledge, perceptions, motivations, culture, training, experience, fear of failure, fear of punishment, fear of death, fear of loss, situational awareness, understanding of technical limitations, and the uniqueness of orbital dynamics assure that the outcome of any space war cannot be known with certainty. Even the space war objectives of the adversary probably cannot be known for certain: e.g., command decapitation; deny battlefield imagery, degrade weapons deliver accuracy; simply show resolve, precursor to nuclear attack; etc. Lack of historical precedence in space wars makes this even more difficult. Another example: the space war that occurred between Russia and the United States in 2014 over the Ukrainian conflict [485] was technically won in space by the US, but ultimately lost on the ground due to Russian cyberattacks against the American banking system. This is also a prime example of how both space and terrestrial wars can be readily linked militarily, economically, politically, and diplomatically.

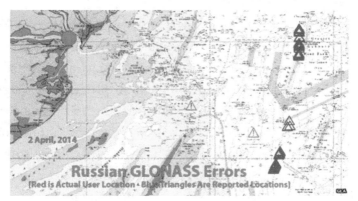

---

[485] United States Loses First Global Space War to Russians. Paul Szymanski. 2014. Available at https://www.slideshare.net/SpaceStrategos/united-states-loses-first-global-space-war-to-russians-with-illustrations.

Figure 17. Russia experienced a system-wide failure of its entire GLONASS navigation system on April 2, 2014, shortly after the beginning of armed conflict between Russia and Ukraine in the Donbas region. Paul Szymanski.

I can readily imagine a scenario where one nation takes a small portion of its space engineers and scientists and devotes them to developing a covert space weapon system. For example, China currently has at least 100,000 people working in space. Take just 5 percent of these and devote these 5,000 engineers and scientists for ten years to a covert project whose sole purpose is to fool a USSF captain in a space watch center (e.g., Combined Space Operations Center - CSpOC) at 3 a.m. on a holiday morning into thinking that everything is all right when he is about to lose billions of dollars of space systems. Who do you think will win this contest—5,000 adversary PhD scientists and engineers working for ten years, or some poor captain not long out of college who has little, if any, true space warfighting training, with no doctrinal support structure that has even attempted to sensitize him to space warfare attack indicators, consequences, or fundamental strategic issues?

Previously I argued that one learns more from failure than from success, especially with major wars. I will now argue the opposite as a devil's advocate. Obviously, the United States has not learned how to successfully fight insurgencies, given the multiple failures of sixty years of past conflicts in these categories. Maybe democracies have difficulties understanding other cultures and are also limited by "moral concerns" that adversary insurgencies appear to have little problems with. On the other hand, the United States and its allies have been preparing for decades for low-level insurgency kinds of conflicts and maybe this explains why NATO is performing so badly in the Ukrainian conflict—we forgot we had to be able to conduct modern high-intensity warfare: "Western Way of War."

I believe there are even more "moral concerns" with space wars that may limit US military preparedness and capability for space war. One of the drivers for the creation of US Space Force may have been to educate the US public on the inevitability of military challenges in space.

How to Win

1. **Situational Awareness Dominates**
2. **Pre-Conflict Positioning**
3. **Decisive Political Will**
4. **Effective Doctrine**
5. **Define Winning**
6. **Emphasize Strategic & Political Post-War Consequences**

How to Lose

1. **Uncertainty and Confusion Leads to Self-Deterrence & Delays Responses**
2. **Military Space Assets are in the Wrong Positions**
3. **Ignoring Future Political Impacts**
4. **The Space War Is Lost on the Ground**
5. **Only Consider Tactical But Not Strategic Aspects of Space Warfare**

Figure 18. How to Win or Lose a Space War.

FOUNDATIONAL PRINCIPLES FOR CONDUCTING SPACE WARS

This section provides some crucial

CRITICAL SPACE WARFARE ISSUES

1. Currently, there is way too much emphasis on "tactical" actions in space at the expense of "strategic" sensitivities. Since satellites cover the Earth and space war is considered very politically sensitive, even tactical actions in space have strategic consequences. One can attack a satellite anywhere on Earth that is near its orbital ground track. This makes any space war a world war that does not have boundaries inclusive of warring country theaters of operation.

2. Like submarine warfare and secretive covert special actions, attacks in space can be largely hidden from public view. They can even be hidden from allied nations and your own government agencies. If the USSF and Space Command conduct an attack on an adversary space system, they do not need to notify the State Department, or other US agencies. Countries are just like

children—they will do anything they want if they can get away with it without consequences from their parents (or the United Nations or their own citizens). In some senses this ability to engage in space warfare with discretion can be good, as it provides a means for countries to show will, intent and resolve against each other without their own populations getting incensed and forcing their governments into unwanted conflicts.

3. Wartime actions have potential peacetime consequences such as generating space debris, inspiring unwanted limiting outer space treaties in the aftermath of conflict, and triggering shifts in alliances.

4. Adversary nations can only employ space systems that are in current operational regions of concern, pre-conflict, due to extreme energy needs & long timelines for orbital changes. You essentially fight with what you have at the start of the space conflict in a particular region of space.

5. Satellite systems almost exclusively generate and transmit information—thus a space war is an information war. When you attack a satellite; you are actually attacking the information that is generated or transmitted by that satellite. If you want to deny an adversary the ability to image the battlefield, you must now consider both satellites and remote drones on the battlefield that are performing the imagery mission, if not someone else on the ground with binoculars. And ultimately you are not just attacking the mission of the satellite; in reality you are attacking the adversary commander's mind that is employing that information to task military forces on the battlefield. Since you are attacking the adversary commander's mind, it is very difficult to simulate and model the ultimate effects of attacks on space systems compared to terrestrial attacks that destroy enemy war-making capabilities.

6. Currently, since there are no major colonies in space, the main purpose of space forces is to support terrestrial forces. That means space warfare planning must intimately sync with terrestrial planning processes and terminology, along with the timing pace of the ground battle.

7. You are not fighting the war—you are fighting the peace. The whole purpose of the war, whether terrestrial or space-based, is essentially to change the adversary's mind. Every action in space can have severe effects on the timing and consequences of the peace process afterward, and ultimately geopolitical re-alignments. You can win the space war but lose the peace—something that the United States has been losing on the ground in its many military conflicts since World War II.

8. In every conflict you are essentially teaching your adversary how to better counter you in the next conflict. Thus, you should be mindful of the types of space weapons you may employ in one conflict, because you can be assured your adversaries will learn from this and make that weapon system less capable the next time around. Also, employing certain categories of space weapons may influence space weapons ban treaties post-conflict. Every time you employ a space weapon, you must fully consider all of the possible consequences—military, diplomatic, political, scientific and economic—both during the conflict, and years later post-conflict.

9. Adversaries of the United States realize how important space is to US conduct of military operations on the ground. Thus, before any adversary will initiate major military operations on Earth, they will, if they can, take out the US's eyes and ears in space to prevent a timely and well-thought-out response. It takes days and weeks to set up a major attack in space by maneuvering and concentrating space weapons at key choke points in orbital space. If the United States and its allies have good space

situational awareness and space domain awareness, then they should be able to frustrate the pre-positioning of adversary ASATs, either by attacking these marshaling points, or simply reporting this attack build-up to the United Nations to warn of the impending terrestrial attacks that will occur after the space attacks begin. It is conceivable that if a country loses its military space capabilities, then it would not even bother to conduct the terrestrial attacks. Maybe in the near future, most wars will be fought in space and not on Earth, so there would be close to zero human casualties rather than the heavy loss of life and destruction of cities on Earth that is occurring in Ukraine.

— Space Situational Awareness (SSA) / Space Domain Awareness (SDA) & Timely Algorithms / Displays
- **Surprise is Easy In Space**

— Pre-Conflict Positioning
- **You Fight With Only What is Available in Local Region of Space**

— On-Orbit Maneuverability (Also, Continuous Thrusting Electric Propulsion to Confuse Targeting?)

— Command Decisiveness
- **Major Space Wars Over With In 24 – 48 Hours**

Figure 19. Prime War-Winning Characteristics.

Critical Questions for Space Attacks

- Will Space Systems be Under Attack In the Near Future?
- Are Space Systems Currently Under Attack?
- Who Is Attacking?
  - Maybe Another Adversary is Trying to "Stir the Pot"
- What is the Adversary Attack Strategy?
  - Counter Command & Control
  - Counter ISR
  - Show of Intent & Will for Deterrence
  - Does it Support Future Adversary Terrestrial Attack Plans
- What Damage Has Been Caused?
  - Does it Really Matter to Current Terrestrial War Planning?
- What Is Optimal Blue Response?
- What Are the Post-War Consequences to These Attacks?
  - Allies Hate You for All of the New Space Debris
  - New Limiting Space Treaties Post-Conflict
  - You Just Educated Your Adversary on How to Beat You in the Next Space Conflict

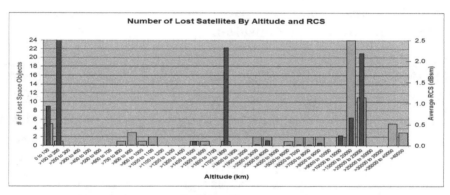

Figure 20. Catalog of Undetected Space Objects by Altitude and Radar Cross Section (RCS - Size) (Paul Szymanski)

ABOUT THE AUTHORS

PAUL SZYMANSKI

**World Famous Scholar and Space Expert
Is Now an Independent Consultant**

Mr. Szymanski is an internationally acclaimed expert on space strategies and space warfare. He is a major contributor to United States military space doctrine as an independent consultant. Szymanski has more than fifty years of experience in all fields related to space control, including policy, strategy, simulations, surveillance, survivability, threat assessment, long-range strategic planning, and command and control. In the past he has worked with the White House National Security Council (NSC), Congress, the US Air Force, US Army, US Navy and Marines as well as civilian agencies like NASA, DARPA, and FEMA. His contributions range from working for the Air Staff at the Pentagon (Secretary of the Air Force - AQSC) to systems development at the Space and Missile Systems Center (SMC - ASP/XRJ) in Los Angeles, technology development at the Air Force Research Labs (AFRL/RD/RV/RI/RH and as a member of the Independent Assessment Team general officer programmatic review board) in Albuquerque, New Mexico (USA) to operational field testing (China Lake Naval Test Center, California). Through this vast experience, he has a unique perspective of understanding all the divergent issues associated with each step of procurement processes.

In addition, Szymanski supported the NATO Supreme Allied Commander Transformation Group and has worked in critical space control programs (non-NRO) for 27 years, developing new concepts, analyses and simulations while managing technical programs critical to national US security. He has administered or participated in multiple architecture studies that provided senior decision-makers with long-term strategic planning road maps and were being briefed to the Secretary of the Air Force, Secretary of Defense, Joint Chiefs of Staff, Congress, and the NSC.

Paul is also the founder of the Space Strategies Center. His works have been featured in the Strategic Studies Quarterly of the Air University of the US Air Force, Aviation Week and he has been a frequent speaker at international conferences and exhibitions on satellite and space missions throughout the world. In total he has presented over 140 lectures and written publications in the last few years alone. He is also publishing seven books in the next two years on the topic of outer space warfare which will serve as the foundation for modern space warfare planning and strategies.

Paul Szymanski is available for lectures, seminars, board membership, and executive consulting.

Space Warfare Group Membership Statistics: The Space Warfare discussion group on LinkedIn that Paul Szymanski developed is probably the most senior discussion group in the country, if not the World, with an interest in critical space warfare topics. It consists of **25,117 hand-picked members** on LinkedIn with experience in **Space Warfare** and Space Domain Awareness (SDA), or at least have expressed an interest in these topics, and includes: 756 members from military colleges (including the former Superintendent of the Air Force Academy), 1,612 from private and Government think tanks, 1,293 from public universities, 228 from government intelligence agencies (including the NASIC Chief Scientist and the former NRO Chief Scientist), 33 from DARPA, 386 from the **Joint Chiefs of Staff**, 590 from NATO, 166 from NORAD-USSTRATCOM, 2,171 **General officers, Admirals or equivalents** (one to four stars), including former: **Supreme Allied Commander in Europe**, NATO Supreme Allied Commander Transformation, NATO Assistant Secretary General, **Commanders (2) of US Army in Europe**, Commander of US Air Force in Europe, Commander of US Army in Japan, Commander & Deputy Commander of Special Operations Command in Europe, Commander of US Army Forces Africa, Commander of US Army Pacific, Commanders (3) of US Forces in Japan, **Commander of US Central Command**, Commander of the Air Force Special Operations Command, Commanders of Air Combat Command (2), **NATO Commanders (2)**, Commander of NORAD-USNORTHCOM, Commanding Generals of the 82nd Airborne Division, 10th Mountain Division (2), 1st US Army, US Army South (2), US Army Special Operations Command, Director of the National Security Space Office, Commander of the Space and Missile Systems Center (SMC), **Commander of Navy Installations Command**; Commander of Naval Air Systems Command, Chief of Naval Research, Commander, Air Force Research Laboratory, also current: **Commanders of US Army Space and Missile Defense Command (3)**, Commander of AFMC, Director of DISA, Superintendent of the US Air Force Academy, Marine Corps Commandant and then **Chairman of the Joint Chiefs of Staff**, also two former Chairmen of the Joint Chiefs of Staff, Chief of Staff of the French Army, 435 from the Secretary of Defense office (including one **former Secretary of Defense, two current Ministers of Defense (Australia & France),** and 74 **current and former Under/Assistant Secretaries of Defense**), 1 current and two former Secretaries of the Air Force, **19 Under/Assistant Secretaries of the Air Force, 1 former Secretary of the Army**, Vice Chief of Staff of the Army (3), **24 Under/Assistant Secretaries of the Army**, two Assistant

Secretary of Homeland Security, ten **Assistant Secretaries of the Navy**, Deputy Chief of Naval Operation, **past and current Commanders of the 3rd, 4th, 5th (2 commanders), 6th (2 commanders) and 10th fleets, Naval Surface Forces Atlantic (2 commanders), Naval Air Forces Atlantic, Commanders of Pacific (2 commanders) and Korea Naval fleets, Commanders of NAVWAR (2 commanders), and 2nd, 7th and 8th Air Forces (3 commanders),** 3 Assistant Secretaries of DOE, **four Assistant Secretaries of the Treasury**, three Under Secretary of Commerce, two from the National Military Command Center, **693 Congressional House & Senate staffers**, 2,298 from specific military space agencies, 716 from various other military services, **221 diplomats & ambassadors,** 128 from the State Department (including eighteen **Assistant Secretaries of State**), 47 from Air Force Research Labs (AFRL), 6,710 from various space-related defense contractors, **360 from the White House and NSC staffs**, 215 from NASA (including their Chief Scientist), 77 **astronaut**s, 42 from The Vatican Observatory, and 128 from the United Nations, among others.

MICHAEL S. DODGE

Michael S. Dodge currently serves as an Associate Professor & Graduate Program Director in the Department of Space Studies at the University of North Dakota. Prof. Dodge received his LL.M. degree in Aviation & Space Law from McGill University in the fall of 2011 (thesis: "Global Navigation Satellite Systems (GNSS) and the GPS-Galileo Agreement"). Before attending McGill, he obtained his JD in 2008 from the University of Mississippi School of Law, where he was also the first recipient of the Certificate in Remote Sensing, Air, and Space Law. He obtained dual degrees in BS (Biological Sciences) and BA (Philosophy) in 2005, from the University of Southern Mississippi.

Prof. Dodge teaches several courses for Space Studies, including Space Politics and Policy (SpSt 560), Space Law (SpSt 565), Remote Sensing Law and Policy (SpSt 575), and Space & the Environment (SpSt

545). These courses include a multitude of historical, political, and legal facets to space activities, and cover subjects such as legal issues in space exploration; regulation, privacy law, and constitutional concerns surrounding the use of remote sensing technology; licensing and regulatory requirements for space activity; the historical and evolutionary nature of space policy (both nationally and internationally); public international law; and domestic United States legal governance of space activity.

Prof. Dodge's research has included GNSS law, remote sensing law & regulation, environmental regulation of outer space, concepts of sovereignty and ownership rights in space, and the nexus of remote sensing technology with global humanitarian law and disaster relief law. Future studies include examination of future environmental regulatory structures for orbital space, as well as domestic United States legislation and its relationship with the precept of non-appropriation in outer space, including an analysis of the ownership of celestial resources from potential asteroid mining operations.

BRYANT A.M. BAKER

Bryant A.M. Baker is a Judge Advocate for the United States Air Force where he has held positions as a Special Victims' Counsel, Chief of Civil Law, and Chief of Operational Law for both the Air Force Global Strike and Space missions. He has degrees from American University's Washington College of Law, North Dakota University's Space Studies Department, Brigham Young University, and Utah Valley State College. He is also a legal advisor to the Space Propulsion Synergy Team, member of the International Institute of Space Law, and active participant in the American Bar Association's Space Law Forum. He is licensed to practice law in the state of Maryland. The views and opinions expressed in his chapter are those of the author alone and do not necessarily reflect those of the United States Department of Defense, the United States Air Force, or any other government agency.

CHRISTOPHER KUKLINSKI

Mr. Kuklinski is a native of Plymouth Township, Pennsylvania (a suburb of Philadelphia).

He currently serves as the Technical Director for the Director for Global Operations at United States Strategic Command (USSTRAT-COM). During his 34-year military and government civilian career, he has gained extensive operational experience in nuclear, space, and command and control operations to include:

- Nuclear Operations: Ground Launch Cruise Missiles at Florennes Air Base Belgium and Comiso Air Station Italy; and Intercontinental Ballistic Missiles at Ellsworth Air Force Base South Dakota;
- Space Operations: Titan II/Titan IV (space launch) at Vandenberg Air Force Base California; and Defense Support Program (missile warning) at Buckley Air Force Base Colorado;
- Command and Control Operations: Headquarters Air Combat Command Langley Air Force Base Virginia (force deployments); and the National Military Command Center (NMCC) Pentagon, Washington District of Columbia.

He holds Bachelor of Arts degree in Architectural Studies and Fine Arts History from the University of Pittsburgh. He also holds a Master of Arts Degree in Education from Chapman University, a Master of Business Administration from the University of Nebraska at Omaha, and a Master of Arts Degree in War Studies from King's College London. Additionally, he earned multiple professional business certifications from the University of Notre Dame, graduated Air War College, Air Command and Staff College, and Squadron Officer School; and is a Senior Executive Fellow from the John F. Kennedy School of Government at Harvard University.

COLONEL CHRISTOPHER R. DINOTE

Christopher DiNote has served over twenty-two years in the United States Air Force and Air National Guard. He has deployed for Operations Enduring Freedom, Iraqi Freedom, and Noble Eagle. Chris is a 1999 graduate of the United States Air Force Academy and a 2003 graduate of the United State Air Force Weapons School. He holds an MA in Military History from Norwich University (2016), and a Master's in Strategic Studies from the Air War College (2017). Chris is currently serving an extended active-duty tour in the Florida Panhandle, where he lives with his with wife and daughter. He has published non-fiction through the Air University's Vigilance Horizons Intelligence, Surveillance, and Reconnaissance Task Force as well as the USAF Weapons School's *Weapons Review* academic journal. Chris has coauthored short works of military science fiction with his wife Jaime DiNote and Philip "Doc" Wohlrab for Baen Books, and as a solo author for Midlands Scribes Publishing.

COLONEL RYAN SANFORD

Colonel Sanford commands the 412th Operations Group at Edwards Air Force Base. Previously, he was a Pol-Mil Strategist on the Joint Staff. He is a graduate of the US Air Force's School of Advanced Air and Space Studies, the US Air Force Test Pilot School, and the US Army's School of Advanced Military Studies. He holds four graduate degrees in fields ranging from mathematics to flight test engineering to military strategy and security studies. Additionally, he is currently completing a graduate certificate in wilderness management. He flew the F-15E operationally and in combat and recently commanded a flight test squadron. Moreover, he has logged pilot-in-command time in over 30 different aircraft types.

LIEUTENANT COLONEL (R) BRAD TOWNSEND, PHD

Lieutenant Colonel Townsend (US Army) is the author of the book *Security and Stability in the New Space Age: The Orbital Security Dilemma* (Routledge Press 2020). He holds a PhD and MPhil in military strategy from the US Air Force's Air University School of Advanced Air and Space Studies. A 2002 graduate of the US Military Academy, he also earned an MS in astronautical engineering from the Air Force Institute of Technology and an MS in space operations management from Webster University. He previously served as a space policy advisor on the Joint Staff, and is now a Senior Engineer within the System of Systems Engineering Office at the Engineering and Technology Group of The Aerospace Corporation, supporting DOD Space.

JOHNATHON MARTIN AND BRANDON BAILEY

Johnathon Martin works for the Department of Defense, is a PhD student studying space warfare, and holds master's degrees in space systems engineering and engineering management. Brandon Bailey is a Senior Cybersecurity Project Manager at the Aerospace Corporation and has won numerous awards for his cybersecurity efforts, including NASA's Exceptional Service Medal in 2019. They are both recognized experts in cybersecurity for space systems. The views expressed here do not represent those of the US government or of the Aerospace Corporation.

MICHAEL UNBEHAUEN

Michael Unbehauen is the founder and president of Acamar Analysis and Consulting, an independent think tank and consulting firm specializing on geopolitics and missile defense. He is also a Space Operations Officer in the US Army Reserve where he supports US Strategic Command (USSTRATCOM) in the fields of strategy, policy and plans for global integrated missile defense. During his active-duty military career, he was the lead planner for Air and Missile Defense Theater Security Cooperation in Europe, as well as the commander of a strategic US missile defense radar station in Israel. He further served as the planning officer of the 100th Missile Defense Brigade (GMD) which is tasked with conducting the national security mission to defend the United States against the threat of an intercontinental ballistic missile attack.

DAINIUS T. BALČYTIS

Dainius T. Balčytis is a security researcher focusing on emerging threats and warfare foresight. His professional experience includes employment by the European Commission, University of Aberdeen and volunteering with the UK Army Cadet Force. He holds double Masters from the University of Aberdeen in History-International Relations (MA) and in European Politics and Society (MSc). He is also co-founder and research coordinator at ETAFIN project mapping global risks. In addition to this, he has a strong interest in simulations, having designed and conducted wargames on topics related to insurgency, unconventional warfare, space conflict and pandemic containment.

Index

Printed in the USA
CPSIA information can be obtained
at www.ICGtesting.com
LVHW082010110124
768645LV00005B/121